Edited by

PHILIP WEEKS

Buckeye PRESIDENTS

Ohioans in the White House

THE KENT STATE UNIVERSITY PRESS

Kent and London

© 2003 by The Kent State University Press, Kent, Ohio 44242

All rights reserved

Library of Congress Catalog Card Number 2002003879

ISBN 0-87338-727-9

Manufactured in the United States of America

07 06 05 04 03   5 4 3 2 1

Library of Congress Cataloging-in-Publication Data

Weeks, Philip.

Buckeye Presidents : Ohioans in the White House / Philip Weeks

p. cm.

Includes bibliographical references and index.

ISBN 0-87338-727-9

1. Presidents—United States—Biography.

2. Ohio—Biography.

I. Weeks, Philip. II. Title.

E176.1 .W366 2002

973'.09'9—dc21

2002003879

British Library Cataloging-in-Publication data are available.

Buckeye
PRESIDENTS

Dedicated gratefully

to Jerome Mushkat, who better than anyone else

taught me about, and demonstrated to me

how to teach and convey,

the sum and substance of United States history.

As always,

for Jeanette and Michael. And to Heather.

And C. C., you were always there with a smile,

then you slipped away so quickly.

Contents

Preface

The Mother of U.S. Presidents—an impressive claim, and one that applies legitimately to only two of the nation's fifty states, Ohio and Virginia. Between them they have provided the republic with fifteen of its presidents. One of the fifteen, William Henry Harrison, is a hybrid who is properly associated with both Ohio and Virginia. His experience reflected that of many Americans during the early decades of U.S. history: born in one of the thirteen British colonies, grew up during the tumultuous Revolutionary era, and then in early adulthood relocated beyond the Appalachian chain to settle and pursue a new life in America's first West. In addition to Harrison, seven Ohioans have piloted the United States from the White House: Ulysses S. Grant, Rutherford B. Hayes, James A. Garfield, Benjamin Harrison, William McKinley, William Howard Taft, and Warren G. Harding. An equal number of Virginians have been the nation's chief executive: George Washington, Thomas Jefferson, James Madison, James Monroe, William Henry Harrison, John Tyler, Zachary Taylor, and Woodrow Wilson.

The presidents associated with Virginia and Ohio directed the affairs of the United States during two critical eras. During the nation's formative period, from the birth of the federal republic in the 1780s through 1850 and the mounting hostility between North and South, seven of the nation's twelve presidents were from the Old Dominion. In the six decades following 1865 and the end of America's Civil War, as modern America emerged, seven of the nation's twelve presidents were Buckeyes. Each helped guide the United States in its transformation from a rural, agrarian, diplomatically isolationist society into a wealthy and powerful commercial and industrial nation, one that became an increasingly major player in global geopolitics. Ohio was so dominant and maintained such a compelling hold on national and presidential politics from the Civil War through World War I that when Republican Warren G. Harding of Marion ran for the presidency in 1920 his opponent was none other than another Ohioan, Democrat James Cox of Dayton.

All eight Buckeye presidents were consequential participants in state and national affairs prior to their ascendancy to the White House. Four were governors of states or territories: William Henry Harrison (Indiana), Rutherford B. Hayes (Ohio), William McKinley (Ohio), and William Howard Taft (Philippines). Six served in the U.S. Congress: William Henry Harrison, Hayes, James A. Garfield, Benjamin Harrison, McKinley, and Warren G. Harding. Six of the eight also had military service. Five were generals in the U.S. Army: William Henry Harrison, Ulysses S. Grant, Hayes, Garfield, and Benjamin Harrison (McKinley had a lesser rank, rising from private to major during the Civil War). To make a living outside of government, some were attorneys (Hayes, Benjamin Harrison, McKinley, and Taft), others were college professors (Garfield, Benjamin Harrison, and Taft), one was an editor and publisher (Harding), and another was a farmer and a store clerk (Grant). Taft, subsequent to his White House years, became chief justice of the U.S. Supreme Court, making him the only American to hold the top post in two of the three branches of the U.S. government. The average age of these eight men upon taking the presidential oath was fifty-four. The youngest was Grant, who was forty-six; the oldest was William Henry Harrison, at sixty-eight, the last president born a British subject. Four of the eight Buckeye presidents did not live to see the conclusion of their terms: William Henry Harrison and Harding died of natural causes while in office, and assassins killed Presidents Garfield and McKinley.

Buckeye Presidents is introductory—not definitive, illustrative—not encyclopedic. It seeks to provide general readers and students with an overview of significant aspects of the lives and times of eight men from Ohio who each became the president of the United States. The book draws on the expertise of eight specialists who have written chapters profiling these chief executives. Of specific value, each chapter presents a synthesis of the author's reflection on recent scholarship about his or her subject and scholarship during the era in which the president lived, as well as the author's own area of academic competence. In most instances, the author of the chapter brings the experience of having already published an important biography about their subject. Each scholar has also included a section of suggested readings, which is placed at the end of his or her chapter; these recommendations will aid readers who wish to expand their knowledge of these eight presidents and their America.

Acknowledgments

I would like to express my appreciation to the authors for taking time out of their demanding professional schedules to participate in this endeavor. It was a pleasure to work with Joanna Hildebrand Craig of The Kent State University Press as she moved this book to publication. And it is wonderful to have the opportunity again to salute in print my best friend, my wife Jeanette, especially at the time of our thirtieth anniversary.

PART I

The Early Republic

The National Story

On the morning of April 30, 1789, a large crowd gathered outside Federal Hall in New York City. Standing on the building's porch, George Washington put his hand on a Bible and was asked, "Do you solemnly swear that you will faithfully execute the office of President of the United States, and will to the best of your ability, preserve, protect and defend the Constitution of the United States?" "I solemnly swear," he replied. With that, the first president of the United States took office, and a new era in the nation's history began. Installing a smoothly operating national authority, establishing a workable federal court system, and addressing the country's economic problems occupied the federal government during Washington's first term. Foreign affairs became the most important concern for Washington during his second term, and it remained central for the first three chief executives who succeeded him: John Adams, Thomas Jefferson, and James Madison.

The foreign affairs policies of the young republic from the early 1790s to the War of 1812 were shaped by three principal objectives. First, the United States planned to settle the nation's first West, the lands west of the original thirteen states and beyond the Appalachian mountains, and secure its western borders. The initial borders of the United States stretched east to west from the Atlantic Ocean to the Mississippi River and north to south from Canada to Florida. Although the Spanish, who controlled the Mississippi, and the British, who possessed Canada, proved problematic in realizing the first objective, it was America's first natives who presented the greatest challenge.

Natives in America's first West and the more remote areas of the South were determined to hold onto their ancestral lands at all costs. Americans, as they surged outward from the Atlantic seaboard and across the Appalachian chain, were just as resolute in their determination to settle a vast western domain from tribal lands. Because Indians resisted, Americans considered them a dangerous impediment to the nation's territorial and economic aspirations. They demanded that the national authority solve the "Indian Question" permanently. In the face of this demand and the country's aggressive thrust westward, the pattern most representative of U.S.–Indian relations was set early. It was subject to the ebb and flow of events and to swings in federal approaches from drafting peace policies to waging war, but through it ran a strain of unremitting American determination to dislodge the indigenous peoples of the western lands.

As settlers overran tribal lands, pushing steadily toward the Mississippi valley, new states emerged both north and south of the Ohio River. South of the river, Kentucky and Tennessee joined the federal republic in 1792 and 1796, respectively. North of the river, the United States government decided to use this region as a laboratory for developing policies and procedures on how to fashion territories from the wilderness and the conditions under which territories would enter the Union as new states. To that end, Congress organized the vast area beyond the Ohio into the Northwest Territory and passed land ordinances in 1784, 1785, and 1787 that articulated an array of policies for the orderly survey, sale, settlement, and establishment of government there. The first state planned by the U.S. government and carved from the Northwest Territory was Ohio in 1803. In succeeding years the nation's westward surge never slackened, and by 1840 one-fourth of the American people lived between the Appalachians and the Mississippi.

The young republic's second foreign policy objective called for the territorial expansion of the United States. Some dreamed of adding Canada or perhaps various Caribbean islands, such as Cuba. Many were especially interested in pushing the national boundaries beyond the Mississippi River, achieving this by making the Louisiana Territory part of the United States. That huge territory, stretching nearly two thousand miles from the Mississippi to the Rocky Mountains, could provide more land for a growing American population. Control of the Louisiana Territory by the United States would also mean control of the Mississippi River and the port of New Orleans. The Mississippi was the most important trade route for Americans settling the lands west of the Appalachians. Acquisition of the Louisiana Territory offered the added benefit of significantly advancing the first foreign policy goal—securing the western borders of the republic.

Spain, which had owned the Louisiana Territory since 1763, relinquished it by secret treaty in 1800 to France, ruled by Napoleon Bonaparte. Bonaparte had come to power the previous year during the turbulent French Revolution. Under his political rule and military leadership France became the greatest power in Europe. Word of the treaty reached Thomas Jefferson late in 1801. The president recognized the grave danger facing the United States and its western settlers with Bonaparte in control of the Mississippi

River and the vital port of New Orleans. Hoping to solve the problem peacefully, the United States offered up to $10 million for that city. Napoleon, then preparing to resume his war in Europe against the British, countered by offering to sell the entire territory to the United States for $15 million. His offer was readily accepted. Jefferson's Louisiana Purchase doubled the size of the republic without any violence—adding to it about 828,000 square miles—and secured the republic's western line of settlement and the strategic Mississippi River.

Finally, the young United States was determined to avoid being drawn into the war between Great Britain and France. The French Revolution had broken out in 1789 when the French overthrew the monarchy and established a republic. In 1793 the new French government beheaded the country's monarchs and unleashed a reign of terror on its citizens using the guillotine, then it declared war on Great Britain and other European countries. Soon war engulfed all of Europe. The United States realized it could not benefit by siding with either Britain or France; in fact, it could be severely damaged by such involvement.

President Washington declared American neutrality, yet for the next decade the United States could not be free from the turmoil in Europe. The United States felt affronted and vulnerable as Europe refused to take its sovereignty seriously. France and Britain harassed American merchant shipping on the high seas and ignored the maritime rights and neutrality of the United States as it tried to trade with both of these countries. At the same time, British agents in Canada intensified the ill will by distributing guns, ammunition, and other supplies to the Indians in the Northwest Territory, urging them to block the westward movement of the young republic and resist American settlement on their lands.

Anger and resentment mounted steadily among Americans. Many agreed with a group of young politicians, hailing mainly from the frontier areas of the South and West, that Britain's actions dishonored the young republic. These "war hawks" argued that armed conflict was the only means to redress the grievous insult and restore honor. President Madison attempted to maintain peace, but at last on June 1, 1812, he asked Congress for a declaration of war against Great Britain.

The president's decision offered possible benefits as well as significant risks. The United States hoped to guarantee forever the maritime rights of neutral nations on the high seas. Equally important, victory would restore the nation's sense of honor. The war would permit the United States to invade British Canada, and they hoped to annex more territory for the republic. The war also would provide a pretense for attacking and removing the Indians remaining in the northwest and the south. However, a British victory might cost the United States some of its land, such as the Louisiana Territory, and it could cost the United States the ultimate price—its independence.

Fighting in the War of 1812 produced mixed results. Although the British might properly have claimed victory on the East Coast because they burned the White House and the U.S. Capitol in 1814, they and their Indian allies lost completely in the Northwest and the South because of the superb leadership of such American military commanders as William Henry Harrison and Andrew Jackson. The Treaty of Ghent did nothing to resolve the problems that had caused the war, however, and both sides agreed to return to the state of affairs that had existed before the war. There would be no winner or loser. But before news of the treaty reached the United States, General Jackson, "Old Hickory," won a smashing victory against the British army at New Orleans. The battle restored the nation's sense of honor and pride. Americans basked in a deep sense of patriotic self-satisfaction; the world now had to take the young United States and its rights seriously. After all, hadn't it stood up to mighty Europe, endured, and at the end triumphed?

A spirit of unity and nationalism infused American life following Jackson's victory at New Orleans, but by 1820 that mood was fast disappearing. Severe sectional and political disputes arose between 1819 and 1834 over permitting slavery in the Louisiana Territory, protective tariffs to safeguard the nascent American Industrial Revolution, and rechartering the Second Bank of the United States. These disputes increasingly threatened to break up the federal Union less than a half-century after its birth. "Like a fire bell in the night," the aged revolutionary Thomas Jefferson said with alarm about the divisiveness and the talk of dissolution, "[it] awakened and filled me with terror."

Andrew Jackson dominated American politics during this period. Forming the Democratic party following his defeat by John Quincy Adams for the presidency in 1824, the nation again elected Old Hickory its president four years later. During his two terms in the White House, Jackson took a firm stand against the right of any state to nullify federal laws or to secede from the Union. He also supported a policy of separation to solve the Indian Question: southern tribes would be colonized, by force if necessary, beyond the Mississippi and the areas of expected white settlement. Martin Van Buren, Jackson's handpicked presidential successor, executed the separation policy, forcibly removing the Cherokees, Chickasaws, Choctaws, Creeks, and Seminoles from their southern homelands to the Indian Territory (essentially, modern-day Oklahoma).

Many Americans opposed Andrew Jackson and his policies. They formed the Whig party in the 1830s and went to war politically against the Democrats. The Whigs hoped to forge an alliance between eastern commercial interests and those of the settlers in America's first West. The party favored high protective tariffs, a strong national bank to aid the business community, and the federal government's support for internal improvements, such as roads and canals, to assist the trans-Appalachian West. The greatest conflict among the Whigs arose over the question of whether the U.S. government, if the republic obtained additional territory, should restrict or permit the extension of slavery into those lands. Within two decades that issue would not only destroy the party, but it also would severely divide America.

Van Buren, emulating his mentor Old Hickory, sought reelection in the 1840 presidential race, but the Whig party defeated him and placed one of its own in the White House for the first time: military hero William Henry Harrison.

William Henry Harrison

Ninth President of the United States, 1841

KENNETH R. STEVENS

I t was cold on the morning of March 4, 1841, as participants assembled for the inaugural parade of president-elect William Henry Harrison. Though the Whig party of Baltimore had offered a carriage and a team of four matched horses for the occasion, the sixty-eight-year-old Harrison chose to ride a spirited white charger. Despite the chill, the general wore no overcoat and carried his hat so he could acknowledge the cheers of the spectators as he made his way along Pennsylvania Avenue toward the Capitol. To his right and left rode Maj. Henry Hurst and Col. Charles Stewart Todd, both of whom had served as his aides at the Battle of the Thames during the War of 1812. Behind them followed an escort of mounted assistant marshals. Then came Tippecanoe Clubs with banners and bands, some with log cabins on wheels, and many decorated with cider barrels and coonskins or other symbols of the frontier to honor this man from America's first West. Representing industry was a large platform drawn by six horses that bore a working power loom. From Georgetown, next door to Washington, D.C., marched the faculty and student body from the Jesuit college there.

At the Capitol, where an estimated 50,000 spectators had gathered, a fortunate thousand were admitted to the Senate Chamber gallery to watch newly elected senators and the vice-president-elect, John Tyler, take their oaths.

Then came the grand moment. At thirty minutes after noon, the dignitaries processed from the Senate Chamber, through the Capitol building, and out to a platform constructed at the east front of the building. Harrison took his place next to Chief Justice of the United States Roger B. Taney, with other Supreme Court justices, senators, the corps of ambassadors, and ladies seated around them. When Harrison rose, the multitude cheered, then listened as he delivered his inaugural address over the next hour and a half, speaking into a cold northeast wind, still without benefit of overcoat, gloves, or hat, while his warmly dressed auditors huddled against the icy gusts. At the close of his speech, the chief justice administered the oath of office.

When the official festivities concluded, Harrison repaired to the White House to receive hundreds of well wishers, and that night, despite the length of the day, he attended a ball where many toasts were proposed for the success of the new Whig administration. Thus, says the chronicler Benjamin Perley Poore, the "Democrats surrendered the power which they had so despotically wielded for twelve years," and the Whigs "took the reins of government."

Exactly one month later, on April 4, 1841, Harrison became the first president to die in office.

William Henry Harrison began life as a child of privilege. The first Harrison arrived in Virginia about 1634, acquired land, and served in the House of Burgesses. William Henry's father, Benjamin Harrison V, was a member of the First and Second Continental Congresses, signed the Declaration of Independence, served in the Virginia legislature, and in 1781 defeated Thomas Jefferson to become governor of Virginia.

William Henry, Benjamin's third son, was born at the family estate at Berkeley, Virginia, on February 9, 1773. At fourteen, he was sent to Hampden-Sidney College, a small Presbyterian school in Hanover County, but, for reasons that are not clear, his stay there was brief. Historians have speculated that a "religious phrensy [sic]"—as Thomas Jefferson styled it—that swept the school so disturbed the staid Episcopalian Harrisons that he was withdrawn. In 1790, Harrison, still but seventeen, was sent to study medicine with Dr. Andrew Leiper in Richmond, but there the impetuous youth joined an abolition society, which must have been a severe trial to his slave-owning father. The next year he was sent to Philadelphia, then the nation's capital, to complete his medical studies at Pennsylvania University under the direction of the eminent Dr. Benjamin Rush. When he reached Philadelphia, however, he learned that his father had died. Harrison attended the medical school for a time, but when Virginia governor Richard Henry Lee was in the capital, Harrison asked him to help him secure a commission in the army. It was accomplished within twenty-four hours, and on August 16, 1791, Harrison was appointed an ensign in the First Regiment of Infantry, with orders to recruit soldiers and lead them to Fort Washington, on the Ohio frontier near Cincinnati.

Army service in the Northwest Territory, the vast area north of the Ohio River, was a formative experience for the young officer. Between 1785 and 1789, the Ohio tribes had signed land cession treaties with the United States, but Indians complained that their councils had not approved the agreements and resisted American encroachments. In September 1791, Arthur St. Clair, the governor of the Northwest Territory, led 1,400 men north from Fort Washington. Near the east bank of the Wabash River, a hundred miles north of Cincinnati, Indians, supported by the British, attacked St. Clair's army at dawn on November 4, 1791. Six hundred of St. Clair's men and fifty-six female camp followers were killed in the worst defeat ever suffered by an American army at the hands of Indians in a single battle. The survivors retreated in disarray through the wilderness. Harrison arrived at Fort Washington just as the remnants of St. Clair's army reached the post. It was a sight that the young ensign never forgot.

Over the next few months, Harrison grew into a competent officer. At first his fellow soldiers scorned him because he had obtained his commission through political favoritism. According to his own account, he spent his time reading Cicero's *Orations,* books on military tactics, and other worthy tomes. In 1792, Congress enlarged the army to 5,414 men, and President Washington appointed Revolutionary War hero "Mad Anthony" Wayne commander of U.S. forces in the West. Wayne made Harrison, newly promoted to lieutenant, one of his aides.

In August 1794, Wayne led 2,000 regulars and 1,500 Kentucky volunteers, under Maj. Gen. Charles Scott, against the Ohio Indians. Fought near a British fort by present-day Toledo, the Battle of Fallen Timbers raged for an hour, with Harrison in the thick of the action, before the beaten tribesmen ran for the protection of the British post, only to find its gates closed. For the next three days, U.S. forces burned and pillaged Indian towns and fields in the area. Then, following the Maumee River to its confluence with the St. Marys and St. Joseph Rivers in Indiana, they established Fort Wayne on the site of the Miami Indian town of Kekionga, before moving on to Greenville.

On August 3, 1795, ninety-two chiefs, representing twelve tribes, and twenty-seven whites, including Harrison and General Wayne, signed the

Treaty of Greenville, in which the Indians ceded 25,000 square miles of land in northern and western Ohio in exchange for $20,000 in goods and a $9,500 annuity, or less than one-sixth of a cent per acre. Harrison would later apply Wayne's questionable methods of dealing with Indians—the rituals of awarding medals to chiefs, ornate rhetoric, exchanges of wampum, smoking calumet pipes, and tippling alcohol—when concluding his own land cession treaties.

Harrison was assigned to a blockhouse at North Bend on the Ohio River, fourteen miles downriver from Cincinnati. North Bend was the home of Judge John Cleves Symmes, a prominent citizen and landowner, and Harrison soon developed a romance with the judge's daughter, Anna. Symmes complained to a friend that, though Harrison came from a good background, "he has no profession but that of army." A year later the judge still expressed reservations because his son-in-law could "neither bleed, plead, nor preach, and if he could plow I should be satisfied." Despite the judge's misgivings, William Henry and Anna enjoyed a loving relationship spanning forty-five years.

After his marriage, Harrison decided that the army offered few opportunities for an ambitious man. In 1798, he resigned his commission and won appointment as secretary of the Northwest Territory, maintaining the territory's records—including laws, land claim decisions, an account of the governor's actions for Congress, and returns of land surveys. He was also authorized to serve as acting governor when necessary. That year a census revealed an increase in population that, by the Northwest Ordinance of 1787, allowed the territory to advance to second grade. That meant it could establish an elected general assembly that could select a nonvoting delegate to Congress. Harrison ran for the position and was elected over Arthur St. Clair Jr., the son of the territorial governor, by a close vote of eleven to ten.

Harrison's most significant accomplishment as a member of the 6th Congress involved federal land policy. During the Confederation period, Congress had established the basic western land policy of the United States when, in 1784, 1785, and 1787, it passed land ordinances establishing policies for the orderly survey, sale, settlement, and government of the Northwest Territory. At this point, the only offices for public land sales were at Pittsburgh and Cincinnati. The laws favored wealthy individuals who could buy large amounts of land for speculation or break it into smaller lots to sell at higher prices.

The people of the Northwest wanted land available in smaller tracts, and Harrison represented their interests well. At his suggestion Congress appointed a committee to reexamine the land law and named Harrison to chair it. In the Land Act of 1800, Congress adopted Harrison's recommendations to reduce the minimum sale from 640 acres to 320 acres and to open additional land offices in Ohio at Chillicothe, Marietta, and Steubenville. The price remained two dollars per acre, but the time for payment was increased from one year to four. The measure had an immediate impact on flagging land sales. By the end of the year nearly 400,000 acres were sold, and another 340,000 were sold in 1802. Historian John D. Barnhart in *Valley of Democracy* credits the Land Act for the large migration to Ohio, which would lead to statehood in 1803.

Harrison also proposed the partition of the Northwest Territory. President John Adams, on May 13, 1800, approved a bill dividing the Ohio Territory from the remainder, called the Indiana Territory, along a line due north from the confluence of the Great Miami and Ohio Rivers. One week later Adams appointed Harrison governor of the Indiana Territory, at that time a huge expanse that included not only the present state of Indiana but also Illinois, Wisconsin, and portions of Michigan and Minnesota (and for a brief time after the Louisiana Purchase of 1803, the area as far west as the Rocky Mountains).

Harrison also represented the private interests of his father-in-law, who owned considerable land in the Northwest Territory. The Land Act of 1785 required that one section of every township be set aside for supporting public schools, but John Cleves Symmes had never fulfilled that obligation. The territorial legislature had instructed Harrison to initiate legal proceedings against his father-in-law if necessary, but Harrison made no efforts to do so.

Harrison arrived at the Indiana territorial capital of Vincennes in January 1801 and settled into the life of a frontier gentleman. He purchased several hundred acres of land and built an elegant brick house to accommodate his busy professional and social life and to provide room for his growing family (the Harrisons' fifth child, John Scott, was born in October 1804). The house, which he named Grouseland, still stands today.

Territorial governors exercised considerable power. At first Harrison, along with three appointed judges, made all laws by decree. After the territory advanced to second grade in 1805, the elected territorial legislature enacted laws, but Harrison retained an absolute veto and the power to appoint almost all territorial officials; and though President Jefferson had the authority to name the territory's legislative council, in fact he left the matter to Governor Harrison. For Harrison and his supporters, as Andrew R. L. Cayton has shown in *Frontier Indiana,* politics was a "hierarchical business" that "operated essentially as a personal faction, acquiring and exercising power through a vertical face-to-face system of patronage."

Harrison made enemies because of his exercise of power. In 1805 an anonymous critic—whom most historians identify as Isaac Darneille—published several letters under the pseudonym Philo Decius, denouncing the governor as "a whimsical and capricious executive" who appointed his cronies to office and ruled against the land claims of those who dared to oppose him. Another adversary was John Badollet, the register of the land office in Indiana, who protested to Treasury Secretary Albert Gallatin that Harrison had cheated settlers and Indians out of their land, tried to prevent the election of Jonathan Jennings as territorial delegate to Congress, and circulated petitions for his reappointment as governor at "abodes of intemperance" and among crowds at horse races. Harrison, he said, was a "moral cameleon [sic]" who could assume "a variety of appearances to answer his purposes, vulgar with the lowest order of mankind, polite . . . fascinating with the more refined."

Jennings proved Harrison's most formidable opponent. A Pennsylvanian who arrived in Indiana in 1806, Jennings served as the territory's delegate in Congress from 1809 until 1816, when Indiana attained statehood. In 1810 he introduced a resolution in Congress—which did not pass—that would prohibit the selection of the governor's appointees to the territorial House or the legislative council. The next year Jennings proposed that Congress allow sheriffs in the territory to be elected instead of appointed by the governor. Throughout his political career, which included service as the new state's first governor from 1816 to 1822 and another stint in the U.S. House from 1822 to 1831, Jennings remained an implacable foe of Harrison, whom he denounced as a member of the Virginia aristocracy.

There were also allegations that Harrison used his office to speculate in public lands, that he bribed others not to bid on public lands and accepted bribes for not bidding on public lands himself. In fact, Harrison, like many other officials, speculated in land despite his official position. There was no rule that prevented such activity, but Secretary Albert Gallatin considered it "extremely improper" and eventually issued an instruction forbidding land superintendents from being involved in speculations.

The question of slavery in the Northwest Territory was another controversial issue. Article VI of the Northwest Ordinance of 1787 had prohibited the introduction of slavery into the territory, but Harrison and others—particularly Virginians raised on plantations—wanted to suspend or repeal Article VI. They argued that the introduction of slavery would encourage the territory's population growth and economic development.

In December 1802, a convention at Vincennes, called and presided over by Harrison, petitioned Congress to suspend Article VI for ten years. When Congress was not forthcoming, the governor and the territorial judges promulgated a law that reduced black servants brought into the territory to a condition little short of slavery. After Indiana advanced to second grade, the territorial legislature, with Harrison's support, again petitioned for the suspension of Article VI and passed an act declaring that black servants could be brought into the territory under "voluntary" agreements.

Harrison's efforts to extend slavery into the territory aroused strong opposition. Some argued that slavery was destructive of government based on republican principles. One critic insisted that slave ownership would destroy the virtue necessary to maintain a republic because it produced "an overbearing and tyrannical spirit, entirely opposite to republican simplicity and meekness." As Nicole Etcheson shows in *The Emerging Midwest,* many Americans who had relocated from the Upland South—who knew the plantation system—opposed slavery in the Northwest because they believed it denied them economic opportunity and created "an uneven distribution of wealth and power." For them slavery contradicted the ideal of the economically self-sufficient, politically independent yeoman farmer.

Harrison's opponents sought unsuccessfully to have him replaced. In February 1803, citizens of Clark County asked the administration to appoint a governor more attuned to the "principles of liberty." When Harrison was due for reappointment in 1809, citizens of Harrison County informed Congress that because most people in the territory opposed slavery, they desired a governor who also opposed it. Though Harrison's foes could not block his reappointment, the next year Congress extended the franchise to all twenty-one-year-old white male taxpayers who had lived in the territory for a year and made officials appointed by the governor, except for justices of the peace and militia officers, ineligible for the territorial legislature. Back in Indiana the territorial legislature repealed the law that held black servants in conditions close to bondage. To reduce Harrison's personal influence, they relocated the territorial capital from Vincennes to Corydon. Harrison's rule was being overtaken by democracy; though he remained Indiana's governor until March 1, 1813, his power was substantially eroded.

Among Harrison's most important duties as governor was his position as superintendent of Indian Affairs. Most of Indiana belonged to a multitude of tribes—the Delaware, Piankishaw, Potawatomie, Miami, Wea, and Eel River Indians along the Wabash River; the Shawnee, Wyandot, and Chippewa in the north; Kaskaskias in Illinois; Kickapoos in the center of the territory; and the Sauk and Fox on the northern prairie. Tribal land claims often overlapped, but they shared much of the area as common hunting grounds. Both President Jefferson and Governor Harrison sought to dispossess the tribes of the land they occupied. Between 1803 and 1809 the governor signed eleven treaties with representatives of various Indian tribes, by which they surrendered millions of acres of land to the United States. He accomplished this through a mixture of coercion, bribery of corrupt chiefs, purchases of land from tribes that did not properly own the land they were selling, and recognition of Indian leaders who were not recognized by the tribes themselves.

Harrison's demands for treaties came at a pace that stunned the tribes. At Fort Wayne, on June 7, 1803, the Delaware, Shawnee, Potawatomie, Miami, Eel River, Wea, Kickapoo, Piankishaw, and Kaskaskia ceded land, the salt spring at Saline Creek on the Ohio, and tracts for way stations on the road linking Vincennes with Clarksville and Kaskaskia, Illinois. Later that summer, the Eel River, Wyandot, Piankishaw, Kaskaskia, and Kickapoo gave up more land. There were additional treaties with the Delaware and Piankishaw at Vincennes in August 1804, with the Sauk and Fox at St. Louis in November 1804, and with the Miami, Eel Rivers, and Wea on August 21, 1805. At the close of 1805, the Piankishaw surrendered their claim to land in southeastern Illinois, giving the United States title to thousands of acres along the Ohio River above the mouth of the Wabash.

Harrison's predatory methods aroused Indian resentment. The most formidable opponents to emerge were the Shawnee brothers Tecumseh and Tenskwatawa. Tecumseh was born, probably in 1768, at or near Chillicothe, on the Scioto River in Ohio; his younger brother Lalawethika, who later adopted the name Tenskwatawa, was born in 1775. Tecumseh became a warrior known for his bravery and intelligence. He was an adept hunter and fighter, who with other Shawnees raided white encampments along the Ohio River, struck frontier settlements in Kentucky, joined Cherokees to make war on Americans in Tennessee, and fought bravely against U.S. forces at the Battle of Fallen Timbers. Much admired among his people, he had become a chief by the time of the 1795 Treaty of Greenville.

Lalawethika was another story. He was boastful, lazy, and often drunk, but in 1805 he experienced a transformation. After falling into a deep trance one night, he spoke of a vision of paradise. Changing his name to Tenskwatawa (the Open Door), and called by many "the Prophet," he said Indians should return to the communal society and traditions of their past. And he declared that although the Master of Life had created Indians,

Americans were children of the Evil Spirit. If the Indians did what the Master of Life ordered, he would "overturn the land, so that all the white people will be covered" and Indians alone would inhabit the earth.

In August 1805 Tenskwatawa and his disciples moved from the headwaters of the Whitewater River in eastern Indiana to Greenville Creek in western Ohio, near where the tribes had signed the treaty in 1795. The Prophet's teachings spread over the frontier like wildfire—much to the distress of Governor Harrison, who believed the Shawnee brothers were tools of the British. In April 1806, Harrison issued a challenge to Tenskwatawa. "If he is really a prophet, ask of him to cause the sun to stand still—the moon to alter its course—the rivers to cease to flow—or the dead to rise from their graves. If he does these things, you may then believe that he has been sent from God." Harrison's challenge was a mistake, for scientists—as the governor should have known—had predicted a solar eclipse on June 16. The Prophet boldly asserted that the midday sky would darken that day and, as the eclipse began, emerged from his house and declared: "Did I not speak the truth? See, the sun is dark!" After this, representatives from Indian tribes all over the Old Northwest visited Greenville to hear his message.

In April 1808 the Prophet and Tecumseh moved to a new settlement called Prophetstown at the confluence of the Tippecanoe and Wabash Rivers in northwestern Indiana. That August, Tenskwatawa and several hundred of his followers visited Harrison at Vincennes, where he informed the governor that he wanted to unite the Indians but wished to live in peace with the whites. The following month, at Fort Wayne, Harrison met with representatives of the Delaware, Potawatomie, Miami, and Eel River and persuaded them to cede more than three million acres of land in Indiana and Illinois in exchange for annuities and $5,200 worth of trade goods.

Harrison had gained more land at Indian expense, but it came at a cost. Tecumseh and the Prophet had warned Indians that the whites intended to take all their land, and the Treaty of Fort Wayne seemed to confirm their assertion. Resentment spread among the tribes. In August 1810, Tecumseh and Harrison met at Grouseland. At their first conference, Tecumseh said that the Americans were pushing the tribes to war by taking their lands. "I do not see how we can remain at peace with you if you continue to do so," he warned. The Fort Wayne agreements were not valid, he said, because the land belonged to the tribes collectively rather than individually, and no single tribe could sell what belonged to them all. When Harrison denied that the United States had taken advantage of the Indians, Tecumseh stood and called the governor a liar, and his warriors suddenly took up their weapons. Harrison drew his sword and a squad of soldiers came forward. For a moment it seemed that fighting would erupt.

That night Harrison assembled the militia in case the Indians attacked, but the next day Tecumseh apologized and the conference resumed. Tecumseh insisted that the land ceded in the Fort Wayne treaty should be returned or he would execute the chiefs who had signed it. Harrison replied he would inform Jefferson of Tecumseh's words but cautioned that the president would not agree to the terms. Harrison informed Washington, in June 1811, that the Indians had demonstrated "uncommon insolence."

In late July 1811, scouts reported that Tecumseh was descending the Wabash River with fifty-three canoes of warriors. Other Indians—more than three hundred in all—were reported moving toward Vincennes overland. Harrison gathered the available regular army troops and called up militia. By the time Tecumseh arrived on July 27, Harrison had an eight-hundred-man force ready, but only verbal sparring took place at the meeting. The chief informed Harrison that he had united northern tribes under his direction and would visit the southern tribes for the same purpose as soon as he left Vincennes. The Shawnee's frankness would prove a serious mistake. After Tecumseh departed, Harrison wrote Secretary of War William Eustis that "his object is to excite the Southern Indians to war against us," but "his absence affords a most favorable opportunity for breaking up his Confederacy."

By September 1811, Harrison had gathered an army of 1,000, including the 4th Infantry Regiment of the regular army, 400 Indiana militia, eighty mounted Indiana riflemen, and two companies of Kentucky volunteers comprising about 120 men, plus a dozen spies and guides. On September 26 the force headed north from Vincennes. At the site of modern-day Terre Haute, they built Fort Harrison. They resumed the march on October 29, crossing to the west bank of the Wabash (which had more open prairie and was less susceptible to ambush), and stopped at Vermillion Creek to construct another fort. By the morning of November 6, Harrison's army was only a mile from Prophetstown. The Prophet sent messengers to suggest a meeting the next day and proposed that Harrison camp on the Tippecanoe, a tributary of the Wabash about two miles west of Prophetstown. Harrison accepted the proposal. The campsite formed a triangle on a height overlooking the prairie.

Harrison ordered the men to sleep with weapons ready and posted sentries in all directions, but apparently he did not expect the Indians to attack. The Prophet, however, told his warriors that rain would ruin the soldiers' powder, but theirs would not be affected; he told them that the darkness would hide the warriors, but the white soldiers would be visible. The most important thing, he told them, was that Harrison must die.

That night a cold rain began to fall as the Indians took their positions. They could see Harrison's men silhouetted against the light of their campfires. Harrison had just risen when the predawn attack began. He called for his horse, a gray mare—which the Indians had seen him riding the day before—but it had broken loose in the confusion. Instead he mounted a dark horse. That mischance may have saved his life: the warriors who were to slay Harrison killed another officer who was astride a light horse. The fighting was furious, but as dawn broke and their ammunition ran low, the Indians fell back. The next day Harrison entered Prophetstown, which had been abandoned, and set the town on fire. The army then began its nine-day march back to Vincennes, arriving on November 18, 1811.

Harrison reported to the secretary of war that the victory at Tippecanoe was "complete and decisive," but he may have claimed too much. His 1,000-man army suffered 188 casualties, at least 62 of them fatal, against an Indian force that certainly numbered no more than 700 and that may have amounted to only 300. Despite the fact that they were outnumbered and lacked the soldiers' firepower, the Indians had inflicted heavy damage.

The Indiana territorial legislature passed resolutions praising Harrison's ability and heroism, but critics soon emerged. Years later Harrison's supporters in the presidential campaigns of 1836 and 1840 would hail him as the hero of Tippecanoe, whereas others would again disparage his performance there.

Defeat at Tippecanoe did not end Indian resistance. The warriors driven from Prophetstown scattered throughout the Northwest Territory and continued depredations against soldiers and settlers in Iowa, Michigan, Ohio, and Indiana. Harrison urged Washington to authorize another offensive against the Indians, but President Madison and Secretary of War Eustis held back. With war against Great Britain imminent, it was not the time to undertake further action against the Indians. Tecumseh, upon his return from his unsuccessful mission to the Southern tribes, now turned to the British. He, with his remaining followers, crossed the Detroit River into Canada and put himself under the command of the British army; a British victory might result in an independent Indian state in the northwest.

Harrison's record regarding the American Indian peoples was mixed. In his 1810 annual message to the Indiana legislature, he reflected a typical attitude among white settlers when he asked: "Is one of the fairest portions of the globe to remain in a state of nature, the haunt of a few wretched savages, when it seems destined, by the Creator, to give support to a large population, and to be the seat of civilization, of science, and true religion?" He was aggressive and ruthless when it came to driving them from their lands, and his success in extinguishing Indian land titles was an important component of his political support. Yet in other matters, Harrison seemed to have compassion for the Indians. For example, he tried to limit the sale of alcohol to tribespeople at the request of their leaders. And when Indians complained about white traders who cheated them, Harrison made efforts to ensure that traders obtained proper licenses. Like his mentor Jefferson, Harrison had an ambivalent attitude toward Indians: he was sympathetic toward their plight but more than willing to take advantage of it.

The Battle of Tippecanoe in November 1811 was the opening event in the war between the United States and Great Britain, which was declared in June 1812. Although historians continue to debate the causes of the War of 1812, Westerners at the time blamed their problems with Indians on British interference, rather than their own rapacious land grabbing, and they saw in this new war with England an opportunity to deal with Indian resistance once and for all.

Harrison was ambitious for command, but at first he was overlooked. By August, when he was appointed a brigadier general in the regular army, war news was grim. After the American garrison at Fort Dearborn (the site of modern-day Chicago) surrendered to a force of British and Indians on August 15, Indians massacred the soldiers and civilians evacuating the post. The next day at Detroit, American general William Hull surrendered without firing a shot to a force of British and Indians, posing a grave threat to the people of Ohio and elsewhere.

On September 17, 1812, Harrison was given command of the Northwestern Army, and on March 3, 1813, he was promoted to major general. The rise of his army career marked the end of his tenure as a territorial governor. Harrison had orders to retake Detroit and invade British Canada. His difficulties were formidable; the greatest of these was supply. The army needed artillery and ammunition, clothing for the soldiers, and food, but the supply system depended on inadequate contractors. And when supplies finally did arrive, they had to be transported through a wilderness. Another problem was that most of his troops were state militia, not soldiers of the regular army. As a politician, Harrison knew how to work with militia soldiers—he praised them profusely after Tippecanoe—but they were poorly trained and distressingly undisciplined.

Harrison began his effort to retake Detroit by concentrating a force at the Maumee River rapids in northwestern Ohio, seventy miles south of

William Henry Harrison was the hero of the Battle of Tippecanoe against Tecumseh's Indian confederation and of the Battle of the Thames against the British during the War of 1812. The nation was stunned when he died one month after his inauguration in 1841. Library of Congress.

their goal. There, on the south bank, he ordered the construction of Fort Meigs, a supply depot and strong defensive position built under the direction of Capt. Eleazer D. Wood, a graduate of the U.S. Military Academy. On May 1, 1813, British general Henry Procter began a siege of Fort Meigs, employing British troops and Indian forces led by Tecumseh. When Harrison received word that Gen. Green Clay's Kentucky militiamen were near, he ordered them to cross the river and take the British batteries there. Many of the Kentuckians were captured or killed in the failed effort. Fort Meigs held, however, and Procter lifted the siege on May 9. In July Procter began a second siege, but by month's end, that too was abandoned.

After giving up on taking Fort Meigs, British forces besieged the lightly garrisoned Fort Stephenson at the lower falls on the Sandusky River, south of Lake Erie. Harrison ordered the post's commander, Kentucky's Maj. George Croghan, to burn the fort and retreat if he could. Croghan replied that he had received Harrison's order too late to execute it. Harrison curtly informed Croghan that he was relieved of command, but the defiant officer brilliantly defended his position, which caused the general some embarrassment. It also checked the British and their allies, who now withdrew from northern Ohio.

From the time he took command of the army, Harrison considered command of Lake Erie the key to victory in the Northwest. On September 10, 1813, U.S. naval officer Oliver Hazard Perry, while patrolling western Lake Erie, met the British fleet under Capt. Robert Barclay at Put-in-Bay. After a fierce battle and the surrender of Barclay's entire fleet, he sent Harrison the message, "We have met the enemy and they are ours." Shortly thereafter, Perry's ships transported 5,000 of Harrison's soldiers across the western end of the lake to the Ontario Peninsula of Canada.

When Harrison's army reached Malden on September 27, it saw that General Procter and his Indian allies under Tecumseh had burned their fort and begun a retreat eastward for the safety of the Niagara frontier. Harrison reoccupied Detroit and, after waiting four days for the arrival of Kentucky mounted troops under Governor Isaac Shelby, began the pursuit of Procter's army. Harrison overtook Procter and Tecumseh on October 5 near Moravian Town on the Thames River. Mounted Kentuckians charged, and the British line broke. General Procter himself fled soon after the engagement began, but Tecumseh's men continued to fight bravely.

Among the Indians killed that afternoon was the great leader Tecumseh. Exactly how Tecumseh met his end is shrouded in myth and mystery. Tecumseh's friend, the Potawatomi chief Shaboni, stated in an 1839 interview that he saw Kentuckian Col. Richard M. Johnson kill the Shawnee chief. Some Indians later claimed that they had buried his body in the forest as they retreated. Several participants at the scene, however, identified a slain warrior as Tecumseh. One who viewed him later wrote that even in death he appeared majestic. Even so, soldiers scalped the corpse and some cut pieces of skin from his back and thighs for souvenirs.

The Battle of the Thames was significant. In October 1813 Harrison concluded an armistice with tribal representatives at Detroit, and the following July, in a formal peace agreement at Greenville, Ohio, the Indians promised to support the United States in the war against Great Britain. After the Battle of the Thames, Harrison traveled east. After visiting the Niagara region, he went to New York City, where he received cheers and applause when he attended the theater and was given a dinner at Tammany Hall, where they toasted the "deliverer of our western frontier." More accolades followed at Philadelphia, and in Washington there were speeches celebrating his accomplishments and a visit to the president's house. On January 9, 1814, he was back in Cincinnati, his military career over; on May 11, 1814, he resigned his commission effective at the end of the month.

No sooner had Harrison resigned than assaults on his war record began. It was at the time—and still is—controversial. Senator William H. Crawford of Georgia, for example, wrote Albert Gallatin that the defense of Fort Meigs hardly merited the praise it had received. The United States could never win the war, he said, as long as its troops were commanded by such "old women and blockheads."

Another attack came during discussion of Senate resolutions introduced in 1816 to honor Harrison and Governor Isaac Shelby of Kentucky with gold medals for their war service. That revived an old accusation by Congressman Joseph Desha of Kentucky, who had served at the Battle of the Thames, that Harrison had not wished to pursue the British and had done so only when urged by Shelby. A motion passed to strike Harrison's name. Harrison was outraged. He sent a letter to Desha demanding to know if he was "the author of a calumny, which was the principal, if not the sole cause of that vote of the Senate . . . which expunged my name from the resolution of thanks." Desha backed away only slightly. He recalled that, at the time, Harrison had expressed doubts that it was worth pursuing Procter, but when the other officers expressed the desire to do so, he had "cheerfully acquiesced." Harrison received more unequivocal testimonials from others, including Governor Shelby, who said that no one could have made "greater exertions" than Harrison to overtake Procter. Two years later the proposal to award medals to Harrison and Shelby was renewed and passed, but questions continued to dog him.

In 1816 Robert McAfee, a veteran of Johnson's mounted Kentuckians, published his *History of the Late War in the Western Country,* which wa[s] full of praise for Harrison's leadership—and which in fact had been s[u]mitted to Harrison for his approval before publication. The book offe[rs]

Gen. James Winchester and Maj. George Croghan, who felt the account slighted their accomplishments. In September and December 1817, Winchester published several articles in the *National Intelligencer* defending his record and criticizing Harrison. Croghan also objected in private letters to Harrison, and their disagreement would become an issue during the 1836 and 1840 presidential campaigns when they were published in the Democratic *Washington Globe*.

Also suspiciously close to the presidential campaigns of 1836 and 1840, former secretary of war John Armstrong Jr. published his two-volume *Notices of the War of 1812*, which provided an unfavorable assessment of Harrison in every respect. When critics complained that the work seemed timed to work against Harrison's candidacy, Armstrong replied, "If the prevailing monomania has dressed up one of my blunderers, and exhibited him in a suit of old tattered Regimentals, as a fit successor for George Washington—is it my fault?"

But much of this controversy lay in the future. On leaving the army, Harrison retired to North Bend, Ohio, where he took up the life of a gentleman farmer. By this time he and Anna had a large family to support—nine children. Harrison had purchased his father-in-law's house, which was located on a great bend of the Ohio River. The original house had been constructed from logs, but it had been enlarged over the years. The estate consisted of 2,800 acres, and on them the general cultivated corn, wheat, fruit trees, and hay for livestock. He also raised cattle, sheep, hogs, turkeys, and chickens. Timothy Flint, a well-known itinerant minister, described Harrison as a gracious host who "kept an open table" for visitors. There was, Flint recollected, "something imposing in the dignified simplicity of his manners" that agreed with the spirit of republicanism.

Political life, however, constantly tugged at Harrison, partly because it offered him the opportunity to defend his military record. When John McLean resigned from Congress in 1816, Harrison successfully ran for his place. Harrison supported legislation of interest to his Ohio constituents, voting for federally funded internal improvements and a tariff to protect the developing iron industry in Ohio, in which he had invested. He also consistently supported slavery. He voted against restricting slavery from the Arkansas Territory and against the Tallmadge amendment, which would have prohibited slavery in Missouri.

The former soldier was mostly interested in military affairs. He advocated relief for disabled veterans, pensions for the widows and orphans of war veterans, opposed a measure that would limit claims for damage to property during the war, urged a land grant bounty of 160 acres for those who had enlisted before December 24, 1811, and spoke in favor of back-pay claims. His greatest effort was a plan to reorganize the militia. Harrison chaired a committee that proposed a national system of military training in every school in the United States and compulsory training camps to be held each year. His report was full of praise for the militia system as the bulwark of free society, but Congress took no action on his proposal. Reelected, during the 15th Congress Harrison pressed, again unsuccessfully, to secure passage of his militia plan.

One of the controversial issues Harrison faced while serving in the House involved Andrew Jackson's unauthorized invasion of Florida—then Spanish territory—in 1818. Jackson had forced the surrender of Spanish garrisons, killed Indians and burned their villages, and executed two British subjects—merchant Alexander Arbuthnot and army officer Robert C. Ambrister—who had aided the Seminoles. A great debate took place in the House of Representatives over whether Jackson should be censured, and Speaker of the House Henry Clay spoke in favor of the measure. The debate placed Harrison in a delicate position, for Jackson was a fellow officer and veteran of the War of 1812, and Clay had often assisted Harrison in his career. In the end Harrison tried to split the difference, voting to condemn Jackson's execution of Arbuthnot, but not the execution of Ambrister. He was the only member of the House to take this stand, and undoubtedly it pleased neither Jackson nor Clay.

In 1819, at the close of the 15th Congress, Harrison returned to Ohio—where he was elected to the state senate. He was an effective legislator, supporting construction of a canal to connect Lake Erie and the Ohio River, encouraging tax exemptions and loans for businesses, favoring the development of a public school system, and proposing a memorial to Congress to provide debt relief for landowners. As always, he was vitally concerned with militia issues. Additionally, antislavery sentiment was growing in Ohio, but Harrison continued to support the "peculiar institution" by voting against a resolution denouncing slavery and its extension into Missouri.

Another contentious issue of the day was the Bank of the United States (BUS). Harrison had favored the BUS when it was established in 1816, and he had served on the board of directors of its branch in Cincinnati, but when hostility to the federally chartered bank became rampant in Ohio he modified his views. While serving in the 15th Congress he had voted for a bill to repeal the BUS, and now, as a member of the Ohio Senate, he again had to confront the issue. The state legislature in February 1819 voted to impose a yearly tax of $50,000 on branches of the BUS in th state. The U.S. Supreme Court had ruled in March 1819, in *McCulloc*

Maryland, that states could not tax the Bank of the United States, but many did not accept the Supreme Court's assertion that it was the final arbiter of the Constitution. When the Ohio legislature adopted resolutions declaring that the state was not bound by the Supreme Court, Harrison objected because, though he opposed the Bank and believed it was unconstitutional, he also considered the decision binding. His position—a curious mixture of nationalism and states' rights sentiment—demonstrated his skill at straddling issues.

Throughout much of the 1820s Harrison sought, with remarkable persistence, political office and political appointment. He ran unsuccessfully in 1820 for the Ohio governorship. In 1821 and 1822, his name was put forward to no avail for the U.S. Senate. In 1822 he also lost a U.S. House election to James W. Gazley, a Cincinnati lawyer. The House contest led to renewed discussion of Harrison's war record and a charge of nepotism because Harrison's son, John Cleves Symmes Harrison, had been appointed receiver at the Vincennes Land Office. Moreover, when antislavery advocates criticized Harrison, he trimmed, claiming that as a young man he had joined an abolition society. Later, when he wished to distance himself from the abolitionists during the presidential campaign of 1840, he would claim it had not been an abolition society, but a "humane society."

In 1823 he asked President Monroe to appoint him minister to Mexico—a post that went to Ninian W. Edwards of Illinois. When Edwards resigned after a short time, Harrison again expressed his interest, but President John Quincy Adams awarded the job to Joel R. Poinsett of South Carolina.

Success finally came in 1824, when the Ohio legislature sent Harrison to the U.S. Senate. As usual he demonstrated his interest in military affairs. Senator Harrison was appointed chair of the Committee on Military Affairs and also served on the Committee on the Militia. He prepared reports on the conditions of forts and arsenals, examined claims for bounties and back pay, and proposed pay increases for officers and enlisted men. He advocated a bill for the relief of surviving officers of the Revolution, and he opposed a proposal to drop the U.S. Military Academy appropriation from the budget.

When Maj. Gen. Jacob Brown, the army's highest-ranking officer, died on February 24, 1828, Congress considered abolishing the rank, but Harrison's Committee on Military Affairs strongly opposed such action, and the measure was defeated. No sooner had that been accomplished than Harrison's supporters began to lobby for his appointment to the position, but the job went to Brig. Gen. Alexander Macomb, the commandant of the U.S. Military Academy.

Another opportunity appeared as the election of 1828 neared: there was no obvious vice-presidential running mate for President John Quincy Adams. Characteristically, Senator Harrison wanted the nomination, but the Republican caucus, meeting at Harrisburg, Pennsylvania, settled on Secretary of the Treasury Richard Rush. When the post of U.S. minister to Colombia became available that same year, Harrison pressed his case. "This person's thirst for lucrative office is absolutely rabid," an exasperated Adams complained. "Vice-President, Major-General of the army, Minister to Colombia—for each of these places he has been this very session as hot in pursuit as a hound on the scent of a hare." Despite the president's objections, Harrison's support in the Ohio, Indiana, and Kentucky congressional delegations carried the day, and he received the appointment.

Harrison sailed for South America in November 1828, along with his seventeen-year-old son, Carter, and Edward Tayloe, a young Virginian and Harvard graduate, who would be the secretary of legation. That same month Jackson defeated President John Quincy Adams. Because Jackson would assume office on March 4, 1829, and would want to appoint his own ministers, it was likely that Harrison's stay in Colombia would not be a long one.

Harrison arrived in Cartagena on December 14, 1828, and began a forty-day journey by boat and mule to Bogotá. His early impressions of Colombia were negative; in his first dispatch, on December 23, 1828, he informed Secretary of State Henry Clay: "The affairs of this country are not only in a most unsettled state, but . . . still more gloomy and ominous of future distress." The government appeared, he said, to be a "complete Military Despotism."

The political situation in Colombia was indeed troubled. The Republic of Gran Colombia had been formed in 1821 by the union of New Granada, Venezuela, Quito, and Panama. Simón Bolívar, known as the Liberator, was president, but he spent much time away from the capital on military campaigns. During his extended absences opposition leaders decried his authoritarian ways and demanded a constitutional government. In Venezuela dissenters called for a federal system that would allow greater autonomy. Yet another faction wanted a centralized government, with Bolívar as president for life and the right to name his successor. And some hoped simply to install Bolívar as monarch. Harrison's predecessor, Beauford T. Watts, had openly supported Bolívar, without whose leadership, he enthused, Gran Colombia would return to chaos and darkness. Bolívar was so pleased with the sentiment that he had the letter published, much to the embarrassment of the United States.

Secretary Clay had admonished Harrison to avoid similar errors. Ironically, Clay gave Harrison a supercilious letter to deliver to Bolívar urging him to adhere to republican ideals. Clay said he had no doubt that Bolívar would explain "the parts of your public conduct which have excited any distrust" and that he preferred "the true glory of our immortal Washington to the ignoble fame of the destroyers of liberty." Not surprisingly, Colombians found the letter offensive.

Nevertheless, Colombian foreign minister Estanislao Vergara received Harrison graciously and described him to Bolívar as "a man who inspires confidence." But the pleasant relations diminished once Harrison began to complain about alleged mistreatment of Americans in Colombia. Conditions in the country distressed Harrison. The people were oppressed by taxes. There was no freedom of press, and political opposition was not tolerated. Local government had been replaced by appointed officials. Bolívar was restoring Catholic Church property in order to win its support. Worst of all were rumors that the Liberator wished to assume the title of emperor and to choose his successor from one of the royal houses of Europe. Since the Monroe Doctrine of 1823, the United States had maintained that it would regard any attempt to extend the European political system—meaning monarchy—to the new world as a threat to its peace and security. The doctrine was, to be sure, an imperious and self-indulgent announcement, but it surely never occurred to most Americans, and certainly not to Harrison, to question it.

Harrison became Jackson's first removal from a diplomatic post. At the end of May 1829—when Harrison had been in Bogotá less than a month—he learned that President Jackson had replaced him with Thomas P. Moore, a Democratic congressman from Kentucky. Unfortunately, despite Clay's advice, Harrison already had become embroiled in Colombian politics. On June 22, he sent the State Department an encoded dispatch, enclosing a copy of one of Bolívar's letters that he had surreptitiously obtained. Subsequently, he acquired other materials from Bolívar's opponents. Early that fall, he reported that Bolívar had proposed himself as president for life with the right to name his successor. But opposition was developing. Word reached Bogotá on September 25 that Gen. José María Cordova had indeed begun a revolt.

In the meantime, Moore, the new U.S. minister, arrived in Bogotá on September 21, 1829, and five days later Harrison presented him to the Colombian government and announced the end of his mission. Having taken leave of his official duties, Harrison took it upon himself to lecture Bolívar in a long letter, urging him to spurn dictatorship and maintain a republic. "Are you willing," asked Harrison, "that your name should descend to posterity, amongst the mass of those whose fame has been derived from shedding human blood, without a single advantage to the human race? Or, shall it be united to that of Washington, as the founder and the father of a great and happy people? The choice is before you." It is hardly surprising that the Colombians resented Harrison's paternalistic missive—or that they retaliated.

While waiting for the vessel that would return Harrison to the United States, Harrison and Tayloe visited the country estate of British consul-general James Henderson outside Bogotá. Extraordinary news from the capital reached them there: Henderson, Mexican minister José A. Torrens, and Harrison had been accused as accomplices in a conspiracy to overthrow Bolívar's government. Oddly, no further action was forthcoming. In fact, Harrison and Tayloe were invited to a state dinner, which they declined to attend, to welcome Moore.

More serious accusations followed. Harrison and Tayloe left Bogotá, on October 13, to visit the salt works at Zipaquirá, about thirty-five miles north of Bogotá. That night they were informed that Harrison—along with Henderson, Torrens, and Albert Gooding, a North American resident of Colombia—were suspected of involvement in a plot to assassinate members of the state council. The three diplomats were ordered to leave the country immediately.

On January 9, 1830, Harrison boarded the brig *Montella,* and he arrived in New York on February 6. In Washington Harrison denied he had involved himself in Colombian politics. In his defense he published his *Remarks of General Harrison, Late Envoy Extraordinary and Minister Plenipotentiary of the United States to the Republic of Colombia, on certain charges made against him by that government* (1830). Although he was not guilty of the crimes of which he was accused, his behavior had left him vulnerable to such charges.

Historians have been critical of Harrison's conduct in Colombia. One scholar of U.S.–Latin American relations, Eugene R. Huck, labels Harrison "the most inept of all of the ministers to Colombia before 1850," and Francisco J. Urrutia, who served in the Colombian delegation in Washington, wrote that Harrison's "passionate and impulsive" personality made him unfit to be a diplomat. Harrison was, in fact, a typical American diplomat of his time, connected politically though lacking experience or training in diplomatic affairs.

His diplomatic career at an end, Harrison returned to the farm at North Bend in April 1830. The next few years were difficult. He owed back taxes and about $20,000 to creditors. In October 1830 his son John Cleves Symmes Harrison died $12,000 in debt, leaving a wife and six children who moved in with the retired general. In the spring of 1832 the Ohio River flooded his land, and the summer brought drought. By the end of 1833 he was so desperate that he contemplated recruiting some of his former soldiers for an expedition up the Missouri River to the frontiers of Mexico. Finally, in 1834, four years after his return to Ohio, he secured the position of clerk of the Court of Common Pleas for Hamilton County. The former territorial governor, major general and war hero, U.S. representative, senator, and diplomat, had been reduced to a minor government functionary. In light of this, his return to national prominence before the decade was out is one of the great success stories in American political history.

The great problem the Whig party faced as the 1836 presidential contest neared was an excess of candidates to oppose Jackson's chosen presidential successor, Martin Van Buren. Among the possibilities were perennial Whig standard-bearer Henry Clay of Kentucky, New England favorite Daniel Webster, Tennessee's Hugh Lawson White, and William Henry Harrison, whom the Old Northwest advanced. One force that had propelled Harrison back into politics was an instinct to defend his military record. The object of his displeasure was Kentuckian Richard M. Johnson, who in 1836 was running for the vice-presidency on the Democratic ticket.

Johnson had turned his participation at the Battle of the Thames in 1813 into a political asset. Although he had never claimed credit for killing Tecumseh, several participants at the battle said they had seen him fire the fatal shot, and that reputation helped secure him election to the U.S. House of Representatives, then the U.S. Senate. Such adulation offended Harrison; in September 1834, he had declined an invitation to celebrate the Battle of the Thames at Indianapolis because he believed it made Johnson his equal.

The road to the White House began on December 14, 1834, when the *Pennsylvania Intelligencer* suggested Harrison as a presidential candidate; and in January 1835 a political meeting at Harrisburg, Pennsylvania, recommended him for the chief executive's office. Harrison wrote his friend Gen. Solomon Van Rensselaer on January 15, 1835: "Some folks are silly enough to have formed a plan to make a President of the United States out of this *Clerk* and Clod hopper!"

The momentum continued to build in the summer of 1835 when Harrison traveled down the Ohio River—visiting Madison, New Albany, Louisville, and Vincennes—and received a hero's welcome. In fall 1835 support for Harrison's candidacy grew even stronger. Throughout the country he was celebrated for his heroic deeds at Tippecanoe and the Thames and compared to Cincinnatus, the Roman general who had returned from the field of valor to stay on his farm until called upon by the people to political leadership.

Political conventions in New York and New Jersey nominated the general as well, and he was also popular in Pennsylvania, Kentucky, Maryland, Delaware, and Virginia. In February 1836, a meeting of more than a thousand Whigs in Ohio nominated Harrison for the presidency, calling him "the gallant defender of his country in the hour of danger." Harrison, in other words, was the one candidate who could draw support across the nation's sections—north, south, and west.

Slavery and the lobbying of Congress by abolitionists were also issues. During the congressional session of 1835–1836 Congress adopted the infamous "gag rule" that petitions relating to slavery would be tabled without further action. In speeches and responses to questions from voters, Harrison said that Congress had no authority over slavery in the states or in the District of Columbia, and that he opposed antislavery petitions to Congress.

Democrats also charged that Harrison had voted to sell whites into slavery—a reference to Harrison's support, while he served in the Ohio senate, for a law that would allow the binding out of paupers who were unable to pay fines.

The Whigs' inability to agree on a single candidate in the 1836 presidential contest proved fatal: it split the vote and Van Buren won, though Harrison made a strong showing in several states. In Ohio, Harrison defeated Van Buren by 104,958 votes to 96,238.

Harrison was, as R. Carlyle Buley notes in *The Old Northwest: Pioneer Period, 1815–1840,* "the first son of the Northwest to have important presidential possibilities." His supporters saw him as another Andrew Jackson, a candidate whose military record could appeal to the people. And just as ordinary Americans rallied to Jackson when they believed that corrupt politicians had stolen the presidential election of 1824 from him, they now identified with Harrison because ambitious politicians tried to dishonor his heroic military record.

The 1836 campaign was hardly over before the Whigs began to prepare for the election of 1840. Two weeks after Van Buren took office on March 4, 1837, the country was plunged into the greatest financial depression it had ever experienced. Banks and businesses failed, unemployment rose and wages fell, and farmers received low prices for their crops and produce. The causes of the immense depression were complex, but the Whigs blamed Jackson and Van Buren.

Whigs sensed that they could win in 1840; however, they had to avoid the pitfall of splitting their votes again among multiple candidates. Harrison's strongest rivals for the nomination were Henry Clay and Daniel Webster. Webster concluded that he could not win the nomination and withdrew. The contest between Harrison and Clay was fiercely waged. When the Whig national convention assembled on December 4, 1839, at Harrisburg, Pennsylvania, Clay seemed to be the favorite—on the first ballot of the delegates, he received 103 votes to Harrison's 91 and Gen. Winfield Scott's 57—but the Clay forces were outmaneuvered. At the instigation of Harrison's supporters the convention adopted a unit voting rule: each state would form a committee of three delegates, and the majority vote of the committee would be reported as the vote of the whole state. The decision—described by Missouri's Thomas Hart Benton as a combination of "algebra and alchemy"—doomed Clay's chance for the nomination. Although he commanded a plurality of the delegates, Clay could not win a majority of the committees. On the final ballot, the vote was 16 for Scott, 90 for Clay, and 148 for Harrison. To win votes in the South, the convention nominated John Tyler of Virginia, a former Democrat who had broken with Jackson, for vice president. It was the team of "Tippecanoe and Tyler, too."

The Whig convention did not construct a platform, a fact that has been incorrectly interpreted as proof that the Whigs did not stand for anything. Part of the problem was that the Whigs were a collection of wildly disparate groups: those who supported a national bank and those who opposed it; proslavery Southerners, antislavery Northerners, proslavery Northerners, and many in the party who were ambivalent about slavery; those who advocated high protective tariffs and those who sought low tariffs; those who wanted sale of the public lands at the lowest prices and those who wished to limit land sales; Masons and Anti-Masons, and others. And all of these united in their opposition to Andrew Jackson and the Democratic party he established. As New York Whig congressman Millard Fillmore pointedly asked: "Into what crucible can we throw this heterogeneous mass . . . so as to melt them down into one mass of pure Whigs of undoubted good metal?"

Some Whigs were stunned by Harrison's selection. Many thought him too feeble. One embittered Clay supporter wrote the Kentuckian that some good might result from Harrison's nomination: the presidency under Jackson had become so powerful that it was perhaps just as well "to place a man upon it who will degrade it by his imbecility."

Harrison's selection pleased the Democrats, who had a low estimate of his abilities. When the nomination was announced, the editor of the Democratic *Baltimore Republican* mocked: "Give him a barrel of hard cider and a pension of two thousand a year, and, our word for it, he will sit the remainder of his days in a log cabin by the side of a 'sea coal' fire and study moral philosophy." This sneer soon became the most powerful symbol of the Whig campaign.

The election of 1840 was a boisterous affair. A Whig meeting at Columbus, Ohio, in February 1840 passed resolutions in support of Harrison. And in conjunction, despite rain, the party held a parade with delegations carrying banners supporting the hero of Tippecanoe and transparencies depicting events from his life. Cuyahoga County Whigs marched with a ship on wheels that bore the likeness of Harrison on its mainsail, while another group pulled a log cabin complete with coons on the roof and a barrel of hard cider at the door—all the while singing verses composed especially for the campaign. The log cabin became such a potent egalitarian symbol that politicians who had not had the opportunity to live in such rusticism lamented the fact. Daniel Webster said that he had not lived in a log cabin, but his father had. "If ever I am ashamed of it . . . ," he said, "may my name and the name of my posterity be blotted forever from the memory of mankind!"

The Democrats held their convention at Baltimore and renominated Van Buren and Johnson. They adopted a platform calling for strict construction of the Constitution and opposition to a national bank, to federal assumption of state debts, and to federally funded internal improvements. In an effort to combat Harrison's popularity, the Democrats charged that he had been a member of the discredited Federalist party—a charge he denied, saying he had always been a Jeffersonian Republican.

The Democrats again attacked Harrison's military record, including the unpleasant correspondence between Harrison and George Croghan over the defense of Fort Meigs and the scurrilous charge that the women of Chillicothe had sent Harrison a petticoat. They continued to praise Vice President Johnson, as the real hero at the Thames. It is worthy of note, perhaps, that Johnson wrote a letter in Harrison's defense during this time.

As in 1836, slavery was the most sensational issue. It was frequently alleged that Harrison was an abolitionist, though Harrison, hoping to secure the Southern vote, strenuously denied it. He had never been an abolitionist, he said, despite the fact that while running for Congress in 1822 he had claimed membership in an abolition society during his youth. Harrison tried to appease antislavery sentiment by skillful obfuscation and fence straddling.

In a speech at Carthage, Ohio, on August 20, 1840, he defended the right of constituents to send antislavery petitions to Congress. At the same time, he said, exercising this right in regard to the slavery question was inappropriate interference in the domestic institutions of the Southern states.

Part of the Whig strategy was to contrast Harrison's manly qualities with what they portrayed as Van Buren's effeminacy and love of luxury. Rarely has a president been subjected to the kind of personal abuse that Van Buren endured. The Whigs had hated Jackson, but they ridiculed Van Buren. All over the country they chanted:

> Let Van from his coolers of silver drink wine
> And lounge on his cushioned settee;
> Our man on a buckeye bench can recline
> Content to drink hard cider is he.

In vain, Democrats protested and tried to portray Harrison as the real aristocrat in the campaign. But the damage was done. Thus was the son of one of Virginia's greatest landowners transformed into a humble frontier farmer and Van Buren, the son of a New York innkeeper, made into an aristocrat.

Part of the explanation for this development can be attributed to Whig journalists across the nation and part to the level of literacy among Americans. A revolution in newspaper publishing occurred in the United States during the nineteenth century. In 1790 the United States had fewer than a hundred newspapers; by 1840—thanks to the invention of the rotary steam press, the use of less expensive wood-pulp paper, and America's high literacy rate (91 percent among whites, according to the 1840 census) there were 1,577 newspapers. Of course, newspapers had always been partisan, but the Whigs raised them to a new level. One of the most important figures in this development was New York publisher Horace Greeley, who began publishing the *Log Cabin* in 1840. The paper was an outright campaign sheet, filled with stories about Harrison and campaign songs. Soon dozens of other Whig newspapers, almanacs, and songbooks copied the formula. Many campaign biographies, such as the *Sketches of the Civil and Military Services of William Henry Harrison* by Charles Stewart Todd and Benjamin Drake, extolled Harrison's virtues and accomplishments.

The Whigs triumphed in the election: Harrison won nineteen states to Van Buren's seven, and he crushed the president in the electoral college, 234 to 60, though the popular vote was closer than the electoral votes would have suggested. Perhaps more significant, 80 percent of eligible voters participated in the election of 1840, nearly double the number that had voted in 1836. The Whigs had learned effective campaign techniques to turn out voters, and American politics would never be the same.

As inauguration day, March 4, 1841, neared, some felt that Harrison lacked the capacity to serve as president. South Carolinian John C. Calhoun wrote a friend that Harrison seemed "quite unconscious" of the duties and responsibilities that awaited him and had neither the physical nor mental powers necessary for the job. Clay informed a correspondent before the inauguration that when he saw Harrison in November 1840, shortly after the election, he seemed "much broken" physically. Harrison, said Benjamin Brown French, a clerk in the U.S. House of Representatives, seemed to be "a warmhearted, generous and kind man, but not a man of very superior talents, and of great egotism." Nor were foreign visitors impressed. Adolphe F. Bacourt, the French minister to the United States, reported that the president-elect was "a vain man, without mind or talent, who will be a puppet in the hands of flatterers, and those who wish to control him will ruin the country while quarreling amongst themselves. However, they say he is an amiable man, rather vulgar, and having the mania of quoting the Greeks and Romans, whom he knows nothing about, but thinks it good taste to appear to know."

In his hour and a half inaugural address, Harrison made a number of promises that reflected Whig political philosophy. He pledged to serve a single term, to be sparing in the use of the veto, and not to abuse the power to appoint and remove officials. He hinted that he would support an act of Congress reestablishing a national bank, reiterated his view that Congress had no authority over slavery in the states or in the District of Columbia, and said that his administration had no plans to assume the debts of the states. He urged Americans to avoid the baneful effects of partisanship. Harrison's speech also confirmed his penchant for ostentatious references to Greeks, Romans, and classical history.

Once he took office, the new president was absolutely beset by office seekers. Harrison accepted their applications, stuffing them in his pockets, then his hat. When his arms were filled an attendant was summoned to carry them all. French saw the president in the market on Saturday, March 26, and wrote that he seemed "like a broken-down old man. . . . He has been almost worried out of his life by applicants for office ever since he arrived in this city, . . . from accounts I had of him I came to the conclusion two weeks ago that he was deranged." When a friend of French called upon the president, Harrison complained of a headache and said that he was *"bothered almost* to death with visitors. I have not time to attend to my person, *not even to change my shirt,* much less attend to the *public* business. I must leave this House Sir. I must go and lock myself up somewhere where I can have some peace . . . [and] be exempted from these interruptions."

Many observers feared that his administration would be dominated by a struggle between Daniel Webster and Henry Clay for control of the Whig party. Because Webster was named secretary of state, he seemed to pull ahead. One observer wrote New York governor William Henry Seward that the president had "thrown himself almost entirely into Webster's hands." Webster, for example, had only to suggest Ohio's Thomas Ewing for secretary of the treasury and it was done. Clay was bold enough to admonish Harrison that any delay in calling a special session of Congress to deal with finances of the country would lead to the "imputation of vascillating [*sic*] counsels." He even prepared a proclamation for Harrison to sign.

There is evidence that Harrison would not have been the weakling that so many critics believed he would be. Harrison curtly dismissed Clay. "You use the privilege of a friend to lecture me," he said. "I take the same liberty with you—You are too impetuous. Much as I rely upon your judgment there are others whom I must consult . . . in many cases to determine adversely to your suggestions." The rebuke outraged Clay.

Harrison also took a stand against Webster. The president wished to name his friend John Chambers of Kentucky as governor of the Iowa Territory, though Webster had promised the job to James Wilson, one of his New Hampshire supporters. At a cabinet meeting, Webster informed Harrison that they had decided that Wilson should receive the governorship. Harrison replied "Ah! That is the decision, then, is it?" Harrison wrote a few words on a scrap of paper and handed it to Webster with the instruction to read it aloud to the whole group. The embarrassed Webster read the words: "William Henry Harrison, President of the United States." When he finished Harrison stood and said "And William Henry Harrison, President of the United States, tells you, gentlemen, that, by [God], John Chambers shall be Governor of Iowa." And so it was.

The end for Harrison came suddenly. During a morning walk, he was caught in the rain. After some rest he began to feel better, and he might have survived had not physicians been called. By the time they finished their ministrations, which included bleeding, blistering, and doses of arsenic, the president was beyond recovery. About 12:30 A.M. on April 4,

1841, Harrison said, "Sir, I wish you to understand the true principles of the government. I wish them carried out. I ask nothing more." Then he was gone.

The nation was stunned. The calamity of a president dying in office had never visited the United States before. The Reverend William Hawley of St. John's Episcopal Church conducted a service at the White House, and thousands lined Pennsylvania Avenue as the president's body was conveyed to the Capitol to lie in state. Harrison was entombed in the vault at the Congressional Cemetery in Washington. Later his remains would be taken to his beloved farm at North Bend, Ohio, where they rest today. President Tyler proclaimed a national day of humiliation and fasting in memory of the deceased chief executive. Across the country memorials were held, statesmen and worthy citizens delivered eulogies, and hundreds of sermons were preached by ministers. Many felt the president's death was a divine rebuke to the nation. The sermon delivered by John Codman in Dorchester, Massachusetts, was typical: the nation's sins—slavery, intemperance, treatment of the Indians, infidelity, violation of the Sabbath, dueling, worldliness, financial speculation, and party spirit—had brought the judgment of God upon the United States.

Not everyone lamented Harrison's passing. In Nashville, former president Jackson acridly gave thanks that a "kind and overruling providence has interfered to prolong our glorious Union and happy republican system which Genl. Harrison and his cabinet was preparing to destroy under the dictation of the profligate demagogue, Henry Clay. . . . *The Lord ruleth, let our nation rejoice.*"

In Washington, House clerk French wistfully noted, "One little month has passed away[;] . . . he for whom millions rent the air with shouts . . . whom thousands listened to with eager upturned faces, is but as a clod of the valley. What the political effect of this National bereavement is to be upon the country time, alone, will show. I can only predict, and I do predict that it will be the cause of a tremendous political excitement, . . . that it will render certain the triumph of Democracy in the next election." He was a good prophet. The presidency of John Tyler—whose Whig credentials were always suspect—would prove one of the most tumultuous in the history of the United States. The entire cabinet, except for Secretary of State Daniel Webster, would resign when Tyler vetoed Congress's proposal for a national bank. His efforts to bring the Republic of Texas into the union as a state would rend American politics. In 1844 James K. Polk of Tennessee reclaimed the presidency for the Democrats from the Whigs.

William Henry Harrison's brief administration left little mark on the history of the presidency. At sixty-eight he was the oldest man to ever hold the presidency (a record he held until the election of Ronald Reagan) and he was the first president to die in office. Because he served such a short time, he is generally omitted from consideration when presidential ranking polls are taken. Whether he would have been an effective president is not certain, but there is no doubt that he had a great impact on the history of the young republic between the time he enlisted as a young ensign in the U.S. army during the Washington administration and the time he took office in his own right as the ninth president of the United States.

Further Reading

The best biography of the ninth president is Dorothy B. Goebel's *William Henry Harrison: A Political Biography* (Indianapolis: Historical Bureau of the Indiana Library and Historical Department, 1926), which is well researched and balanced. Freeman Cleaves, *Old Tippecanoe: William Henry Harrison and His Time* (New York: Charles Scribner's Sons, 1939), is favorable toward Harrison. James A. Green, *William Henry Harrison: His Life and Times* (Richmond, Va.: Garret and Massie, 1941), is a laudatory study by an open admirer of the Hero of Tippecanoe. Reginald Horsman, "William Henry Harrison: Virginia Gentleman in the Old Northwest," *Indiana Magazine of History* 96 (June 2000), is an excellent historiographical examination of Harrison's background and career.

Harrison's administration of the Indiana Territory is covered extensively in John D. Barnhart and Dorothy L. Riker, *Indiana to 1816: The Colonial Period* (Indianapolis: Indiana Historical Bureau and Indiana Historical Society, 1971).

For additional information about Tecumseh and the Prophet, see R. David Edmunds, *The Shawnee Prophet* (Lincoln: Univ. of Nebraska Press, 1983), and *Tecumseh and the Quest for Indian Leadership* (Boston: Little, Brown, 1984). Edmunds argues that Tecumseh has remained an important figure in American history and legend because whites have romanticized his life, although the Prophet's personal qualities were not appealing. John Sugden's *Tecumseh: A Life* (New York: Henry Holt, 1997) is an excellent sympathetic account of the Shawnee warrior.

A good, brief discussion of Harrison's tenure as minister to Colombia is Randall O. Hudson's "American Diplomacy in Action: William Henry

Harrison in Colombia," *Wichita State University Bulletin* 49 (August 1973): 2–16. Hudson concludes that Harrison had few qualifications for the post he held, other than political influence and that he was "interfering, demanding, unconscious of, or unconcerned with, local customs or manners."

The classic study of the presidential campaign of 1840 is Robert G. Gunderson, *The Log-Cabin Campaign* (Lexington: Univ. of Kentucky Press, 1957). A brief account is Kenneth R. Stevens, "The Triumph of Old Tip: William Henry Harrison and the Election of 1840," *Traces of Indiana and Midwestern History* 2 (fall 1990): 14–21. Readers who wish more information about archival sources and historical writing about Harrison should consult Kenneth R. Stevens, *William Henry Harrison: A Bibliography* (Westport, Conn.: Greenwood Press, 1998).

PART II

Sectional Conflict, War, and Peace

The National Story

At the time of William Henry Harrison's death in 1841, the western frontier of the United States had reached the Missouri and Arkansas Rivers on the eastern edge of the Great Plains. By that time reports from the far West had already spread eastward about the abundance of fertile, almost empty lands beyond the Rocky Mountains and the Sierra Nevada. During the 1840s thousands of people ventured across the Great Plains, through American Indian lands, and settled in the Oregon country, California, and other western areas. These new residents, not wishing to live under British or Mexican rule, began to call for the United States to annex the western areas, with military force if necessary, and an increasingly large following in the United States supported them.

Territorial expansion became the major issue in the presidential election of 1844. James K. Polk of Tennessee, the Democratic party's candidate, ran as an outspoken expansionist and a vigorous proponent of American manifest destiny. His victory over the Whig candidate, Henry Clay, made rapid territorial expansion inevitable. Almost immediately the United States demanded the entire Oregon country from Britain and threatened war. The British, not eager to fight a war over a wilderness so far from home, offered a compromise. Great Britain and the United States agreed to divide the Oregon country at the forty-ninth parallel of latitude. The British retained that portion north of the compromise line, now part of western Canada; Americans acquired sole right to the territory south of it, down to the northern border of California.

The United States annexed the Republic of Texas in March 1845, making it the twenty-eighth state of the Union. In the spring of 1846, escalating American-Mexican tension over the exact southwestern border of Texas erupted in war. Troops of the United States put the capstone on more than a year of successful, sometimes brilliant campaigning when Mexico City fell to them in the autumn of 1847. The Treaty of Guadalupe Hidalgo in 1848 ended the conflict and required the Mexican government to sell the United States the entire area from New Mexico to California. The treaty added 1.2 million square miles of land to the area of the United

States, with this the country's east-west boundaries extended from the Atlantic to the Pacific Ocean.

The fruits of the Mexican War proved exceedingly bittersweet. Certainly the foremost consequence was that it overheated sectional animosity by raising an enormously divisive question: Should Congress open these lands to slavery or ban them from it? Events in newly acquired California soon compelled the U.S. government to provide an answer for this daunting question.

Non-Indians sparsely settled California under Mexican control, whereas a substantial indigenous population, numbering approximately 100,000, lived there. One of the non-Indian settlers was John A. Sutter, an immigrant from Switzerland who reached California in 1839 and developed a large ranch near Sacramento. In 1847 Sutter hired some workers to build a sawmill. The following January James Marshall, the crew's supervisor, and some of his Indian workers spotted some gold in the river that powered the mill. As the news spread locally, gold hunters from San Francisco swarmed the area. When news of the discovery reached the East Coast, an avalanche of gold-hungry individuals headed for California in 1849 to strike it rich.

The Forty-Niners changed California overnight. Mining camps blanketed the area, where fortunes made in a day of gold-hunting were lost in a single night of gambling. Lawlessness and violence became all too common. White miners not only murdered each other, they turned California into a killing field, indiscriminately hunting down Indian men, women, and children to eliminate potential competition for riches. Over the next decade, California's native population plummeted to approximately 30,000 persons.

In the fall of 1849 California wrote a state constitution and applied to the U.S. Congress for statehood, bringing the controversy over the expansion of slavery to a head. If California was admitted as a free state, as it requested, this would upset parity—the numerical balance of free and slave states in the Union. It might also set a precedent of slavery's exclusion from the rest of the territory won in the Mexican War.

Soon thereafter Congress begun debating the questions of California statehood and the extension of slavery into the remaining territory acquired from Mexico. It was not long before tempers rose to dangerous levels, causing furious debates that sometimes ended in fistfights between the statesmen. It could have turned far uglier, had Senator Henry Foote of Mississippi fired the revolver he pulled against a colleague on the Senate floor on April 17, 1850. Trying to avert a national catastrophe, Senator

Henry Clay made an eloquent plea for civility and concessions. He offered to his Northern and Southern colleagues a package of compromises, later known as the Compromise of 1850. Under the most important terms of the package, California would be admitted as a free state. The question of slavery in the rest of the Mexican War territory would be decided by the Democratic party's doctrine of popular sovereignty, that is, by the settlers who lived there.

Gen. Zachary Taylor, one of the American military heroes from the recent war with Mexico, in 1848 became the second and last member of the Whig party to be elected president. Taylor had spent his entire adult life in the U.S. Army. Although a Southerner and a slaveholder, he was an impassioned nationalist who countenanced nothing that might threaten his beloved Union. Taylor, after he took office, opposed all of the terms of the compromise package except for California's entry as a free state. He declared that he would veto the rest of it. But before Taylor could act, he died suddenly on July 9, 1850. His vice president, the new chief executive, Millard Fillmore, supported the whole package. It became law in September without presidential opposition. Most members of Congress were convinced, or at least prayed, that the compromise would settle forever the most important issues dividing the North and the South.

Friction between the two sections of the country, dormant for a few years, reappeared and escalated during the second half of the 1850s. One event built on another as the decade passed, straining sectional antagonism to the breaking point. The Kansas-Nebraska Act; the Dred Scott decision by the U.S. Supreme Court; antislavery books such as *Uncle Tom's Cabin;* John Brown's raid on the arsenal at Harpers Ferry, Virginia, which intended to incite a huge slave insurrection in the South—all divided the country further along sectional lines. Then came the presidential election of 1860 and a crisis that lengthened into the American Civil War. Abraham Lincoln's victory and the ascendancy to power of the Republicans, a purely Northern party dedicated to preventing the extension of slavery, posed a threat too great to many Southerners. Quickly, South Carolina carried out its long-standing threat to secede. Before Lincoln took office in March 1861, a half dozen more states of the Deep South dissolved their ties with the federal union. At Montgomery, the state capital of Alabama, these seven states quickly established a Southern nation, the Confederate States of America.

Fighting broke out in April 1861 when Confederate forces attacked and forced the surrender of Fort Sumter, a federal installation guarding the harbor of Charleston, South Carolina. Lincoln declared the Deep South to be in a state of rebellion and immediately issued a call for 75,000 army volunteers to crush it. Four states of the Upper South, seeing Lincoln's call as an act of war, also seceded from the United States and joined the Confederacy. War fever swept across both the North and South when people heard the news of Fort Sumter. People cheered. Bands played. Flags waved. Men quickly rushed to join the army so they would not miss the war. In Ohio 30,000 men volunteered for military service within days of the fall of Sumter. By war's end the Ohio adjutant general calculated that more than 346,000 men had served in the armed forces of the United States. A number of Ohio-born men played roles as commanding officers in the conflict: among them Generals Ulysses "Sam" Grant, William Tecumseh Sherman, Don Carlos Buell, James A. Garfield, Benjamin Harrison, Rutherford B. Hayes, Irvin McDowell, James B. McPherson, and William Rosecrans.

Northerners and Southerners alike expected the war would be but a few glorious battles with minimum casualties; people repeatedly fixed estimates of its probable duration at sixty days. In a short time, however, as Americans grimly battled Americans, terrible reality settled over the land like a pall. Americans made war upon each other from 1861 to 1865. When the guns at last fell silent, one substantial area of the country lay in ruins, one group of Americans had been absolutely defeated in war, and some 620,000 Americans — 2 percent of the country's population — rested prematurely in their graves.

The combination of military, political, social, psychological, cultural, familial, sectional, economic, industrial, demographic, constitutional, and racial consequences wrought by the Civil War made it a pivotal event in the national experience. In its aftermath, the U.S. government faced two monumental problems: reunification and emancipation. What must Southerners and the eleven former Confederate States do to reestablish their relationship with the United States? The government also had to figure out what the status of black people would be in white postwar America. The 1865 Thirteenth Amendment to the Constitution ended slavery forever in the United States, giving human dignity to some four million people who before that amendment had been chattel. Emancipation, by its radical nature, raised a number of serious questions. Was emancipation an end in itself, or were more rights needed or warranted? Were the former slaves to be made citizens of the United States? Would they be required to serve a probationary period, like newly arrived immigrants pouring into the United States? How would the former slaves earn a living in a ravaged South? In other words, what did freedom really mean?

While the United States wrestled with these two huge issues, it simultaneously had to confront a dangerous problem out west. The relentless westward push of humanity and enterprise that followed the Civil War rolled across the remaining Indian land like a tidal wave, with Americans clamoring for more and more of the republic's heartland. That region seethed with activity. Ranchers moved in with growing herds of longhorns, launching great cattle empires. Pioneer families, lured by the Homestead Act of 1862, arrived to establish farms on the sod of the prairies. Miners continued to scour western rivers and mountains for a fleck of gold or silver that might open the door to fortune. Construction crews pushed to extend rail lines further onto the western plains and to finish a transcontinental railroad. The settlement of the trans-Mississippi West in the years 1865 to 1900 marked the largest migration of people in the history of the United States. Americans settled more land in those years than in any period of their history. For western Indians, however, the claiming of the "last frontier" by Americans became an episode of apocalyptic proportion.

Faced with unyielding pressure to support and defend Americans, their interests, and their aspirations, the U.S. government applied a new solution to the Indian Question: Concentration. This policy called for the drastic reduction of Indian landholding in the West and the compulsory relocation of tribes to federal reservations where permanent residency, under strict governmental, judicial, and cultural control, would be enforced. Indian resistance to the policy of Concentration, and Washington's commitment to it, resulted in the titanic struggle of the 1860s and 1870s known as the Plains Wars. When it ended with the subjugation and concentration of western tribes, their way of life passed into darkness.

As the territorial frontier was disappearing from the American West, another change was taking place in the United States: the growth of big business and the maturation of the American Industrial Revolution. Before the Civil War, Americans had been largely a nation of farmers. Now the republic strove to become one of the world's leading industrial powers.

The United States was particularly fortunate to have everything it needed to become an industrial giant in the post–Civil War period. The nation had an abundance of natural resources such as coal, iron, and oil. Great sums of money, often amassed during the Civil War, were available for speculation, investment, and development. Industry formulated the means for mass production through new methods of manufacture. It enjoyed a federal government that did not interfere in the affairs of private business, yet that also safeguarded American commerce from foreign competition by protective tariff legislation. Industry also could draw upon a large supply of workers: Americans who had given up farming and moved to cities to live and work and others who came from overseas to forge new lives in America. The growth of American industry depended as well on the talents and hard work of business leaders who organized and managed the burgeoning industries, people such as Gustavus Swift and Philip Armour in meat packing, Andrew Carnegie in steel, and John D. Rockefeller in oil.

Ideas and inventions flourished in this stimulating and transforming environment. They significantly changed the way Americans lived and worked. Alexander Graham Bell developed the telegraph and telephone. Melville Bissell invented the carpet sweeper. Christopher Sholes aided businesses with the typewriter, as did James Ritty with his contribution of the cash register and William Burroughs with a new adding machine. Transportation on railroad trains became safer after George Westinghouse introduced his air brake. And Thomas Edison, with more than a thousand patents, could invent nearly anything—from electric lighting to the phonograph.

Ulysses S. Grant

Eighteenth President of the United States, 1869–1877

BROOKS D. SIMPSON

In spring 1877 Ulysses S. Grant, fresh from two terms as president of the United States, paid a visit to Georgetown, Ohio. What he found was not all that different from the hamlet he had left in 1839 to attend the U.S. Military Academy at West Point, New York. His old house was still standing; there, across the street from his old bedroom window, was the tannery his father ran that had so repulsed him as a boy. If he looked up the street, he could still see Dr. Bailey's home: it had been Bart Bailey's inability to survive at West Point that had opened up a slot for young Ulysses. He met old friends and listened to their stories; away in the town cemetery, not too far from the old schoolhouse where Grant had gone to school, lay Thomas Hamer, the congressman who had appointed him and who later predicted great things of the young officer serving in the Mexican-American War. Yet the visit left Grant restless. The town and the people were not what they once were, and of course neither was U. S. Grant. "The change I saw in them was so great," he informed Hamilton Fish, who had served for eight long years as Grant's secretary of state, "that I had no desire to tarry." It was time to move on again.

Although Grant was the first Ohio-born president, few people actually thought of him as a native of the state. Ohio's governor failed to give him command of one of its regiments at the outset of the American Civil War in 1861; when Republicans nominated him for president in 1868, it was as

Ulysses S. Grant of Illinois; when he died in 1885, it was New York City that provided his resting place. And yet at various times throughout his life, people and events in Ohio played important roles in shaping his course. He would find several of his most loyal lieutenants in the Civil War from Ohio, including William T. Sherman, James B. McPherson, and Philip H. Sheridan (although Sheridan's place of birth remains a subject of discussion). As he rose to prominence in the Civil War, he survived the slings and arrows of the Cincinnati press (as well as the efforts of his father to defend his eldest son in print). In 1867 the state elections in Ohio dealt Radical Republicans a setback, easing the way for Grant's nomination for the presidency in 1868; four years later dissident Republicans launched the ill-fated Liberal Republican movement by meeting in Cincinnati. In 1875, the pleas of Ohio Republicans anxious about the party's prospects in the closely contested state election helped persuade President Grant to turn down the request of Mississippi's Republican governor for federal forces to intervene to stop political terrorism. Rutherford B. Hayes's subsequent victory in the gubernatorial race that year positioned him to win the Republican presidential nomination in 1876, and four years later another Ohioan, James A. Garfield, defeated Grant's bid for a third term in the White House.

Born April 27, 1822, in the sleepy hamlet of Point Pleasant, Ohio, within sight of the broad Ohio River and less than two dozen miles upriver from Cincinnati, Hiram Ulysses Grant (it appears that the Hiram soon faded from use) was the firstborn of Jesse Root and Hannah Simpson Grant. Eventually Ulysses would be joined by five siblings, two boys and three girls. Jesse Grant was a man on the make in the early nineteenth century, who sought to make his fortune as a tanner. In pursuit of that goal he relocated his family to Georgetown, the county seat of Brown County. During the next several decades the irrepressible Jesse became a leading Whig in the community, shedding his earlier allegiance to the Democrat Andrew Jackson, and even won a term as mayor. Moreover, he loved to boast about his eldest son, and soon townspeople who had tired of hearing of "my Ulysses" looked for ways to get back at the father through ridiculing the boy. Young Grant did his chores, went to school (where he showed some talent in mathematics), took on odd jobs, and developed quite a reputation as a horseman who put his skills to good use in hauling property and passengers around southwest Ohio. However, he had no intention of following his father into the tanning business; he found revolting the sight of blood and the stench of the hides.

The region of Ohio where Grant grew up developed quickly, propelled in part by the growth of Cincinnati. His father's enterprising nature took advantage of these opportunities, and in time the tannery business expanded into the founding of a general store located in Galena, Illinois. If the Ohio River helped shape the commercial activity of the region, it also served as a line marking the boundary between slavery in the lands south of it and freedom in the states above it. Jesse Grant was an outspoken opponent of slavery, and in sending his eldest son to Ripley to go to school, he was entrusting him to the Reverend John Rankin, another impassioned opponent of slavery and a prime operative on the Underground Railroad. The school's location was not far from the place later made famous by Harriet Beecher Stowe in her bestseller *Uncle Tom's Cabin* as the location where Eliza made her way across the icy Ohio to freedom.

Ever aware of the worth of a dollar, Jesse decided that his boy needed to get a good education, first at a series of local boarding schools, including Ripley, and then as a cadet at the U.S. Military Academy. That took some doing: Jesse had learned that another local boy, Bart Bailey, had failed to make the grade at the academy, and he scrambled to secure the slot for his son. However, when Senator Thomas Morris said that he had no appointments to bestow, Jesse found himself forced to apply to Congressman Thomas L. Hamer, who had fallen out with Jesse over political matters several years before. Whatever Hamer made of Jesse's request, he held nothing against Ulysses, and so he had no problem filling out the nomination papers, although he did so hastily, as it was his last day as a congressman. And so, in May 1839, Grant made his way east to West Point, New York. Almost immediately government red tape and a bureaucratic mistake gave him the opportunity to evade his destiny. He had always been known as Ulysses; just prior to his departure he had decided to transpose his first and middle names—Hiram and Ulysses—to avoid having people laugh at the initials HUG. However, Congressman Hamer, unaware of the young man's given name and pressed for a middle initial, had hurriedly inserted an "S" after Hannah Grant's maiden name in making out the nomination papers. Grant quietly accepted the change, although for years to come he would profess he had no idea what the "S" represented.

During his four years at West Point, Grant demonstrated anew his great skill in mathematics and as a horseman. In most of his other academic endeavors he was solid but not superb, and in foreign languages he was simply dismal. Moreover, his occasional lack of interest in matters of deportment and dress led to him earning sufficient demerits to lower his class rank. Still, of the thirty-nine cadets who survived the rigorous four years (barely more than half of the entering class), Grant stood twenty-first. The new lieutenant applied for assignment to the mounted dragoons; instead he found himself assigned to the infantry and posted to Jefferson Barracks, just south of St. Louis, Missouri. In all, it was not a bad assignment, as the installation was a short ride from the plantation of his roommate, Fred Dent. Grant's visits to the plantation increased in frequency after he met Fred's sister Julia, and within a relatively short time the two fell in love, much to the chagrin of Julia's father, a crusty old slaveholder with the honorific title of colonel. It was only when Grant learned that his regiment was about to be transferred to Texas, however, that the lieutenant fully realized where his heart lay. Securing an extended leave, he rushed to the Dent plantation and proposed to Julia. It would be another four years before the couple would be married.

Grant rejoined his regiment in Louisiana and then accompanied it to Texas, where it formed part of Gen. Zachary Taylor's expeditionary force, assigned to the duty of protecting American interests along the disputed Texas–Mexico border. Inevitably this force brushed up against its Mexican counterpart, and at the end of April 1846 one nasty clash led to the initiation of full-scale hostilities between the United States and Mexico. In later years Grant would protest that the Mexican War was immoral, but such observations are absent from his contemporary correspondence. More than anything, he was frustrated to be separated from Julia during the conflict. He saw action at Palo Alto and Resaca de la Palma as Taylor's forces secured northern Mexico. Grant next distinguished himself at Monterrey, when, clinging to the side of his horse, he dashed down the city streets to hurry ammunition to the front. He also befriended Tom Hamer, the congressman to whom he owed his nomination to West Point, who now arrived in Mexico as a brigadier general of volunteers. Hamer thought highly of the young officer from Ohio and promised him a position on his staff. That idea came to a sudden end, however, when Hamer fell victim to dysentery and died. Weeks later Grant's regiment was reassigned to the command of Gen. Winfield Scott, who planned to land a force at the port of Vera Cruz on the Gulf of Mexico, and from there to march westward to the capital, Mexico City. Grant found his skills as a quartermaster and commissary officer taxed to the utmost, but he responded ably, gathering supplies and food as Scott's columns advanced. Once more he came under fire, scrambling over the walls at El Molino del Rey, then helping to crack the enemy position at San Cosme when he directed the placement of a howitzer in a church belfry. The next day Mexico City fell to U.S. forces.

Grant's combat experience during the Mexican-American War was rendered all the more unusual given that during most of the conflict he served as his regiment's quartermaster and commissary officer. The training he received in those positions proved invaluable when it came to managing the needs of a much larger force. Yet, as fellow officer James Longstreet observed, "You could not keep Grant out of battle." His coolness, courage, and ingenuity under fire were remarkable. Grant took the measure of his fellow officers, noting characteristics and traits that would later inform his assessment of their skills during the Civil War. He also spent time observing the style and strategy practiced by Generals Taylor and Scott and found much to admire in both. In later years officers speculated that Grant modeled his approach to informality in uniform upon the example set by Taylor, whereas the Vicksburg campaign of 1863 resembled Scott's ambitious plan to take Mexico City.

Once hostilities with Mexico ceased, Grant hurried to St. Louis in 1848 and married Julia on August 22. The Grants then embarked upon the life of a peacetime army officer and spouse, shuttling between posts in upstate New York and Detroit, Michigan, before Ulysses received orders in 1852 to accompany his regiment across the Panamanian isthmus to assignment on the Pacific coast of the United States. Already the mother of one son, Julia was pregnant with a second child, so Grant advised her to return to St. Louis rather than risk the perils of the journey. In light of the heavy mortality rate that the column suffered, this was a wise decision; for the rest of his life Grant remembered but rarely spoke of the horrors of crossing the isthmus, and his experience led him to advocate the digging of an interoceanic canal in the region. For nearly two years Grant went from post to post in the Far West, missing Julia and his two sons, growing ever more depressed and bored, battling ill health and irritating superiors, and at last seeking solace in alcohol before deciding to resign from the army in 1854.

Returning to his wife and sons in St. Louis, Grant struggled in civilian life, first as a farmer, then as a real estate agent, and finally as a minor civil servant. Ill health and bad luck dogged his efforts to make a living. Neighbors complained that he was too easy with the Dent slaves and hired hands who helped him out. In 1859 Grant went so far as to free William Jones, the one slave he had obtained from the Dents, at a time when the money Jones would have brought at the auction block would have been advantageous for the financially hard-pressed Grant family. Finally, Jesse

Grant came to his eldest son's rescue, offering him a position at his general store in Galena, Illinois, alongside his younger brothers. Desperate, Grant accepted the offer with pain, and in 1860 the family, now six strong, with sons Fred, Ulysses Jr., Jesse, and daughter Ellen, moved to Illinois. A year later the Civil War broke out and the Grants' lives would change dramatically.

Ulysses S. Grant was the only man in Galena with professional army training. With the nation at war, his neighbor John Rawlins noted a change in the old captain: "I saw new energies in Grant. . . . He dropped a stoop shouldered way of walking, and set his hat forward on his forehead in a careless fashion." Believing himself qualified by experience for command of a volunteer regiment, Grant nevertheless found it difficult to secure a position, and at first he had to rest content with serving in the state adjutant's office in Springfield and as a mustering officer for Illinois's new recruits. He sought opportunities whenever he could find them, at one point journeying to Cincinnati in an unsuccessful attempt to secure a position under Maj. Gen. George B. McClellan, whom Grant during his final year at West Point had known as a plebe.

Fortune finally smiled upon him when Illinois governor Richard Yates, aware that the officers and men of the 21st Illinois Infantry despised their commanding officer, decided that Grant was an ideal candidate to restore order in the rowdy regiment. Within weeks of receiving his commission the new colonel whipped his recruits into shape and led them across the Mississippi into Missouri, a border slave state that President Lincoln was determined to deny the Confederacy. Later he wrote Julia that her home state contained "great fools . . . [who] will never rest until they bring upon themselves all the horrors of war in its worst form." No sooner had the 21st Illinois Infantry arrived than orders came to oust a group of Confederate raiders under the command of Col. Thomas Harris encamped at Florida, some twenty-five miles away. As his command approached Harris's position, Grant later recalled, "My heart kept getting higher and higher until it felt to me as though it was in my throat. I would have given anything then to have been back in Illinois, but I had not the moral courage to halt and consider what to do: I kept right on." However, when he went forward to observe the enemy camp he discovered that it was abandoned. "My heart resumed its place," he continued. "It occurred to me at once that Harris had been as much afraid of me as I had been of him. This was a view of the question I had never taken before; but it was one I never forgot afterwards. From that event to the close of the war, I never experienced trepidation upon confronting an enemy, though I always felt more or less anxiety. I never forgot that he had as much reason to fear my forces as I had his. The lesson was valuable."

Elevated to brigadier general of volunteers in the summer of 1861—the result of Congressman Elihu Washburne's alert intervention on behalf of an able constituent who also was from Galena—Grant was ordered to Cape Girardeau on September 1. The next day he crossed the Mississippi and took command at Cairo, Illinois, at the confluence of the Mississippi and Ohio Rivers. It was not long before he made his influence felt. On September 6, responding to reports that the Confederates had invaded neutral Kentucky, Grant seized Paducah, at the mouth of the Tennessee and Cumberland Rivers, an excellent point from which to launch an offensive into Confederate Tennessee. Two months later he led a force down the Mississippi and surprised a Confederate encampment at Belmont, Missouri, across the river from the main Confederate defensive position at Columbus, Kentucky. Although eventually the Confederates drove Grant's men back to their transports, the general received credit for his aggressiveness and coolness under fire. But it was not until February 1862 that he got his big chance, when he targeted a brace of Confederate forts just south of the Kentucky–Tennessee border. Fort Henry, on the east bank of the Tennessee River, fell to Flag Officer Andrew H. Foote's gunboats on February 6. Grant then focused his attention on Fort Donelson, a day's march away along the west bank of the Cumberland River, where Gen. Albert Sidney Johnston had posted some 17,000 men. This time the Confederates put up a better fight, driving away Foote's gunboats and actually launching an attack designed to allow the garrison to escape Grant's efforts to lay siege. Grant rallied his forces, counterattacked, and by the evening of February 15 not only had restored his lines but also placed Donelson's defenders in peril. That evening, Gen. Simon B. Buckner, having just inherited command from his two superiors who had fled, contacted his prewar friend Grant to inquire about terms of surrender. "No terms to the damned Rebels!" barked a division commander, Charles F. Smith, who had been commandant of cadets when Grant was at West Point; Grant refined the advice to read bluntly: "No terms except unconditional and immediate surrender will be accepted. I propose to move immediately upon your word." An unhappy Buckner accepted the demand and on February 16 surrendered Donelson, along with some 12,000 men. The capitulation was the largest ever on the North American continent to that time.

Donelson made Grant a national hero. Manipulating his malleable initials, Northerners cheered "Unconditional Surrender" Grant; reading newspaper accounts of how he had directed his men into action with a cigar in his hand, they showered him with countless boxes of cigars, leaving the ever-pragmatic Grant (heretofore a pipe smoker by preference) to decide to diminish the stock by smoking them. However, Grant's fame proved short-lived. His superior officer, Henry W. Halleck, jealous at the praise lavished on his subordinate, had long sought to replace him. Seizing upon the nonreceipt of daily reports from Grant, Halleck called upon the new hero to stay behind while his army advanced southward along the Tennessee River, toward the state of Mississippi. He then chastised Grant's administrative abilities while hinting to others, including commanding general George McClellan, that Grant had "resumed his old habits" — referring to Grant's liquor consumption. Grant protested and asked to be relieved rather than accept such a demotion. Halleck relented when President Lincoln directed Halleck to make his case against the conqueror of Donelson or drop it altogether.

Grant rejoined his command, now known as the Army of the Tennessee, at Pittsburgh Landing, a few miles north of the Tennessee–Mississippi border. His orders were to wait in place until the Army of the Ohio, led by Don Carlos Buell, joined him; then, under Halleck's direction, the combined armies would advance against Corinth, Mississippi, a critical rail junction twenty miles to the southwest. However, the Confederate commander, Albert Sidney Johnston, had a different idea. Still smarting from his setbacks in Tennessee, Johnston gathered his forces at Corinth with the intention of striking at Grant before Buell arrived. Although the noisy Confederates bumbled their way northward, they caught Grant and his men off guard on April 6 in a massive attack that drove the Yankees back through their camps, including one posted around Shiloh Church, and toward the steamboat landing. Grant rallied his forces, directed reinforcements to the scene, and conducted a vigorous defense all day, giving ground grudgingly and at great cost. By the end of the day Grant's men had been forced back to the area around the landing, but the battered and bruised Confederates, having lost Johnston, who bled to death from a wound in the leg, decided to pause for the day. That night, as reinforcements arrived in the driving rain, Grant sought shelter under a tree near the landing from both the weather and the screams of the wounded and dying. When division commander William T. Sherman, wounded several times in the fighting, remarked on the tough going that day, Grant agreed, puffed on his cigar, and added: "Lick 'em tomorrow, though." He was as good as his word, and by day's end on April 7 the Confederates withdrew in the face of a Union counterattack orchestrated by Grant with support from Buell. Grant had turned back the Confederacy's last major bid to regain control of West Tennessee and break the momentum of the Federal offensive.

The Battle of Shiloh proved a tough ordeal for Grant. Although he had been cool and calm under pressure, his overconfidence blinded him to the possibility of a Confederate attack. The result was the bloodiest battle in United States history to date. In two days of combat, the Federals had some 13,000 men killed, wounded, and missing, the majority from Grant's command; Confederate losses exceeded 10,000. Sherman, in charge of security, had minimized reports of Confederate activity prior to the battle, even reassuring Grant that there was no danger of an enemy offensive. Instead of pointing a finger at Sherman, however, Grant praised his performance on the battlefield and drew closer to the trusted lieutenant—who had friends in high places, including his father-in-law, the elder Ohio political statesman Thomas Ewing Sr. and his brother, U.S. Senator John Sherman. These connections were particularly valuable because of the heavy criticism now directed Grant's way by the press, especially in Cincinnati. Was Grant surprised by the Confederate attack at Shiloh? Had he been intoxicated? Jesse rushed to defend his son in print, which further escalated the controversy. Although Halleck absolved Grant of responsibility to his superiors, in reshuffling his command structure he placed Grant in the awkward position of second-in-command, minimizing Grant's responsibilities and input to the point that after the fall of Corinth at the end of May 1862, Grant sought a transfer elsewhere. Fortunately for Grant, Lincoln called Halleck to Washington to serve as general in chief, leaving Grant in command of Federal forces in West Tennessee. He pondered his options as he looked to strike deep into the Confederate heartland to deprive the enemy of the resources and morale needed to wage war. He decided on Vicksburg, Mississippi, a heavily fortified Confederate stronghold controlling the middle stretch of the Mississippi River. Its capture would be a major blow to Southern prospects for victory and would help isolate Confederates west of the river. After turning back a Confederate effort to retake Corinth in October 1862, Grant commenced planning to take the city.

Capturing Vicksburg would prove a daunting challenge, and not simply because of the rugged and difficult terrain or the Confederate defenders. One of Grant's subordinates, the political general John A. McClernand of Illinois, was angling for an independent command to lead a downriver expedition from Memphis to Vicksburg. Relying upon his connections with Lincoln and his political value to the Republican president as a War Democrat, McClernand succeeded in securing somewhat ambiguous and carefully worded orders to raise a force to do just that—provided Grant judged that he could spare the men to do it. Although Lincoln did not make Grant privy to the plan, Halleck, distrusting McClernand, began urging Grant to move ahead with whatever force he could lay his hands on. In turn Grant, suspicious of McClernand, decided to advance before McClernand arrived at the front. The result was a premature offensive two-pronged strike in December 1862. However, when Confederate cavalry raids severed Grant's supply lines, he was forced to abandon his overland advance, allowing the Confederates to concentrate on driving off Sherman's water-borne force north of Vicksburg at month's end. Finally on the scene, McClernand first moved his makeshift force along the Arkansas River to capture a Confederate post, then remained west of the Mississippi. At the end of January, Grant took charge of the operation against Vicksburg, relegating McClernand to corps command.

Throughout early 1863 Grant struggled to find a way to use the rivers, swamps, and bayous around Vicksburg to his advantage. However, efforts to divert river channels through canals for his troop transports and gunboats or to open up passages through the morass north of the city utterly failed. Meanwhile, the general's problems mounted. Grant's critics had a field day as public faultfinding grew; rumors of incompetence and intoxication circulated; McClernand connived to secure his superior's removal in order to replace him. Through it all, Grant never lost confidence that he would take Vicksburg.

With the advent of spring, the roads dried and Grant and Adm. David Porter worked together to frame a plan whereby Porter's gunboats and transports would run the gauntlet of Vicksburg's batteries under cover of darkness and journey southward down the Mississippi to meet Grant's columns and ferry them across the river. Once safely on its east bank, Grant planned to unite with Nathaniel Banks's troops and together take out both Vicksburg and Port Hudson, Louisiana. Porter's flotilla ran past the batteries on April 16, suffering only minor damage. Some two weeks later, after declining to force a crossing at well-fortified Grand Gulf, Grant ferried his men across the Mississippi further to the south at Bruinsburg and pressed inland into Mississippi, defeating a Confederate force at Port Gibson on May 1 and entering Grand Gulf two days later.

At Grand Gulf Grant welcomed the chance to bathe, change into a fresh uniform, and eat a warm meal; to this point in the campaign his personal baggage had consisted of a single toothbrush. When he learned that Banks would not be prepared to join forces with him for several more weeks, Grant demonstrated the talent for inspired improvisation that was a hallmark of his military skill. He decided to move eastward into Mississippi, looking to isolate Vicksburg; his men would live off the land, with wagon convoys providing other needed supplies and munitions. He would also have to move quickly, for already a Confederate force was forming in central Mississippi under the command of Joseph E. Johnston to assist the defenders of Vicksburg. A week later Grant's army was again on the move, turning back a Confederate force at Raymond (May 12) before entering the state capital at Jackson (May 14). Now positioned between two Confederate forces that united would have outnumbered him, Grant turned westward to confront Vicksburg's defenders, commanded by John C. Pemberton, who now moved out to contest the Union advance. At Champion Hill (May 16) and at Big Black River Bridge (May 17), Grant broke Pemberton's line in pitched battles, forcing the Confederates to take refuge in Vicksburg's fortifications. The Federals pursued, but two assaults (May 19 and 22) failed to dislodge the defenders, and Grant settled down to lay siege to the city while fending off the half-hearted efforts of Johnston to relieve the garrison. Through June, Federal artillery and gunboats shelled the town. Finally on July 3, Pemberton agreed to surrender the city and his army of approximately 30,000 starving men the following day. On July 4, 1863, Grant entered Vicksburg. The United States now controlled the entire Mississippi River.

The Vicksburg campaign showed Grant at his finest. He prepared well, moved quickly, and struck hard, taking advantage of opportunities as they appeared and altering plans to fit circumstances. In the eyes of Lincoln, gracious enough to admit that he had erred in favoring a different approach to capturing the river citadel, the victory removed all doubt about Grant's military ability. The president no longer indulged the machinations of McClernand, whom Grant had finally removed during the siege, ostensibly for violating army regulations.

After Vicksburg Grant contemplated new offensives, particularly against Mobile, Alabama, but Halleck hesitated to give his approval. In September Grant was injured in a riding accident, leaving him bedridden for several weeks. While he was recuperating, U.S. forces suffered an overwhelming defeat in northwest Georgia at Chickamauga (September 19–20). Braxton Bragg's Army of Tennessee followed up its victory by laying siege to the critical rail junction of Chattanooga, Tennessee, occupying the heights overlooking the city, expecting the Federals to either leave or starve. Lincoln called on Grant to take overall charge of military affairs between the Appalachians and the Mississippi. Grant hurried to Chattanooga, found the army on the verge of starvation, set into motion a plan to reopen supply lines, and awaited reinforcements before mounting an attack on Bragg's forces. "We began to see things move," an officer remarked of Grant's arrival. "He began the campaign the moment he reached the field." On November 23, the battle of Chattanooga opened. In a three-day clash (November 23–25), Federal forces broke the Confederate position. Grant's victorious men were "completely and frantically drunk with excitement," wrote an officer, whereas Bragg's fleeing troops dashed "wildly down the hill and into the woods, tossing away knapsacks, muskets, and blankets." Soon after, Confederates pulled back from Knoxville too. East Tennessee had been secured for the United States, and the way to assault Atlanta was open. Critics would later question how much the result was due to Grant's generalship; but in the end it was the result that counted most, and Grant received the credit.

If Vicksburg secured Grant's career, Chattanooga opened the path to supreme command of all U.S. armies. In December 1863 Congressman Elihu B. Washburne of Illinois, who had long served as Grant's political spokesman, introduced a bill reestablishing the rank of lieutenant general; implicit was the notion that the rank would go to Grant, a point made explicit in a short-lived amendment. At first President Lincoln appeared less than enthusiastic about the bill. Initially he had thought that Grant should remain where he was in the west and continue the job he had been doing. Lincoln was also concerned about a possible Grant presidential candidacy in 1864, a theme sounded by several disparate groups, including some Democrats and *New York Herald* editor James Gordon Bennett. Grant had little patience with such talk. "I am not a politician, never was and hope never to be," he informed a former congressman; to become president was "the last thing in the world I desire. I would regard such a consummation as being highly unfortunate for myself if not for the country." When Lincoln learned of such sentiments, he supported the bill, assuring everyone that he would name Grant to the new rank. Traveling to Washington, Grant accepted his commission as lieutenant general on March 9, 1864, becoming the first officer to hold that full rank since George Washington. The next day Lincoln formally named him general in chief.

What had brought Grant to this place? What had made him successful? No one was quite sure, and some attributed it to mere luck. Certainly he did not look the part of a successful general, although that conclusion revealed more about the observer than the observed. Some of that success was doubtless due to his understanding of how one made war. Simply imitating the examples of history was not enough, Grant remarked: "If men make war in slavish observance of rules, they will fail. . . . War is progressive, because all the instruments of war are progressive." Nor did he think it necessary to clutter one's thinking with a detailed knowledge of military history. "The art of war is simple enough," he later observed. "Find out where your enemy is. Get at him as soon as you can. Strike at him as hard as you can and as often as you can, and keep moving on." Sherman once told Grant that he worried about the general's lack of a formal education in military history: "But I confess your common-sense seems to have supplied all this."

That common sense so uncommon in many of Grant's peers, welcome as it might be, was not enough. There was also something almost intuitive about how he applied his conclusions; as Sherman marveled, "he knows, he *divines*, when the supreme hour has come in a campaign or battle, and always boldly seizes it." At pains to inform himself of circumstances and conditions, able to concentrate on what was important, able to improve as circumstances dictated, Grant also possessed a sense of self-confidence that allowed him to weather adversity. Sherman compared it to the faith Christians had in Christ; in a more earthy moment, he proclaimed, "I'll tell you where he beats me and where he beats the world. He don't care a damn for what the enemy does out of his sight, but it scares me like hell!" It was this combination of intelligence and character, rarely called forth in civilian life, that made Grant the general he became in the first two years of the Civil War.

Despite his protestations that he had no political ambitions, Grant had always grasped the interrelationship between military means and political ends; how one waged war depended on exactly what one wanted to achieve. He also understood the central role of slavery in the war and that the progress of Federal armies would erode the peculiar institution. At first the general was reluctant to facilitate this process, protesting that the army should be used neither to protect escaped slaves nor to assist slave owners eager to regain their property. However, in 1862 he embraced congressional initiatives and military policy in gathering black refugees and putting them to work on plantations under Federal protection. The following year Grant endorsed the government's decision to enlist blacks in the U.S. Army, observing that the freedmen "will make good soldiers and taking them from the enemy [will] weaken him in the same proportion they strengthen us." In 1864 he would need all the resources he could lay hands on to implement his strategy for crushing the Confederacy.

The general in chief's grand strategy for 1864 was simple yet compelling. He would unleash a series of simultaneous offensives designed to strike at the Confederate heartland. Sherman would advance on Atlanta from

Chattanooga, with orders to defeat the Army of Tennessee, now commanded by Joseph E. Johnston. Nathaniel Banks would dispatch forces to capture Mobile, Alabama, and then move inland into Alabama and Georgia. In Virginia, Grant would accompany George G. Meade's Army of the Potomac as it sought battle with Robert E. Lee's Army of Northern Virginia, while Franz Sigel's columns would lay waste to Confederate food resources in the Shenandoah Valley and threaten Richmond, forcing Lee to protect his capital and supply lines by either withdrawing or fighting the Army of the Potomac on unfavorable terms. There was little to suggest that Grant sought or even anticipated the prolonged slugfest of appalling attrition that would come to characterize his operations in Virginia in the spring of 1864.

Unfortunately for Grant, generals whose claim to rank rested with their political influence and not their military skill headed three of the key commands for the offensive. Banks, a veteran of Republican and Know Nothing party battles, found himself stranded in Louisiana along the Red River, allowing Confederate forces to concentrate against Sherman in the absence of a threat against Mobile. Initially Franz Sigel, whose German ancestry made him an attractive command choice to Lincoln in an election year, was in charge of the forces earmarked to drive south through the Shenandoah Valley, but an inferior Confederate force turned him back at New Market, Virginia. Finally, Benjamin F. Butler, the well-known Massachusetts Democrat-turned-Republican, headed the newly formed Army of the James with orders to approach Richmond from the east and south. However, Butler squabbled with his subordinates and moved so cautiously that the Confederate forces around Richmond were able to check his progress fairly easily, leaving Lee unencumbered to face Grant.

On May 4, 1864, Grant began his advance, and for some six weeks he and Lee battled it out in a series of brutal fights between the Rapidan and James Rivers, with Grant relentlessly retaining the initiative but finding himself unable to deliver a crushing blow to the Army of Northern Virginia. Lee brilliantly fended off his foe's offensives but could not prevent his opponent from advancing toward Richmond. In years to come, the names of the Wilderness, Spotsylvania Court House, North Anna, and especially Cold Harbor came to represent a war of grinding attrition and immense bloodshed, with nearly 100,000 Northern and Southern soldiers claimed as casualties during forty days of fierce fighting. Grant grimly chewed on his cigar and promised his superiors that he would "fight it out on this line if it took all summer." He decided to cross the James in mid-June in an effort to capture Richmond from the south through Petersburg. However, the final Federal thrust at the Southern capital fell victim

Lt. Gen. Ulysses S. Grant at his Cold Harbor, Virginia, headquarters, June 1864. National Archives, NWDNS-111-B-36.

to a combination of exhaustion, bad luck, and a skilled enemy response, so Grant decided to lay siege to Richmond and Petersburg.

The result was not exactly what Grant desired, but at least the siege had deprived Lee of the initiative; he was bottled up inside his defenses. "This army cannot stand a siege," Lee observed pessimistically. "We must end this business on the battlefield, not in a fortified position." The Confederate commander tried to shake Grant's hold by dispatching a force north through the Shenandoah to the outskirts of Washington, D.C., but this only redoubled Grant's determination to remove the Valley from the conflict. Unable to crack Lee's lines in front of Richmond and Petersburg, most notably during an ill-fated attempt to explode a mine under the enemy entrenchments on July 30, Grant turned to thinning out the Confederate forces by repeatedly aiming blows at both of its flanks, each time coming one step closer to severing Lee's contact with points south. That prevented the Confederate commander from sending reinforcements to assist in the defense of Atlanta, which Sherman finally captured on September 2. Several weeks later Philip H. Sheridan, another Grant favorite, who replaced Sigel, commenced his offensive south through the Shenandoah, defeating Jubal Early thrice in a month's time in dramatic fashion. The series of Union victories, a result of Grant's grand strategy of continuously pressing the Confederacy all along the front until something gave way, helped secure Lincoln's reelection by a healthy majority that November.

With Lincoln reelected, Grant looked to close out the Confederacy. He approved Sherman's plan to abandon Atlanta and march to the sea, his command living off the land while simultaneously gutting Georgia, although his approval came only after Sherman had explained why he could not carry out Grant's preference to take on John Bell Hood. That assignment was left to George H. Thomas, who gathered Federal forces around Nashville to fend off Hood's fall invasion of Tennessee. Although Hood's army suffered significant damage at Franklin on November 30, the Confederate commander pressed northward, and Grant grew impatient as Thomas deliberately planned to take the offensive. Indeed, Grant was intending to relieve Thomas when word came that he had decisively defeated Hood on December 15–16. At the same time Grant learned of Sherman's arrival outside of Savannah; the following month, as Sherman prepared to march northward through the Carolinas, Grant assisted the effort by ordering an amphibious assault against Fort Fisher, outside Wilmington, North Carolina, thus shutting down the Confederacy's last significant port.

As Sherman's men smashed their way through the Carolinas, Grant tightened his grip on Lee. Finally, in late March 1865 Lee sought to break the impasse with a desperate assault on Federal forces, only to be foiled with heavy losses. Quickly Grant responded by launching one last movement against Lee's supply lines; when Sheridan shattered the Rebel right at Five Forks on April 1, Lee hastily evacuated Richmond and Petersburg.

Rapidly pursuing the fleeing Confederates, Grant first prevented Lee from uniting with Confederate forces in North Carolina, then sealed off his escape route westward to the Blue Ridge Mountains at Appomattox Court House. It was over. "There is nothing left to do but go and meet General Grant," he sighed, "and I would rather die a thousand deaths." Lee surrendered on April 9, 1865. Grant's generous terms prevented reprisals, including prosecutions for treason, so long as Lee and his men observed the terms of their parole. Five days later, after attending a cabinet meeting and declining Lincoln's invitation to attend the theater later that day, Grant headed to New Jersey with his wife and one of his sons to visit his other children. That evening the general learned that the president had been felled by an assassin's bullet at Ford's Theater. In years to come Grant would celebrate Lincoln as "incontestably the greatest man I have ever known."

Ulysses S. Grant emerged from the Civil War a national hero, surpassed in stature only by Abraham Lincoln. He was feted at dinners, receptions, and balls by an exultant, victorious nation that wished to lavish adulation and gifts upon the commanding general of the Armies of the United States. Grant received dozens of choice horses, a purse of $100,000 from New York City merchants, a splendid collection of leather-bound and gilt-paged books of every author of note while in Boston, transportation on William Henry Vanderbilt's private railway car, and a well-appointed house from admirers in Philadelphia.

The general also touched base with his past. He visited his parents' house near Cincinnati, where Hannah Grant, in her apron, acknowledged her son succinctly: "Well, Ulysses, you've become a great man, haven't you?" and then went back to her housework. And after a little more than four years after he had left, carpetbag in hand, Grant returned to Galena. There was a parade just for him. The worn army overcoat had been replaced with something a bit more elaborate to go along with his rank of lieutenant general. As Grant made his way down Main Street, he was showered with cheers; spanning Main Street was a banner emblazoned with "Hail to the Chief Who in Triumph Advances," its supports bearing the names of numerous battlefields. Another banner proclaimed, "General, The Sidewalk Is Built," a reference to the general's admission that the only political office he might seek would be that of mayor of Galena in order to build a sidewalk from his house to downtown. Of course, a new house awaited him now, a brick residence high on top of a hill far away from the smaller abode he had once shared with his wife and four children. For the moment, at least, Ulysses S. Grant was home.

With war's end, General Grant addressed various new responsibilities, including the demobilization of the huge Union army and the establishment of a new peacetime regular army. To newspaper reporters he speculated about the possibility of ousting the French-supported regime of Maximilian in Mexico and thus enforcing the Monroe Doctrine, which forbade all foreign interference in the affairs of the Western Hemisphere and which Washington had not enforced during the Civil War. Rarely did he show much interest in what was happening in the defeated South, although he did intervene to halt an attempt to try Robert E. Lee and other Confederate military leaders for treason. At first he endorsed President Andrew Johnson's efforts to bring the South back into the Union quickly and without punitiveness. He was sensitive to criticisms about the behavior of black soldiers on occupation duty in Southern states and the operations of the Freedmen's Bureau, which was largely staffed by army officers. The Bureau, established by Congress just before the end of the war, was to aid refugees and freed blacks by furnishing supplies, medical and educational services, and other types of assistance. At the end of November 1865, at the new president's urging, Grant undertook a two-week tour through parts of the old Confederacy, visiting Virginia, the Carolinas, Georgia, and Tennessee. He returned guardedly optimistic about the prospects for a just peace. Although he concluded that "the mass of thinking men of the south accept the present situation in good faith," he admitted that most white Southerners were not yet ready "to yield that ready obedience to civil authority" that might be expected. Moreover, "it cannot be expected that the opinions held by men at the south for years can be changed in a day, and therefore the freedmen require, for a few years not only laws to protect them, but the fostering care of those who will give them good counsel, and on whom they rely."

Relations between the president and the general in chief deteriorated during 1866, as Grant supported and Johnson opposed the initiatives of congressional Republicans to protect blacks and provide for their equal treatment before the law in the wake of extensive Southern hostility toward them. Grant became increasingly critical of the recalcitrance of white Southerners toward congressional Reconstruction and outwardly deplored outbreaks of white supremacist violence at New Orleans and Memphis, where white mobs and white police indiscriminately attacked blacks. He saw the Civil Rights Act of 1866 and the renewal of the Freedmen's Bureau as essential to rebuilding the defeated South on a just basis. President Johnson had vetoed both bills, but Congress mustered the two-thirds majority necessary to override the veto. Grant was offended by Johnson's efforts to enlist him in support of the president's policy. Moreover, he regretted allowing himself to be persuaded to join Johnson on the chief executive's ill-fated "Swing Around the Circle" speaking tour in August and September 1866, when he asked voters to support his policy and to repudiate that of congressional Republicans. Shocked at President Johnson's vulgar language and his proclivity to trade barbs with hecklers, Grant termed the result "a national disgrace" and expressed his disgust "at hearing a man make speeches on the way to his own funeral." After the Republicans scored resounding victories in the 1866 congressional elections, Grant redoubled his resistance to presidential initiatives and unsuccessfully advised white Southerners to ratify the Fourteenth Amendment, which made blacks citizens of the United States. He also helped Republicans frame the Reconstruction Acts to establish loyal civil governments throughout those former Confederate states not yet readmitted to the Union. That process would take place under military supervision, with the South divided into five military districts, a sign that a growing number of Republicans trusted General Grant to oversee that difficult task.

During 1867, the rift between Johnson and Grant widened further, as the general resisted the president's effort to impair the execution of the Reconstruction Acts. In a shrewd effort to entangle Grant in political controversy, Johnson suspended Secretary of War Edwin M. Stanton and asked Grant to accept the War Department portfolio on a temporary basis until the Senate met to rule on Stanton's status under the terms of the Tenure of Office Act. That legislation prohibited the president from dismissing members of his own cabinet without the consent of the Senate. Grant reluctantly accepted but then found himself unable to prevent Johnson from removing Generals Philip Sheridan and Daniel Sickles from command of the military districts set up under the Reconstruction Acts. As Grant and Johnson wrestled over Reconstruction, voters in several Northern states, especially Ohio, shaped the general's political prospects when they defeated Republican efforts to secure black voting rights at the state level. These electoral setbacks suggested that Radical favorites, including Ohio's own Senator Benjamin F. Wade and U.S. Chief Justice Salmon P. Chase, would not fare well as presidential candidates in 1868; not enough Republican voters shared their commitment to far-reaching social and racial change.

The intensity of the continuing partisan debate over Reconstruction, especially Johnson's willingness to obstruct congressional initiatives, convinced Grant that he should consider accepting the Republican nomination for president. He did not want to see the national government in the hands of the Democratic party, which he associated with support for white supremacy and which he believed was still tainted with disloyalty for its role during the Civil War. Yet the general also wondered whether some Republicans were too eager in their pursuit of Radical Reconstruction. Personally, he had little desire to run for president: he preferred to remain general in chief and enjoy the economic security and public adulation that came with the position. Johnson forced the issue in early 1868, though, when he tried to involve Grant in a plan to thwart the Senate's decision to restore Stanton to the War Department. When Grant refused to cooperate, the president accused him of deception. Infuriated by the denunciation, the general made public his break with the chief executive. Even the hard-to-please Radical congressman Thaddeus Stevens of Pennsylvania, long skeptical of Grant's commitment to Republican principles, concluded that the general was "a bolder man than I thought him to be!" Grant went so far as to support Johnson's impeachment by Congress in 1868, declaring that the president deserved conviction "because he is such an infernal liar."

Johnson survived his impeachment trial in part because several Republican senators looked suspiciously at the economic policies of his would-be successor, Ohio's Senator Benjamin F. Wade. Better to secure the White House through other means, they decided: on May 21 Republicans meeting in Chicago unanimously nominated Grant for president. The general reluctantly accepted. "If this were simply a matter of personal preference and satisfaction I would not wish to be president," he told a friend, adding that "to go into the Presidency opens altogether a new field to me, in which there is to be a new strife to which I am not trained." To his wartime comrade Sherman he explained his thinking: "I could not back down without . . . leaving the contest for power for the next four years between mere trading politicians, the elevation of whom, no matter which party won, would lose to us, largely, the results of the costly war which we have gone through." Accepting the nomination, he concluded with the words that would become forever identified with him: "Let us have peace." The expression embodied the appeal of his candidacy: an end to sectional and partisan bickering and racial friction so that the reunited nation could move forward. The Democrats reinforced this appeal in July when they nominated former New York governor Horatio Seymour and Missouri's Frank P. Blair as their standard bearers. Seymour, a virulent critic of Lincoln during the Civil War, in 1863 had addressed New York City draft rioters as "my friends," whereas Blair announced that the first task facing a Democratic president would be to repeal Republican Reconstruction measures. Watching from the sidelines, frustrated presidential aspirant Salmon P. Chase noted that it was as if the Democrats had responded to Grant's

"Let us have peace" with their own "Let us have war." Another observer concluded, "Grant can do nothing for himself, but Seymour and his men rarely open their mouths that they do not strengthen Grant's hand."

Grant led the Republicans to victory in the 1868 election, running ahead of the party ticket in many areas of the nation. However, a closer examination of the election results revealed that although Grant would have prevailed in the electoral college had the electorate been restricted largely to whites, his popular majority was due to the votes of newly enfranchised blacks in the South because of congressional Reconstruction measures. Grant had understood the importance of securing that vote once civil governments were restored throughout the South. He also acknowledged that the Republican platform of 1868, with its distinction between supporting black suffrage in the North while mandating it in the former Confederacy, smacked of a hypocritical double standard even as it reflected political reality in light of repeated failures to secure changes in Northern state constitutions. Thus Grant threw his support behind a federal constitutional amendment that would abolish race, color, or previous condition of servitude as barriers to the exercise of the franchise. He backed this effort both because that amendment would protect Southern blacks from future revisions in state constitutions and because it would allow Republicans to circumvent the difficulties inherent in securing black suffrage in the North through statewide referenda.

On March 4, 1869, Grant took the oath of office as eighteenth president of the United States. He had kept both his inaugural address and his cabinet selections largely secret. "The responsibilities of the position I feel, but accept them without fear," he announced. "The office has come to me unsought; I commence its duties untrammeled." With the political friction of the Johnson years in mind, he announced that "all laws will be faithfully executed, whether they meet my approval or not"; the new president assured listeners that he would "on all subjects have a policy to recommend, but none to enforce against the will of the people." Then he outlined his own agenda: the reduction of the national debt incurred during the war, the resumption of specie payments through deflating the currency, the need for a new policy toward American Indians "which tends to their civilization and ultimate citizenship," and the ratification of the Fifteenth Amendment, protecting black suffrage as part of a larger policy of bringing an end to the Reconstruction process.

That Grant did not feel beholden to any sections of the Republican party became apparent the next day when he sent his cabinet selections to the Senate for confirmation. He had kept his choices secret from all interested parties, including his wife; a few nominees were not even aware of their selection. The result was a stark contrast to previous presidents' efforts to balance rival factions (although it paid attention to geographical distribution). Heading the list as secretary of state was Elihu B. Washburne, Grant's longtime political mentor; department-store magnate Alexander T. Stewart was to take charge of the Treasury Department; several second-level political figures filled other positions; and people scratched their heads when they saw the name of Philadelphia businessman Adolph E. Borie as secretary of the navy—who was he, anyway? Somewhat astonished, the Senate ratified the slate, but problems immediately surfaced. Massachusetts senator Charles Sumner argued that a 1789 statute prohibiting men with commercial interests from serving as treasury secretary barred Stewart; Washburne decided to resign his post to accept what he really wanted— the position of minister to France. Grant hurriedly named Hamilton Fish to replace Washburne and secured George Boutwell to replace Stewart after Stewart's proposal to put his holdings in a blind trust proved unacceptable. Still, it was Grant's cabinet, not a balancing of party interests, and several senators smarted at the result; a few bore grudges for years. Some of this feeling was evident when Grant battled the Senate over the repeal of the Tenure of Office Act. Originally designed to handcuff Johnson, the legislation now appealed to those senators who wanted to teach the new president a lesson. In response, Grant simply refused to fill lesser offices, threatening to strangle the patronage lifeline essential to political survival for congressmen; eventually the legislation was modified, with the Senate no longer able to restore dismissed officeholders.

This initial clash suggested the uneasiness with which some Republicans viewed Grant's coming to power. After all, it was not clear whether the Republican party had a future. The party had achieved its goal of destroying slavery and preserving the Union; Grant's victory appeared to secure unity between the executive and legislative branches as the federal government put the finishing touches on Reconstruction and the reestablishment of civil governments in the former Confederate states. Republican leaders did not agree on economic policy—namely management of the currency, retrenchment, and tariff policy—and other leaders were demanding that it was time to address new issues, including civil service reform. There was also a sizable war debt to pay off. The new president would also have to wrestle with foreign policy issues arising from the war, most notably how to secure compensation from Great Britain for the damage inflicted by British-built Confederate raiders—the so-called *Alabama* Claims, named after perhaps the most famous of these raiders.

Upon taking office Grant immediately addressed financial policy. Two weeks after his inauguration he signed the Public Credit Act, which committed the federal government to pay off war bonds in gold (or its specie equivalent), not inflated greenbacks, which would be gradually withdrawn from circulation. However, he slipped badly later that year when he found himself entangled in a scheme to corner the gold market. His new brother-in-law, Abel Corbin, introduced him to Jay Gould and Jim Fisk, two New York speculators with more than a whiff of the unsavory about them. Unknown to Grant, Gould and Fisk had hatched a scheme whereby they would use information gained from government sources to drive up the price of gold, corner the market, and make a killing in speculation. Grant encountered Gould and Fisk several times and in each instance resisted their efforts to pump him for information; it would have been far better had he avoided these encounters altogether. Believing that they had persuaded the president not to authorize government sales of gold (which would drive the price of gold down and thus wreck their scheme), Gould and Fisk began buying gold heavily in September 1869 and sought to secure their investment by opening accounts for people close to Grant. When Grant got wind of the plot, he ordered Boutwell to sell several million dollars in government gold, thus effectively foiling the conspiracy as prices collapsed on September 24, 1869—thereafter known as Black Friday. Although a congressional investigation cleared Grant, his immediate family, and other high administration officials of complicity, Corbin and a few officeholders did not get off so easily. The affair raised questions about Grant's discretion in even being seen with such dubious characters and reminded people of how important it was to address the currency question so as to prevent future speculation.

Having drawn attention to the status of American Indians in his inaugural address, Grant looked to institute a new approach based on the establishment of federal reservations where natives would be protected from white violence and exposed to the benefits that white civilization and Christian religion would presumably bring as they were assimilated into American society. He entrusted execution of this approach, soon labeled the Peace Policy, to Ely S. Parker, a Seneca chieftain who had befriended Grant in Galena before the war and served on the general's staff. Grant secured from Congress approval to set up an independent commission to oversee implementation of his policy and then staffed the Board of Indian Commissioners with philanthropists and other advocates of a more conciliatory policy toward American Indians. Initially he hoped to staff the Bureau of Indian Affairs with army officers; when Congress blocked this in 1870,

Grant responded by appointing agents in accordance with the recommendations of leaders of various religious denominations. Before long it looked as if Grant's policy was well on its way to securing peace on the frontier and the eventual integration of American Indians into the dominant society.

The new president also looked to bring Reconstruction to a close. Advocating the ratification of the Fifteenth Amendment, he lobbied Republicans to move forward to secure its enactment. At the same time, he chose to ease the readmission of three remaining former Confederate states (Virginia, Texas, and Mississippi) by calling for a separate vote on proposed state constitutional propositions looking to deny the right to vote and to hold office to large numbers of former Confederates. Voters in those states accepted the state constitutions framed in accordance with the requirements of the Reconstruction Acts while rejecting the proscriptive clauses: by early 1870 Congress had agreed to seat delegations from these three states. Grant agreed that the amount of political violence and fraud in Georgia in 1868 demanded a federal response in the form of remanding the state to military supervision to allow state Republicans to undo the results of Democratic political terrorism. With the ratification of the Fifteenth Amendment in March 1870 and the readmission of Virginia, Texas, and Mississippi, many Republicans agreed with *The Nation,* which observed that it was time to leave the South alone, because "all that paper and words can do for it have been done."

Perhaps the most controversial event of Grant's first term, one with far-reaching consequences, was his interest in annexing the Dominican Republic. Aware of the need to secure ports in the Caribbean and intrigued by the prospect of constructing a canal in Central America connecting the Caribbean and the Pacific, Grant showed interest when representatives of President Buenaventura Baez's regime contacted the president about the possibility that the United States would absorb his country through purchase. Grant dispatched his private secretary, Orville Babcock, to investigate the proposal, and Babcock returned to Washington in August 1869 with a draft treaty of annexation in hand. This seemed premature (and irregular); however, eventually Babcock secured authorization to negotiate a treaty and returned with a document in December 1869.

Grant's interest in annexation went beyond the normal motives of American territorial expansion. The president believed that if the United States acquired the Dominican Republic, Southern blacks might threaten to migrate there if white Southerners continued to fail to respect their rights as citizens. It was an interesting attempt to create economic leverage for the freedmen; however, Grant did not publicize his vision. Instead, his efforts to garner support for the treaty fell short when Senator Charles Sumner, chairman of the Senate Foreign Relations Committee, decided to oppose ratification. Grant, believing that he had already secured Sumner's support, became angry; he was also dismayed when other Republicans, citing several questionable and possibly corrupt aspects of the negotiation and questioning the wisdom of Caribbean expansion, joined Democrats in blocking ratification in June 1870.

Exasperated by Sumner's behavior during the unsuccessful attempt to annex the Dominican Republic as well as his efforts to wreck administration attempts at settlement of the *Alabama* claims against Great Britain, Grant now moved systematically to reward friends and punish opponents, playing patronage politics with a sometimes unseemly passion. He secured approval of a committee to investigate the Dominican Republic with an eye toward refuting Sumner's insinuations of corruption. Senators eager to please him, ready to punish Sumner, or anxious for better relations between the Senate and the executive approved deposing Sumner from his committee chairmanship. With Sumner out of the way, Grant and his secretary of state, Hamilton Fish, negotiated the Treaty of Washington, which called on the United States and Great Britain to submit their differences in the *Alabama* claims matter to an international arbitration board. The following year the board awarded the United States more than fifteen million dollars as compensation for damages inflicted by British-built Confederate commerce raiders; earlier talk by the United States of acquiring Canada from Great Britain as compensation faded in the eagerness to reach an accord.

Grant also moved to smother white political terrorism in the South aimed at blacks, their white allies, and Republican regimes. At first, the president wondered whether vigorous action would render him vulnerable to charges of being a military dictator; however, after moderate responses failed to save Republican regimes in North Carolina and Georgia, Grant urged Congress to pass firmer measures. The result was the Ku Klux Act of 1871, which bore the name of the most prominent of these white supremacist terrorist groups. It empowered Grant to suspend the writ of habeas corpus, mobilize the Department of Justice (established in 1869) in support of arresting and trying violators, and call out the army to restore peace to especially troubled areas. Grant invoked the act that fall in South Carolina, suspending the writ in nine counties. However, public support for intervention was uncertain and sporadic, and limited resources hampered federal efforts to arrest and prosecute violators. Moreover, many Republicans believed they had gone about as far as they could to protect Southern blacks: as one congressman put it, "We have reconstructed, and reconstructed, and we are asked to reconstruct again. . . . We are governing the South too much."

Grant had scored several successes in his first term; he had also laid the groundwork for renomination with his more vigorous use of patronage to bring together a coterie of supporters, especially in the Senate, who served as advocates of administration policy. Democrats appeared disoriented, casting about for new issues in the aftermath of the 1868 presidential election, adopting a "New Departure" strategy in hopes of setting aside the issues raised by the war in favor of contesting economic policies. It was left to disgruntled Republicans—many of whom found in the Grant administration's continuing commitment to Reconstruction a distraction from what they believed were the true issues of economic, monetary, and civil service reform—to mount a challenge to Grant's bid for reelection. Unable to deny him renomination, these dissidents, styling themselves Liberal Republicans, gathered in Cincinnati in May 1872 to select a candidate. They were joined by other administration critics who did not embrace the reformers' vision of change but who found common cause in the need to defeat Grant. Out of this disparate gathering emerged the candidacy of New York newspaper editor Horace Greeley, whose commitment to a true reform agenda was tenuous at best and whose nomination seemed to confirm the observation that the true rallying cry of the Liberal Republicans was "Anything to beat Grant!" Desperate Democrats concurred in Greeley's selection the following month.

Unlike some of his fellow Republicans, Grant was confident that he would secure reelection. In previously calling for the establishment of a civil service commission, the president had blunted the force of one of the Liberal charges; a 10 percent reduction in tariff rates similarly countered demands for free trade. He refused to take to the stump, pointing out that two candidates had previously tried the experiment: "Both of them were public speakers, and both were beaten. I am no speaker and don't want to be beaten." Greeley argued that it was time to pursue a policy of reconciliation toward Southern whites, rendering him vulnerable to charges that a Democratic/Liberal Republican triumph would mark a repudiation of the war and its achievements; *Harpers Weekly* cartoonist Thomas Nast excelled in associating Greeley with the Confederacy, corrupt Democrats, and John Wilkes Booth. At a time of national prosperity marked by foreign policy triumphs and the seeming success of Reconstruction, Grant faced few obstacles, and in November he achieved a sweeping reelection triumph, marred only by the subsequent death of his opponent. As he spoke to the nation upon taking the oath of office a second time on March

4, 1873, he revealed just how much he had been stung by criticism of his performance. Reminding Americans that he had not sought the presidency, he asserted, "I have been the subject of abuse and slander scarcely ever equaled in political history, which today I feel that I can afford to disregard in view of your verdict, which I gratefully accept as my vindication."

Even as Grant was celebrating his reelection, revelations of corruption in Congress tainted the victorious Republicans. Several prominent party leaders were implicated in the Credit Mobilier bribery scheme connected with the building of the transcontinental railroad. Among those named were Grant's outgoing vice president, Schuyler Colfax. In later years critics would associate the scandal with Grant's administration, although the activities under investigation actually took place during Andrew Johnson's presidency. An effort by the outgoing session of Congress to award its members retroactive pay raises also sparked controversy, and what became known as the Salary Grab further tarnished Republicans.

Although these incidents did not directly involve the executive branch, other allegations did cloud Grant's first term. The events that culminated in Black Friday in 1869 raised questions about Grant's sense of propriety; so did several aspects of the negotiations surrounding the plan to annex the Dominican Republic. Even more damaging was the activity of former Grant military aide George K. Leet, who had turned his association with Grant (bolstered by a bland recommendation letter) into an opportunity to profit from the warehousing of goods at the New York Customshouse. Most Republican voters overlooked these charges; Grant's lukewarm support of civil service reform satisfied them that he was doing what he could to end government corruption. In his second term, however, more worrisome challenges arose, commencing with the Panic of 1873 and the serious economic depression that followed. In light of notions of limited governance, Grant could do little to soften the devastating blow. Congressman James A. Garfield quickly dismissed the president's musings about the wisdom of commencing public works programs to give employment to those displaced by the economic downturn. In the aftermath of the crash, some Republicans and a good number of Democrats reconsidered the wisdom of the government's contractionist monetary policy and in 1874 pushed through Congress a so-called inflation bill that would put the brakes on specie resumption and lead to a limited reissue of greenbacks. After much thinking, Grant vetoed the bill, an act cheered by advocates of "sound money" (mainly creditors) and denounced by debtors and others hard hit by the economy. Eventually, in early 1875, Grant signed a measure calling for the resumption of specie payments within four years.

The economic depression also contributed to the erosion of support for the administration's Reconstruction policy. Attempts by Southern Republicans to attract support for the party from Southern whites through economic development programs (especially the building of railroads) withered in the face of the economic panic, as sources of credit dried up, major investment houses failed, and the railroad bond market collapsed. The depression also exacerbated preexisting intraparty factionalism that Republicans desperately needed to overcome if they were to survive Democratic challenges. Conservative forces already had the upper hand in Virginia, Tennessee, North Carolina, and Georgia. Before long, Republican regimes in Arkansas, Alabama, and Texas found themselves vulnerable too. Democrats claimed victory in the off-year elections in 1874 in the South; nationwide Democrats claimed control of the House of Representatives, effectively blocking further Reconstruction initiatives. Economic issues, not justice to the freedpeople or the continuing suppression of white supremacy, were the going concern. Democrats also took advantage of rumors that Grant was interested in a third term to raise again the charges that the president was really little short of a military tyrant bent on absolute power.

The erosion of public support for the Republicans in the North and the continuing collapse of Republican regimes in the South proved formidable challenges to Grant's Reconstruction policy. So did the escalation of Southern white supremacist violence, especially in Louisiana, and an increasingly narrow interpretation by courts of measures designed to stop such violence. In April 1873, some one hundred blacks were indiscriminately slaughtered in Colfax, Louisiana, in the aftermath of a disputed state election in which both Democrats and Republicans claimed to control the state house and the governor's chair. In the absence of a congressional mandate, Grant dispatched federal troops to Louisiana and recognized the Republican claimants; such intervention, however necessary to thwart white supremacist violence, helped to undermine the legitimacy of Republican regimes by demonstrating their dependence on federal intervention to survive in power. The campaign of violence continued in 1874, as Democrats formed paramilitary groups known as the White Leagues in an effort to regain power. In August they assassinated several Republican officeholders at Coushatta. The following month they embarked on an effort to overthrow the Republicans in New Orleans through several days of battle in the streets. Once more Grant intervened; once more he prevented disaster, although in the face of more public criticism. His efforts were further hampered when federal circuit courts in Kentucky and Louisiana declared portions of federal enforcement legislation unconstitutional; the latter case, *U.S. v. Cruikshank,* involved people implicated in the Colfax murders.

The Democratic electoral triumph in 1874 suggested that public support for continuing intervention, let alone sterner measures, was fading. Grant himself held reservations about several Southern Republican regimes, observing in January 1874, "I am tired of this nonsense. . . . The nursing of monstrosities has nearly exhausted the life of the party. I am done with them, and they will have to take care of themselves." He explored efforts to forge coalitions with conservative regimes in several Southern states and urged Southern Republicans to reform themselves or face the loss of administration support. However, he would not countenance political terrorism. Addressing Congress in December 1874, he told critics of his intervention under existing enforcement legislation that he had acted properly, and if enforcement measures could not be invoked in such circumstances, "then they are without meaning, force, or effect, and the whole scheme of colored enfranchisement is worse than mockery and little better than a crime." The solution was simple: "Treat the negro as a citizen and a voter, as he is and must remain, and soon parties will be divided, not on the color line, but on principle. Then we shall have no complaint of sectional interference." But such was not to be the case. In January 1875 Louisiana Democrats attempted a coup d'etat by seizing control of the state legislature, and federal troops under Phil Sheridan had to restore order. Administration critics, overlooking what had precipitated such a response, claimed that Sheridan's action showed the dangers of military intervention in interfering with civil government and possibly forecast the subsequent disruption of the political process elsewhere. At first administration supporters seemed dazed; Grant rallied them when he chose to defend Sheridan in a special message sent to Congress on January 13, 1875: "Fierce denunciations ring through the country about office holding and election matters in Louisiana, while every one of the Colfax miscreants goes unwhipped of justice, and no way in this boasted land of civilization and Christianity to punish the perpetrators of this bloody and monstrous crime."

Powerful words, these, but at best they but momentarily countered criticism of administration policy. Republicans failed to pass sterner enforcement measures, contenting themselves with additional civil rights legislation concerning the prohibition of segregation in certain public places, which would be problematic to sustain. By the beginning of 1875, Republicans could claim to be in power in only four Southern states (Mississippi, Louisiana, South Carolina, and Florida), the first three largely because of a reliance on black votes. Democrats went to work with resolve to eliminate that advantage. First came Mississippi, where Democrats proclaimed that they would triumph in the 1875 elections, "peaceably if we can, forcibly if we must." Unable to devise methods to defend his regime, Republican governor Adelbert Ames wired Grant for help. Ohio Republicans, engaged in a dogfight in their state elections, warned Grant that intervention might well cost them the Buckeye State, long deemed a barometer of political prospects for the following year's presidential race: a Democratic victory in 1876 would bring an end to Reconstruction. "I am somewhat perplexed to know what direction to give in the matter," Grant admitted to his attorney general. "The whole public are tired out with these annual, autumnal outbreaks in the South, and there is so much unwholesome lying done by the press and people in regard to the cause and extent of these breaches of the peace that the great majority are ready now to condemn any interference on the part of the Government." For the moment, at least, he decided against intervention. Republicans narrowly prevailed in the October state elections in Ohio, electing Rutherford B. Hayes governor for a third time; the following month, they went down in defeat in Mississippi, as Democrats there wisely waited until days before the election to step up their campaign of intimidation and violence, leaving too little time for the federal government to respond effectively. Grant later wondered whether he had made the right decision, although in the wake of the 1874 electoral setbacks, more federal intervention would have further damaged Republican chances in the North. Supreme Court decisions the following March gutted key sections of enforcement legislation, rendering intervention even more problematic.

Frustrated by setbacks in his Southern policy, Grant also found himself under fire when the activities of key administration figures came under close scrutiny. His private secretary, Orville Babcock, was implicated in the Whiskey Ring, a scheme to defraud the federal government of revenue (with some of the proceeds making their way into Republican party coffers). When he learned that Babcock was under suspicion, Grant indignantly declared, "Let no guilty man escape"; eventually, however, he grew so angry at what he believed to be the partisan motive behind the inquiry and eventual indictment that he paid less attention to what Babcock might have done. Although Babcock was acquitted of all charges, with Grant offering a deposition in his support, the president moved quickly to displace him from the White House. No sooner had this chapter closed, however, than Grant's secretary of war, William Belknap, hurriedly offered his resignation to avoid impeachment on charges that he had sold post traderships in the West. Here, too, there was some uncertainty as to what exactly happened, with some people pointing the finger at Belknap's second and third wives (who were sisters) as the instrument of the corrupt arrangements; nevertheless, the Democratic-controlled House, ignoring the fact that Belknap had resigned, impeached the secretary, and he escaped conviction by the Senate on the grounds that a public official who had resigned was not subject to the impeachment process. House Democrats launched investigation after investigation in an effort to uncover more evidence of fraud and corruption, with some success in highlighting dealings that were at best dubious, although in these cases the partisan motivation behind these inquiries was apparent.

Other administration initiatives, such as Indian affairs and civil service reform, were foundering as well. Support for Grant's Peace Policy was never very strong, and in 1871 Ely Parker left his post as commissioner of Indian Affairs under fire. What support remained eroded in the aftermath of a renewal of the Indian wars in 1873. In April of that year, Grant's efforts to bring an end to the Modoc War along the California–Oregon border failed when the Modocs assassinated U.S. negotiators. In return, Grant ordered that the Modocs be crushed and the assassins punished. The following year, hostilities erupted along the northern Plains. The discovery of gold in the Black Hills on the Great Sioux Reservation in the Dakota Territory led to pressure to open these lands to white settlers. In 1875 Grant gave in to that pressure. However, a massive offensive against the Sioux in the spring of 1876 turned into disaster when Lt. Col. George Armstrong Custer and portions of the 7th Cavalry met with absolute defeat at Little Big Horn on June 25, 1876. An outraged American public called for a massive military response to put an end to the Plains wars. Grant could not point to his achievements in civil service reform, for the rules promulgated by the commission in 1872 proved insufficient and were not supported by Congress; Grant finally abandoned the effort in 1875. In the wake of such setbacks, administration achievements were ignored, including the peaceful resolution of a dispute with Spain following the seizure by Spanish authorities of an American-built steamer, the *Virginius*, and the subsequent trial and sentencing to death of several crew members, including eight American citizens, for this assistance to Cuban insurrectionaries. Grant and Hamilton Fish fended off cries for war and worked toward an equitable and just resolution of the crisis.

Back in 1875 Grant had declared that he had no interest in a third term; the cloud of corruption that covered the administration in 1876 ensured that the question would not be reopened. However, if Grant could not dictate a successor from among his supporters, those candidates were equally determined to deny the nomination to Grant's critics. As a result, Rutherford B. Hayes emerged as the compromise nominee to battle Democratic Samuel J. Tilden in the fall presidential contest. Perhaps not surprisingly, the South played a central role in the outcome of the contentious battle for the White House. That fall Grant once more found it necessary to quell violence in South Carolina, although he waited until after the October elections to take substantial action. Elsewhere, in Florida and Louisiana, the remaining Republican state regimes were losing their already tenuous grips on power. On election night, it looked as if Tilden had prevailed: only when it was evident that the returns from these three Southern states were in dispute did Grant step forward to ensure a peaceful resolution of the election. In the crisis that followed, the outgoing president moved shrewdly to pose as a nonpartisan arbiter while preserving Republican chances; he was instrumental in securing passage of the legislation establishing the Electoral Commission and assured Democrats that once the vote was complete that he would withdraw federal support from the remaining Republican regimes. When Hayes prevailed, Grant ensured his peaceful inauguration.

Grant's eight years in the White House were trying ones, and he was eager to leave. The experience bore out his prediction that his presidency would diminish his reputation. However, critics who lambasted him as a naive pawn surrounded by corrupt associates and controlled by Congress badly overshot the mark. If he was unable to construct a Southern policy that would serve both sectional reconciliation and justice for black Americans, no one posed a more satisfactory alternative. Although there was evidence of wrongdoing, recent studies suggest that what was notable about the Grant administration was not the amount of corrupt activity but the degree to which it was exposed and investigated. The misadventure in annexing the Dominican Republic overshadowed Grant's achievements in foreign policy, and several students of his presidency now praise the impact of his monetary and economic policies. Yet Grant himself was willing to admit that he fell short: in his last annual message he confessed that he had come to office inexperienced in the ways of politics. "Mistakes have been made, as all can see and I admit," he conceded, although he added that "failures have been errors of judgment, not of intent." It was left to Congressman James A. Garfield, at best an erstwhile supporter of the administration, to admit as Grant's term ended that "no American has carried greater fame out of the White House than this silent man who leaves it today."

All his life, Ulysses S. Grant had liked to travel and explore new places. He had long contemplated a tour of Europe. Now, freed at last from the responsibilities of public office, he had the resources to realize that dream. In May 1877, with Julia and son Jesse at his side and accompanied by newspaper reporter John R. Young, he set forth across the Atlantic. Over the next several months he dined with Queen Victoria of Great Britain, discussed high politics with German chancellor Bismarck, chatted about American Indians with Czar Alexander of Russia, and took in the pyramids of Egypt along the Nile and works of art at several museums. Much to his surprise, he was received not as a private citizen but as a former head of state. Each step of his journey was covered in the American press, and readers began to see Grant once more as a symbol of the republic's greatness. Young carefully drew Grant out to discuss various political issues; the former president's frank assessments about military and political topics made for good if sometimes controversial copy, proving that he was not always the close-mouthed sphinx that had befuddled so many interrogators. Perhaps, some Republicans ruminated, he might make a good standard bearer in 1880.

What began as a simple desire to visit Europe and the Mediterranean soon developed into a world tour, Grant assisted by the welcome discovery that his investments would allow him to satisfy that ambition. After visiting India, the Grants headed toward the Orient, where he met both China's Li Hung Chang and Japan's emperor Mutsuhito, rare encounters for a Westerner. At one point Grant even mediated a dispute between China and Japan over the Ryukyu Islands, helping to avoid the outbreak of war between the two Asian powers. It was not until September 20, 1879, that the Grants returned to the United States, debarking at San Francisco to the shouts of an assembled crowd. For the next several weeks Grant showed his wife where he had lived and suffered during their long and painful separation during his tour of duty on the West Coast in the 1850s. It took the global travelers another three months to complete their journey, and they returned to Philadelphia on December 16, 1879, having been feted and saluted the entire way across the nation.

Grant returned to the United States just as Republicans were casting about for a presidential candidate. Rutherford B. Hayes had declared that he would not run for a second term, and a good number of Republicans, including many of Grant's most loyal supporters, were relieved that the incumbent intended to honor his pledge. Dissatisfied with four years under Hayes, these Republicans, led by New York's Roscoe Conkling and John A. Logan of Illinois, sought to regain control of the White House for their wing of the party, now known as the Stalwarts, by promoting Grant's candidacy. Grant viewed their efforts with ambivalence. Certainly an unprecedented third term in the White House would be a mark of the nation's continuing esteem for him and a rebuke to his critics. Moreover, he had returned from his world tour with a broader understanding of the international scene, which he might be able to put to good use as chief executive. Still, Grant was aware that a good number of Republicans preferred someone else to head the ticket. The list of other presidential hopefuls was headed by James G. Blaine of Maine. John Sherman of Ohio also aspired for a shot at the top spot, as did none other than Elihu B. Washburne, Grant's old patron and spokesperson.

Grant did not want to win the presidency for a third time nearly so much as he feared rejection at either the convention or the polls. Other Republican contenders did what they could to slow down what at first appeared to be the Grant juggernaut, so that by the time the party faithful gathered in Chicago in June 1880 Grant could command a plurality but not a majority of the delegates. Eventually the anti-Grant forces united behind James A. Garfield, who prevailed on the thirty-sixth ballot. Embarrassed by his defeat, at first Grant sulked. Before long, however, Republicans realized that the fall election would be a highly competitive one, with the Democratic nominee, former Union general and Civil War hero Winfield Scott Hancock, Garfield's formidable opponent. Hancock could attract Northern veterans' votes, and he could count on the always solidly Democratic South. Garfield wrote Grant proposing that the two appear jointly at several functions. Grant held off, at first suggesting that perhaps he could fit a few events into his summer travel schedule in the Midwest. But dire predictions of Democratic victory moved the former president to meet Garfield in Ohio on September 27, and over the next six weeks he did for Garfield what he had never done for himself: he stumped for the ticket, warning voters of the turmoil that was sure to follow Hancock's victory. Whether his efforts tipped the balance in closely contested states such as Ohio and New York is best left for speculation; nevertheless, Garfield squeaked to victory in November. Ahead of him was the task of assembling an administration and placating party regulars, including Grant, who intended to extract something as a reward for his activities.

Grant quickly grew displeased with Garfield's cabinet selections and other patronage decisions, grumbling that the new president "is not possessed of the backbone of an angleworm." Following Garfield's assassination during his first year in office, Grant looked for more from the slain president's successor, Chester A. Arthur, who had been a loyal Grant and

Conkling man in the 1870s, only to be disappointed once more. By 1883 he wondered whether the Republican party had any higher goal "except to peddle out patronage to soreheads, in order to bring them back into the fold, and to avoid any positive declarations upon all leading questions." Grant preferred the world of business. Named president of the Mexican Southern Railroad in late 1880, he negotiated with the Mexican government to gain concessions for a railroad that was never completed. In light of previous experience, he showed questionable judgment in associating with Jay Gould, who helped finance the establishment of the company. At first it seemed that Grant's other business endeavor, a partnership in an investment brokerage firm run by his second son, Ulysses, and Ferdinand Ward, would prove more successful. Grant and Ward (the Grant in the firm's name was the general's son) appeared to be prosperous, and many people, encouraged by the former president's reputation for probity, invested funds. However, Ward was fooling everyone: he took investments and used the proceeds to pay out dividends to other investors while pocketing sizable sums for himself. The scheme unraveled in 1884. Ward's final fraud was to persuade Grant to borrow $150,000 from millionaire William H. Vanderbilt. Two days later the firm collapsed. Grant, shattered, moaned, "I have made it the rule of my life to trust a man long after other people gave him up. But I don't see how I can ever trust any human being again."

Plunged into debt, determined to make good his considerable losses, Grant commenced writing articles on several Civil War battles for *Century* magazine's series of war recollections. He also watched as Congress debated whether to restore him to the rank of general of the army on full pay. That fall he suffered another devastating setback when he learned that he had been stricken by throat cancer. Anxious to provide for his family, Grant considered preparing his memoirs for *Century*'s publishers, then accepted Mark Twain's offer to give him seventy percent of the profits to place his book with Twain's own house. Aided by his eldest son, Fred, and his former military private secretary, Adam Badeau, who gathered information and checked facts, Grant embarked on writing his life story. News that Congress had finally passed the bill to restore him to military rank pleased him, but the pain of the growing cancer made dictation a struggle, and he turned to scribbling his thoughts on a pad. Every day the press issued updates on what soon became the longest running deathwatch of a public figure in American history. At one point, when it looked as if he were on the verge of death, Badeau offered to complete the work; Grant, already displeased by what he saw as Badeau's presumptive behavior, dismissed him. Intent on finishing and worried about the impact on his health should he remain in his New York brownstone off Fifth Avenue on 3 East 66th Street, Grant accepted an invitation to relocate in June 1885 to Mount McGregor in upstate New York, less than a dozen miles from Saratoga. Just over a month later he completed work on his memoirs, a few days before his death on July 23, 1885.

Grant's memoirs have long been hailed as a classic of American letters; the clear prose, occasional dry wit, and lucid explanations of campaigns and battles were matched by the tremendous sales of the two-volume work, securing the financial future of his family. Understandably, they recounted his life only through the end of the Civil War, although he offered a few observations about Reconstruction. Here and there he settled old scores or remained silent on personal questions, most notably his rumored fondness for alcohol. And yet to anyone familiar with the pattern of Grant's life, with its extremes of success and failure, the success of the book should have come as no surprise, for anyone who had ever underestimated Ulysses S. Grant eventually had cause to regret it. As a general he stood in the forefront of his craft; if he did not match that success as president, he was far from the stumbling failure portrayed by critics and a number of ill-informed historians who accepted his critics at face value. In many ways Grant was the symbol of his age as well as its foremost hero: as a staff officer noted in 1864, "He is the concentration of all that is American."

Further Reading

Perhaps the best way to commence reading about Ulysses S. Grant is to consult *The Personal Memoirs of U. S. Grant,* 2 vols. (New York: C. L. Webster, 1885–86), which has been widely praised as a masterpiece by critics ranging from Edmund Wilson to Gore Vidal. Essential as well is John Y. Simon et al., eds., *The Papers of Ulysses S. Grant,* 24 vols. (Carbondale: Southern Illinois Univ. Press, 1967), which contains Grant's personal correspondence and official documents.

Surprisingly, there is a dearth of capable single-volume biographies, despite a recent upsurge of interest: readers can choose between William S. McFeely, *Grant: A Biography* (New York: Random House, 1997), a book whose usefulness is marred by numerous factual errors that outweigh the occasional insight; and Jean Edward Smith, *Grant* (New York:

Simon and Schuster, 2001), which provides a reasonable synthesis of much recent scholarship.

For more detailed examinations of Grant's life throughout the Civil War, one should turn to Lloyd Lewis, *Captain Sam Grant* (Boston: Little, Brown, 1950); Bruce Catton, *Grant Moves South* (Boston: Little, Brown, 1960), and *Grant Takes Command* (Boston: Little, Brown, 1969); or Brooks D. Simpson, *Ulysses S. Grant: Triumph over Adversity, 1822–1865* (Boston: Houghton Mifflin, 2000), the first of a two-volume study. Valuable as well are Horace Porter, *Campaigning with Grant* (New York: Century, 1897); Albert D. Richardson, *A Personal History of Ulysses S. Grant* (Hartford, Conn.: American Publishing, 1868); the controversial Sylvanus Cadwallader, *Three Years with Grant* (New York: Knopf, 1955); Kenneth P. Williams, *Lincoln Finds a General,* 5 vols. (New York: Macmillan, 1949–59); J. F. C. Fuller, *The Generalship of Ulysses S. Grant* (London: John Murray, 1929); and T. Harry Williams, *McClellan, Sherman, and Grant* (New Brunswick, N.J.: Rutgers Univ. Press, 1962).

A study that links Grant's wartime and early postwar involvement in issues of strategy, politics, and policy is Brooks D. Simpson, *Let Us Have Peace: Ulysses S. Grant and the Politics of War and Reconstruction, 1861– 1868* (Chapel Hill: Univ. of North Carolina Press, 1991). For Grant's presidency, which is currently undergoing reevaluation, see William B. Hesseltine, *Ulysses S. Grant: Politician* (New York: Dodd, Mead, 1935), and Frank J. Scaturro, *President Grant Reconsidered* (Latham, Md.: Univ. Press of America, 1998), which argues for a more positive view. Grant's Reconstruction policy is covered in William Gillette, *Retreat from Reconstruction, 1869–1879* (Baton Rouge: Louisiana State Univ. Press, 1979), and Brooks D. Simpson, *The Reconstruction Presidents* (Lawrence: Univ. Press of Kansas, 1998); Robert H. Keller, *American Protestantism and United States Indian Policy, 1869–92* (Lincoln: Univ. of Nebraska Press, 1983). Covering Grant's final years are Thomas Pitkin, *The Captain Departs: Ulysses S. Grant's Last Campaign* (Carbondale: Southern Illinois Univ. Press, 1973), and Richard Goldhurst, *Many Are the Hearts: The Agony and Triumph of Ulysses S. Grant* (New York: Reader's Digest, 1975).

Rutherford B. Hayes

Nineteenth President of the United States, 1877–1881

ARI HOOGENBOOM

Sophia Birchard Hayes, mother of Rutherford Birchard Hayes, knew death well from a young age. When she was thirteen, growing up in Vermont, her father died of tuberculosis, and before she was twenty-one two siblings and her mother died of typhus. But Sophia also knew happiness. Prior to her mother's death, Sophia fell in love with Rutherford Hayes Jr., a storekeeper, whom she married in 1813 (six months after her mother's death), and they began to raise a family. Hard times in 1817 led the young family to migrate—a forty-nine-day wagon trip—from Vermont to Delaware, Ohio, where they farmed and operated a distillery. Then in 1821, the couple lost their four-year-old daughter, Sarah, and in July 1822 typhus claimed the life of Sophia's husband. Pregnant, in her third trimester, she was left to care for her younger brother, Sardis, who had a wild streak, as well as her seven-year-old son, Lorenzo, and her two-year-old daughter, Fanny. On October 4, two months after her husband's death, the birth of his namesake, Rutherford Birchard Hayes, added to her heartache, because she did not expect the "sickly, feeble boy" to survive infancy.

Rutherford, or Rud as he was called, did survive. But just as he waxed in strength, his nine-year-old brother Lorenzo, who had always been sturdy, drowned while ice-skating in January 1825. Sustained by the Presbyterian faith that she had embraced after her husband's death, Sophia coped, but she became excessively protective of Fanny and Rud, whom she would not let engage in rough-and-tumble sports until he was nine. Fanny, who was very bright, was Rud's constant companion. He played with her dolls (until he got toy soldiers), and they read together and recited passages from Shakespeare, Walter Scott, and other favorites. Despite their mother's understandably dour outlook on life, Fanny and Rud would joke and pun irreverently, and while loving "each other dearly," Fanny would tease Rud unmercifully while he, frustrated by her quick wit, would sometimes respond with his fists.

For Rud, the trio that he, his mother, and his sister formed was the stable core of his family. Sardis moved away when Rud was four and prospered as a merchant and land speculator in northern Ohio. Although Sardis served as Rud's surrogate father and Rud admired him greatly, he was only an occasional presence. Sophia depended on her brother only for unusual expenses, such as school tuition. To cover day-to-day costs, she took in boarders, rented out the farm, and managed carefully. After Lorenzo's death, she contemplated selling her farm and moving back to Vermont, but depressed land values and emotional ties to her adopted state kept her in Ohio.

Bonds with one's state and section were strong in early-nineteenth-century America. Thanks to his mother's decision to remain in Ohio, Rud Hayes grew up a passionate Buckeye. His love for his home state developed early and never waned. His devotion to Ohio in turn enhanced his devotion to the American Union because Ohio was its creation. To what Hayes called the great charters of the U.S. government—the Declaration of Independence, the Northwest Ordinance of 1787, and the federal Constitution—the citizens of Ohio owed their freedom, equality, schools, republican government, and membership in a viable growing union. Moreover, federal policies regarding land, tariffs, monetary matters, and American Indians, from Hayes's viewpoint, furthered the aspirations of Ohioans. Even as a boy, he did not think that federal power threatened the interests or rights of states, and he rejected the idea that a state could nullify within its borders a law of the United States. With no urging, he would recite Daniel Webster's classic 1830 denial of nullification: "Liberty and Union, now and forever, one and inseparable." When Hayes matured and achieved military and political prominence, he always felt his love of Ohio was fully consistent with defending the Union, enhancing the power of the presidency, and, to secure a more equable society, supporting universal education with federal funds.

The Union shaped Ohio, and Ohio molded Rutherford B. Hayes. He appreciated his New England heritage, but he was proud to be a Buckeye. Hayes was the outstanding boy scholar in Joan Hills Murray's school in

Delaware, Ohio, and at thirteen and fourteen years old he did well in his preparatory studies at the Norwalk [Ohio] Seminary, yet had no strong desire to go to college. Arguing that "all the plow joggers are happier than students," Rud wished to be an Ohio farmer and while at home, when Fanny was off at school, he did little studying. His family, however, wanted to prepare him for a distinguished career, preferably in law or public service. Realizing that he was lazy at home but a fast learner at school, Sophia, Fanny, and Sardis agreed that fifteen-year-old Rud should attend Isaac Webb's Preparatory School in Middletown, Connecticut. There he progressed and was happy, but he was ever aware that he was a Buckeye in a Yankee school. He liked his two Buckeye intimates there "a little 'taller' than anybody else in Connecticut." His Ohio chauvinism was often playful, as when—remembering the woeful condition of Ohio's roads—he claimed that "a Buckeye ride in mud two feet deep" was superior to a Yankee sleigh ride in two feet of snow. The scroll on the coat of arms he designed as a boy was: "R. B. H., Buckeye."

His mother reinforced Rud's identification with Ohio. His Uncle Sardis wanted him to remain in Webb's school for another year and then enter Yale, but she insisted dolefully, "If Rd. lives he is to be a Western man" and called him home to attend Kenyon College in Gambier, Ohio. Growing up as a "Western man," and specifically as a small-town Ohioan, nurtured Hayes's egalitarianism. In Delaware he had encountered no entrenched mercantile or plantation elite as existed in the East or in the South, and despite modest circumstances Fanny and Rud were content. They did envy the "picture and story books" belonging to the children of the town's leading lawyer, but they also felt equal to them in their town's fluid, mobile society. Rud remained faithful to the egalitarian ideal he identified with Ohio. Years later, when residing in Fremont, Ohio, he proudly celebrated "this level country,—level society as well as scenery."

Rud's years at Kenyon College (1838–42) confirmed his unpretentious, friendly nature. Because he was "growing so fast," Sophia outfitted him meagerly, and constant wear reduced his clothes to tatters. His "shabby" appearance—about which he teased his mother—harmed neither his self-esteem (which, in his opinion, was "remarkable") nor the esteem of students and teachers. Northern and Southern students at Kenyon were sharply divided over sectional issues and nearly came to blows on July 4, 1839, yet Rud had associates in both camps, some of whom became his lifelong friends, among them Stanley Matthews of Cincinnati and Guy Bryan from the banks of the Brazos River in the then-independent country of Texas.

Rud did well in college. Kenyon's curriculum emphasized Greek and Latin classics, biblical literature (but not Hebrew), and included natural philosophy (the physical sciences), mathematics, and "mental philosophy," which stressed "habits of study and reflection." Rud profited from his courses, liked his teachers (especially Bishop Charles Pettit McIlvaine, the ex officio president of the college) but probably gained more from his extracurricular activities. Outside of class, he honed his writing and debating skills as a member of the Philomathesian Society, and the college's library records reveal that he read more history, biography, fiction, and poetry than his peers.

Rud's last years at Kenyon were triumphant. As a junior he emerged as a campus leader, respected for his level head and good judgment. With leadership came the resolution of his career goals. In typical bantering fashion, he told his mother that he "would love to be a farmer," but failing that he would spend every cent he could on "a *good* and *complete* education, and . . . practice law in some dirty little hole out West." She knew he was teasing about farming and the dirty hole west of the Mississippi, but was serious and purposeful about education and the law.

Rud remained focused during his senior year despite severe personal strain. His sister Fanny had become gravely ill. She had married following his freshman year, had suffered the loss of her first child during his junior year, and after the birth of her second child during his senior year suffered a postpartum psychosis that institutionalized her for more than six months. He was disturbed but not distracted; he excelled in his studies, served as president of the Philomathesian Society, and was surprised to be named valedictorian of his class because the honor had always been given to a church member, and he neither had nor ever would join a church. Taking it all in stride, he discovered after commencement that he was "the same old Rud" without "a single cubit added to my stature."

To prepare for the legal profession, Hayes for ten "vexatious and tedious" months read law under the tutelage of Thomas Sparrow, a competent Columbus lawyer. He stayed with his fully recovered sister and her family. But Hayes at twenty was still easily distracted when studying on his own. He found the political scene in the state capital, the bookstore under Sparrow's office, the coffee house in the same building as his brother-in-law's jewelry shop, the study of German (so he could read Schiller in the original language), and newspapers more enticing than Sir William Blackstone's *Commentaries on the Laws of England,* whose mastery he regarded as the passport into the legal profession. Lack of progress convinced Hayes and his family that he should attend Harvard Law School.

His expenses were met by the 10 percent interest he received from his share of the recent sale of his mother's Marion County property with supplements from Sardis when necessary.

The reaction of Hayes to Boston in 1843 was as ambivalent as his earlier feelings about Connecticut. He realized that his instructors at Harvard—Justice Joseph Story of the U.S. Supreme Court and Simon Greenleaf—were vastly superior to Sparrow in Columbus. Story was a font of good sense, high ideals, and intense patriotism and frequently digressed to eulogize sages of the law or to tell amusing anecdotes or relate fragments of his own experience. In contrast, Greenleaf was "searching and logical," kept "the subject constantly in view," and, Hayes concluded, a better teacher than Story. When not studying, Hayes visited Bunker Hill, the Boston Navy Yard, and Mount Auburn Cemetery; attended the theater and lectures by literary figures Henry Wadsworth Longfellow, Jared Sparks, and Richard Henry Dana Jr.; participated in political rallies, played ball, and found in the conservative Unitarian Dr. James Walker a preacher worth listening to twice on Sundays in the Harvard College Chapel. Yet Hayes remained a Buckeye who associated primarily with other Buckeyes. In September 1844 at a huge rally on Boston Common for Henry Clay, the Whig party's presidential candidate, Hayes marched "with the Buckeye delegation." He spoke derisively about self-satisfied, fashionable Boston men, with the same kind of cravat, coat, and whiskers, and proud, pious Boston women, none of whom "could be a belle in Columbus." His hypercritical remarks suggest an uneasy, self-conscious, lonely westerner who was not at home in New England.

Hayes never seriously thought of practicing law outside of Ohio. He initially settled in Lower Sandusky in the northwestern part of the state, where his Uncle Sardis lived. Sardis could steer clients his way, and Lower Sandusky was far enough away from Columbus, where his strong-minded mother and sister lived. However, Lower Sandusky turned out to be neither challenging professionally nor stimulating socially. Its belles could not compare with those of Columbus or (despite his earlier disparaging remarks) of New England. By the spring of 1847 Hayes was disappointed in love, bored professionally, and plagued by a bleeding sore throat and ebbing strength. Suspecting tuberculosis, his physician advised him to change his routine, diet, and climate for a year or two. In response Hayes concocted the "wild scheme" of enlisting in the army and going off to war in Mexico for therapeutic as well as patriotic reasons. As a Northern Whig he believed the Mexican war, which had begun a year earlier, was unjust, but as an American expansionist with unrealistic notions about war, he longed to be a part of it, "playing the Vagabond" and sowing his wild oats. But Hayes agreed with his family to take the advice of Cincinnati's leading physician, Dr. Reuben D. Mussey, who upon examining him told Hayes to avoid the "extreme heats of the South" and prescribed cod-liver oil, exercise in the open air, and, when stronger, travel to the North. Following Mussey's regimen, Hayes's throat healed and his strength returned, but after five less-than-challenging years in Lower Sandusky (which he helped rename Fremont), he decided to move to Cincinnati, the West's biggest city.

In the winter of 1848–1849, before settling in Cincinnati, Hayes, accompanied by his Uncle Sardis, visited his college friend Guy Bryan in Texas. This enjoyable and instructive trip provoked his usual ambivalent feelings about places outside of Ohio. He found Texans hospitable but violent, their customs fascinating yet repelling, their state vast with "boundless prairie" and wild with cougars and jaguars roaming along the Brazos River. Initially appreciative, Hayes after a few weeks became more critical of Texas and Texans. Although noting there were "many finely improved sugar plantations" along the Brazos, he judged that the white men on them were "generally dissolute and intemperate," and, unlike Ohio, there were "few villages, no mechanics, no public improvements." After visiting the plantation of a "shrewd, intelligent, cynical old bachelor," Hayes concluded that his way of life had affected his character. "The haughty and imperious part of a man develops rapidly on one of these lonely sugar plantations, where the owner rarely meets with any except his slaves and minions." Hayes— with his Ohio ideas of freedom and equality—doubted (quite naively) "whether a person of Northern education could so far forget his home-bred notions and feelings as ever to be thoroughly Southern" in defending slavery. Although Hayes recognized the skill of individual slaves, he observed that slave labor—lacking incentives—was not only unjust to slaves but also inefficient and aggravating as well as degrading for slaveholders.

Hayes arrived in Cincinnati on Christmas Eve 1849, and, although he would experience some lean years, he found that city stimulating professionally, intellectually, and socially. He shared an office with John W. Herron, who became his lifelong friend (and was later the father-in-law of William Howard Taft, the early-twentieth-century president from Cincinnati, Ohio). Hayes also joined the Cincinnati Literary Society and with its members imbibed ideas laced with "liberal amounts of the local Catawba wine" or "German lager" at Gleissner's in the Over-the-Rhine district, met Ralph Waldo Emerson during his ten-day course of lectures, attended the theater, and flirted with charming "city belles."

Although fascinated by the sophisticated ways of those belles, Hayes, at heart "a country-bred boy," contrasted their "artificial" attractions with the "natural gaiety," "gleesome smile and merry talk" of Lucy Webb from Delaware, Ohio, who was attending Wesleyan Female College. Although Lucy was nine years his junior, the charms of the city belles—especially those of Helen Kelley, the coquettish daughter of railroad president Alfred Kelley—faded as Hayes appreciated more and more the ingenuousness of Lucy. "Must keep a guard on my susceptibles," he warned himself, "or I shall be in beyond my depths." His susceptibles, however, were not too strong. Lucy and Hayes were engaged in June 1851 but, because Hayes felt his income insufficient, delayed their marriage until December 1852.

Lucy was a bright, vivacious, unpretentious woman with strong beliefs in Methodism, temperance, and abolition. She influenced her husband without nagging him about their differences: his unorthodox Christianity, his moderate use of alcoholic beverages, and his less-than-ardent antislavery views. Although not an abolitionist, as a lawyer he soon defended runaway slaves; although he neither acknowledged Jesus Christ as a personal savior nor joined a church, in time he attended Methodist services regularly; and although he was a temperate social drinker, he ultimately became a total abstainer. Lucy, who stressed good works more than blind faith, was satisfied that her husband was a decent man with impeccable morals.

Soon after their marriage, in fairly quick succession Lucy and Hayes had three boys who survived, lost two additional boys in infancy, had a girl at last (much to Hayes's delight), then another boy, and finally their eighth child—a boy—died in infancy. They were indulgent and understanding parents who enjoyed their children. Hayes romped on the floor with his boys, treasured their bright and amusing sayings, and when they were older delighted in their baseball playing, tried to cultivate their minds, advised them not to do anything they would be ashamed to tell their mother, tolerated a visit to Saratoga in racing season, and encouraged them in their careers. It was, however, his daughter Fanny—named for his sister—who was his favorite.

Although not connected directly, marriage, reputation, and prosperity coincided for Hayes. He gained renown and insight, but little income, as a defender of murderers and runaway slaves. In his most celebrated cases, Hayes saved Nancy Farrer from the gallows and prevented the return of Rosetta Armstead to slavery. These and other cases heightened his antislavery feelings and made him a lifelong proponent of prison reform and ultimately an opponent of capital punishment. Because Nancy Farrer, the poisoner of two families, wore a foolish expression and was so homely that she appeared deformed, Hayes convinced a jury that she was mentally unsound. The Rosetta Armstead case was more complex. She was a young slave who entered Ohio while being moved on behalf of her owner from Louisville, Kentucky, to Richmond, Virginia. In Columbus, alert antislavery activists detained her. Her owner journeyed to Columbus and asked her, a minor, to choose between him and freedom. When she chose liberty, he apparently acquiesced but then changed his mind and had her arrested by federal authorities as a runaway slave. She was taken to Cincinnati, where her antislavery guardian (who had been appointed by the probate court at Columbus), sought a writ of habeas corpus in the Hamilton County Court of Common Pleas. Along with Senator Salmon P. Chase and Judge Timothy Walker, Hayes defended Armstead.

The Rosetta Case, as it was called, attracted enormous attention. Not only was Armstead's freedom at stake, but intriguing legal questions were involved. Because her owner was responsible for her presence in Ohio, could she be considered a runaway slave? If not a runaway, did she become free when her foot touched Ohio soil? If still a slave, did her owner manumit her when he offered her freedom and she chose it? Could a minor make that decision? Could a writ of habeas corpus issued by a state court release someone imprisoned by a U.S. marshal? The Ohio court, claiming the right of transit with slave property through Ohio did not exist, issued the writ releasing Armstead, but the U.S. commissioner, charged with enforcing the 1850 Fugitive Slave Act, had her rearrested and held a hearing. Hayes made the closing address at the hearing and, in Chase's words, "acquitted himself with great distinction," arguing that Rosetta Armstead was neither a fugitive nor a slave because she was taken—and did not flee—to the free state of Ohio.

The antislavery cause gave new meaning to Hayes's long-term fascination with politics. During his adolescence, the political scene provided the liveliest entertainment in his small Ohio town, and because his Uncle Sardis was an ardent Whig, Hayes rooted for that party with the same passion latter-day youths have for their favorite ball clubs. In 1840, while at Kenyon, he wrote a partisan Whig history of the "whirlwind" that elected his candidate for the presidency, William Henry Harrison. His ardor for Whig presidential candidates continued in 1844, when Hayes would have cheerfully started his career as a lawyer "without a penny" if such a sacrifice would have elected Henry Clay, and in 1848, when he campaigned "like a trooper" (this time with success) for Mexican War hero Gen. Zachary Taylor. Hayes briefly soured on politics after the Compromise of 1850 seemed to settle the slavery extension issue and neither the Whig nor the

Democratic party was willing to upset the resulting status quo. But the 1854 Kansas-Nebraska Act, throwing open to slavery much of the western land previously closed to it, reinflamed the slavery extension issue and led Hayes in 1855 to join in establishing the Republican party in Ohio. It opposed the extension of slavery from the South into the western territories of the United States. Hayes's ardor for politics returned in 1856 with the nomination of John Charles Fremont as the first Republican presidential candidate. Fremont's defeat "in the first pitched battle" disappointed but did not discourage Hayes, who declared: "However fares the cause, I am enlisted for the war."

Hayes's own entry into politics came in December 1858, when the Cincinnati city council elected him to fill out the term of the city solicitor, who had been killed by a locomotive. Hayes's election by one vote marked the beginning of his reputation for phenomenal luck in politics and war. But his much-touted luck was neither blind nor dumb. He never appeared to be seeking office. Instead, by instinctively and deliberately enhancing his availability, he created conditions conducive to good luck. Eschewing extreme positions, he made himself acceptable to a wide spectrum of voters. Genuinely decent and kind, he was careful not to take his friends for granted nor to offend his rivals. And Hayes's reputation for fairness and integrity made him acceptable to many who did not agree with him on issues. In April 1859 the people of Cincinnati elected him to a full term as their solicitor.

In the early months of the 1860 presidential campaign, Hayes felt curiously detached, but by October he enthusiastically supported the Republican presidential nominee, Abraham Lincoln. Although opponents predicted disunion if Lincoln was elected, Hayes was not afraid to confront the threats of secession by the "ultra South." He concluded, "If the threats are meant, then it is time the Union was dissolved or the traitors crushed out." He believed that the moderate states of the upper South and lower North (especially his beloved Ohio Valley) would not tolerate disunion. Lincoln won the election, and seven states of the lower South seceded during the winter of 1860–1861, organized the Confederate States of America, and prepared to fight for independence if opposed by the U.S. government. At this point Hayes feared a compromise perpetuating slavery more than he feared disunion and civil war. Months of uncertainty ended in April 1861 when Confederate batteries fired on Fort Sumter in the harbor of Charleston, South Carolina. "I like it," Hayes decided. "Anything is better than the state of things we have had." Doubting both his own military capacity and that the war would last, Hayes did not volunteer immediately. In a month, the urge to be part of the war became too great: *"I would prefer to go into it if I knew I was to die or be killed in the course of it, than to live through and after it without taking any part in it."*

Thanks to his political connections, on June 7, 1861, Hayes was commissioned a major in the 23d Ohio Volunteer Infantry. From the start, he enjoyed military life "as much as a boy does a Fourth of July." Moving and acting in concert, the regiment aroused Hayes's emotions and confirmed his long-standing Ohio chauvinism. His skilled and resourceful men, Hayes boasted, were "fully equal to the famous Massachusetts men in a mechanical way. They build quarters, ditches, roads, traps; dig wells, catch fish, kill squirrels." He discovered "a new sensation" in "the affection and pride" he felt for his troops.

The ensuing four years of warfare confirmed Hayes's initial bias in favor of western troops, preferably from Ohio and especially the men of his beloved Twenty-third. In contrast, he found the Army of the Potomac, largely composed of eastern regiments, wanting. The 23d OVI was briefly attached to that army, commanded by George B. McClellan, during the 1862 Antietam campaign. Robert E. Lee's Army of Northern Virginia, capitalizing on its victory at Second Bull Run (August 29–30), invaded Maryland in September 1862 in a bold attempt to win it for the Confederacy. Federal troops, including the Twenty-third, followed in cautious pursuit. Hayes was appalled by the "confusion and disorder" among thousands of straggling Army of the Potomac men, whose officers left their commands "to rest in the shade" and "to feed on fruit." As it moved toward Frederick, Maryland, the crisply marching Twenty-third, Hayes proudly reported, was "always near the front, if not the front."

The Twenty-third was a good outfit. At South Mountain on September 14, General McClellan wished to force through Turner's Gap and attack Lee's scattered divisions. He selected Gen. Jesse L. Reno's corps to outflank the Confederates by penetrating Fox's Gap to the south of Turner's Gap. Reno called on Gen. Jacob D. Cox's division to lead; Cox placed Col. Eliakim P. Scammon's brigade up front, and Scammon picked the Twenty-third, commanded by Lieutenant Colonel Hayes, to spearhead the assault. Shortly after it made contact with the enemy, a heavy volley made its position untenable. With "his eyes shining like a cat's," Hayes ordered a charge, shouting, "Now boys, remember you are the Twenty-third, and give them hell." Having driven the Confederates back in that charge and a subsequent one, Hayes, sensing victory, had just ordered a third charge when a musket ball left a gaping hole in his left arm, breaking the bone but not shattering it.

Unable to set shattered bones, Civil War field surgeons routinely amputated the arms and legs of wounded soldiers. Although Hayes did not lose his arm, he lost much blood, and it was almost a year before he regained his strength. His skill and bravery at South Mountain earned his promotion to colonel of the Twenty-third. Beginning in January 1863 Hayes commanded a brigade and led raids against Confederates in western Virginia. The following year, arduous campaigning in the valleys of Virginia (as a part of Gen. George Crook's Army of West Virginia), where he worked to cut Confederate lines of communication with Richmond, brought Hayes new laurels and confirmed his bias against eastern troops. For example, Hayes attributed the Union victory on May 9 at Cloyd's Mountain to the Twenty-third, singling it out as "*the* regiment," and believed that the 36th Ohio would have done as well if it had led the assault. On the other hand, he had contempt for the Pennsylvania troops of the Potomac Brigade, who "broke and fled" and who after the battle engaged in "infamous and universal plundering."

Later in the summer of 1864, Crook's army became the Eighth Corps of Philip Sheridan's Army of the Shenandoah. Operating near Winchester, Virginia, the Eighth Corps especially distinguished itself at Opequon Creek (September 19) and at Fisher's Hill (September 22), where Hayes commanded a division. Apparently having demolished the Confederates under Jubal Early, Sheridan's forces systematically destroyed the enemy's resources in the valley as it moved north and grew complacent. At Cedar Creek on October 19, Early's small force surprised and badly mauled Crook's Eighth Corps (twice wounding Hayes) before Sheridan rallied his two other corps—the Sixth and the Nineteenth—counterattacked, and turned a disaster into a stunning victory. Before the Battle of Cedar Creek, the men of the Eighth Corps (comprised mostly of westerners) had bragged that they were the "A No. 1" corps in Sheridan's army. After that battle, Hayes believed that jealous, "foolish fellows in the Sixth and Nineteenth Corps . . . got the Eastern correspondents to represent the rout of Crooks's Corps as worse than theirs." After Sheridan's report "restored things gloriously," Hayes felt less defensive and was proud of his leadership and of his division for the way it had re-formed after its initial rout.

Following the Battle of Cedar Creek, the last engagement for both Hayes and the Twenty-third, he was promoted to brigadier general. He was especially proud to have earned it "at the close of a most bloody campaign on the recommendation of fighting generals like Crook and Sheridan." A few days after hearing of his promotion, he reviewed his troops and pronounced the Twenty-third "the crack regiment" but noted poignantly how few of its original members were left. "I could see only six to ten men in a company of the old men. They all smiled as I rode by. But as I passed away I couldn't help dropping a few natural tears. I felt as I did when I saw them mustered in at Camp Chase." The smiles of the veterans and the tears of the general acknowledged an unbreakable bond. To the end of the war, Hayes retained his bias in favor of western troops (idolizing fellow Ohioan William Tecumseh Sherman's army) and his prejudice against the Army of the Potomac ("composed too largely of the scum of the great Cities").

Hayes was mustered out of the army on June 8, 1865, and, after his discharge, was breveted major general for "gallant and distinguished services during the campaign of 1864." Not only had he experienced physical hardship, personal danger, and mental strain, Hayes had proved a worthy warrior: he had been wounded five times (once badly) and had four horses shot under him. In battle, he had "displayed personal daring, self-possession, and efficiency." William McKinley, fellow Ohioan and another future president who was with the Twenty-third all through the war, recalled, "His whole nature seemed to change when in battle. From the sunny, agreeable, the kind, the generous, the gentle gentleman . . . he was, when the battle was on . . . intense and ferocious." Although General Hayes was pleased with his title, he freely admitted, "I never fought in a battle as a general." As a citizen officer who had helped make the army of a free, democratic republic successful, he asserted with pride, "I was one of the good colonels in the great army."

Being a warrior had been hard, but it had given Hayes the experience of a lifetime. It also made him a hero in Ohio, and it shaped his subsequent political career. In 1864, before the war ended and while Hayes was in the Shenandoah Valley, his friends in Cincinnati nominated him for the U.S. Congress. When they asked him to campaign, he shrewdly refused, exclaiming, "An officer fit for duty who at this crisis would abandon his post to electioneer for a seat in Congress ought to be scalped." Hayes realized, however, that this letter, written from the front, would advance his career more than stump-speaking in Cincinnati. He was elected to the Thirty-ninth and then the Fortieth congresses, serving from 1865–1867. In Congress he backed Radical Republican Reconstruction measures establishing governments that guaranteed the vote for African American males in the states of the former Confederacy. Hayes attended regularly, spoke rarely (he thought most congressmen talked too much), and did significant work on the Joint Committee on the Library by facilitating the acquisition by the Library of Congress of the books and papers of the Smithsonian Institution and the collection of American pamphlets, manuscripts, and newspapers amassed by Peter Force.

Hayes did not enjoy being a congressman. He neither relished distributing patronage (because it disappointed more people than it gratified) nor liked running errands in Washington for constituents. But the real drawback was living away from his family for much of the year. By 1867 he was thinking of giving up politics entirely; then Ohio Republicans asked him to run for governor. The Hayes movement was especially strong in the Western Reserve of northeastern Ohio, where the Twenty-third had been recruited. Congressman Hayes, consistent with his lifelong commitment to equal rights, had advocated voting rights for black Americans in the South and was ashamed that they could not vote in Ohio. But that could change, because the state legislature had proposed to extend suffrage to blacks by an amendment to the Ohio Constitution. To become a part of that constitution, the proposed amendment would have to be ratified by Ohio voters in the upcoming election. With voting rights the major issue of the campaign, Hayes had no regrets about accepting the nomination. He was an obscure congressman with little influence, but if he became governor of Ohio he would be the major political warrior in a pivotal state and could strike decisive blows in the ongoing battle for equal rights.

Hayes plunged into the campaign on August 5, speaking once or twice daily. Although he was in an uphill fight against the Democrats, who appealed to racial prejudice, Hayes forthrightly advocated the state Negro suffrage amendment and defended Radical Republican measures reconstructing the Union. Hayes began his set campaign speech by invoking Lincoln's words at Gettysburg, and reiterated that the Declaration of Independence dedicated the nation to equal rights for all men. "Our government," he elaborated, "is not the government of any class, or sect, or nationality, or race." To Hayes, "the plain and monstrous inconsistency and injustice of excluding one seventh of our population from all participation in a Government founded on the consent of the governed in this land of free discussion is simply impossible." Hayes favored not only "impartial suffrage" but also free public schools for all, which would promote popular intelligence, economic progress, and sectional and racial harmony. Hayes believed that he and Ohio Republicans deserved victory because they aimed, like Lincoln, "to afford all an unfettered start and a fair chance in the race of life." The 1867 Ohio election, however, was a major Republican setback. Voters rejected the suffrage amendment to the Ohio Constitution, and the Democrats carried the state legislature and with it a seat in the U.S. Senate. On the positive side, Hayes, rewarded for his heroism in war as much as for his courageous campaign, won in the gubernatorial race by 2,983 votes out of 484,603 cast.

Hayes had little power as governor. Although he could make appointments and suggest legislation, the Ohio governor had no veto power. He could not stop the racist strategy of the Democratic legislature to gain white support through Negrophobia. The legislature, however, did gratify Hayes in one respect. In April 1869 it approved a geological survey of Ohio, which he called the "best thing of my administration." The Republicans renominated Governor Hayes in 1869 by acclamation. In his campaign, he castigated the Democrats for opposing Negro suffrage. He also attacked them for wanting to pay the federal war debt with greenbacks rather than with gold-backed dollars. This time, not only did Hayes win the governorship in another close election, but also the Republicans gained the legislature by a narrow margin.

Hayes hoped that with a slim Republican majority the Ohio legislature would ratify the proposed Fifteenth Amendment to the U.S. Constitution. This radical Reconstruction measure would prevent citizens from being denied the vote "on account of race, color, or previous condition of servitude." Hayes called for its approval in his annual message following his reelection and also urged the legislature to advance education, as well as civil-service, judicial, and penal reform. In addition, this former Civil War general did not wish to forget the veteran, "nor his widow, nor his orphan, nor the thousands of other sufferers in our midst." Hayes observed that civil servants under the patronage, or spoils, system, even "the Warden of the Penitentiary and his subordinates, and the Superintendents of asylums and reformatories and their assistants," were dismissed when their party lost power, no matter how much their experience had enhanced their qualifications. He advocated an amendment to the state constitution requiring that civil servants be appointed for their ability and not for their political services and influence, and that they be given the "same permanency of place" enjoyed by army and navy officers. To secure a judiciary independent from the influence of wealthy individuals and corporations, Hayes suggested that the current system of poorly paid elected judges be replaced by well-paid justices appointed by the governor and confirmed by the state senate.

Hayes's first priority was ratification of the Fifteenth Amendment. He engineered its passage—57 to 55 in the Ohio house and 19 to 18 in the Ohio senate—ironically by securing federal patronage for a handful of "Reform Republicans." The legislature also moved to provide a land-grant college.

Ohio had previously accepted the terms of the Morrill Land Grant Act of 1862, but squabbles over where to locate the school had paralyzed the legislature. The Morrill Act provided generous allotments of federal public lands for states to finance colleges of agriculture and the mechanical arts. In March 1870 the legislature heeded Hayes's pleas and established at Columbus the Agricultural and Mechanical College, which would become Ohio State University. In line with his convictions about civil service reform, Hayes initiated the practice of appointing minority party members to serve on the boards of state institutions and asked—without success—George Hunt Pendleton, his recent Democratic opponent for the governorship, to serve on the new college's board. Loving both history and Ohio, Hayes also began collecting manuscripts relating to Ohio history for the state library.

Civil service reform, humanitarian feelings, faith in education, and experience as a defender of murderers combined to make Hayes a penal reformer. Ever since the dreadful experience of accompanying to the gallows a murderer he had unsuccessfully defended, Hayes approved the death penalty only in egregious cases. During the war he had no sympathy for a bounty-jumping deserter and as governor he allowed it for murderers with criminal records and for those who had killed during a robbery, but he was criticized when he commuted death sentences "on the ground of youth and doubt as to the deliberation and premeditation of the act."

In 1871, during the final year of his second term as governor, Hayes again resolved "to quit the race for political promotion." He believed that the "small questions of today about taxation, appointments, etc." were uninteresting compared with "the glorious struggle against slavery" and not worth the "worry and anxiety" of political life. Hayes thought that his mission in politics—securing equal rights for African Americans—had been achieved with the passage of the Fourteenth and Fifteenth Amendments.

As Hayes retired from the governorship in January 1872, he squelched a movement to make him a U.S. senator in place of John Sherman. Hayes had no strong desire to return to Washington. Scandals at the national level of politics had besmirched the Republican party, and President Ulysses S. Grant—although personally upright—had alienated many liberal reformers by making unsavory appointments and choosing spoils-minded advisers. By 1872 the Liberal Republican revolt against Grant and "Grantism" was in full swing. Although Republican corruption disturbed Hayes, he thought the Liberal Republicans, by opposing Grant, were playing into the hands of the Democrats, who committed the "crime" of rebellion, were "wrong" on Reconstruction, and were "led and ruled . . . by

New York City plunderers." Hayes heeded pleas to strengthen the Republican ticket in 1872 by making a hopeless run for the U.S. House of Representatives. He lost, but Grant triumphed over the combined forces of the Liberal Republicans and the Democrats and secured a second presidential term. The recognition Hayes received for helping his party was paltry and disparaging. After the Grant administration nominated him to the minor post of assistant U.S. treasurer at Cincinnati, Senator John Sherman added insult to injury by temporarily blocking his confirmation. Hayes took pleasure in refusing this meager "reward" and was glad to be out of politics.

Hayes returned to private life but not to the practice of law. In the spring of 1873, at the age of fifty and tired after twelve years of "vagabondizing" as a soldier and a politician, Hayes moved with Lucy and their three youngest children (their two oldest boys were attending Cornell University) into the home his Uncle Sardis had built for them in Spiegel Grove on the outskirts of Fremont. When Sardis died in January 1874, Hayes inherited his considerable land holdings and was occupied in their management and active as a trustee of the Birchard Library, Sardis's gift to Fremont.

Hayes's busy semiretirement soon ended. By the spring of 1875, the Republican party was in disarray, both in Ohio and nationally. The Democrats controlled the state, and the deepening economic depression following the Panic of 1873 had enabled them to gain control of the House of Representatives that would convene in December 1875. Desperate to reverse their party's decline, Ohio Republicans turned to their best vote-getter and nominated Hayes to run for a third gubernatorial term.

"Now that I am in for it I rather like it," Hayes admitted, although he knew that once again he had an uphill fight. To get voters to forget the depression and Republican corruption, Hayes identified the Democratic party with slavery, rebellion, and repression of blacks since the war. He also stressed repudiation of the national debt (by paying it off with inflated greenbacks), corruption (especially Boss Tweed's New York), and Catholicism. In exploiting the Catholic issue, Hayes claimed that the Republicans were right to resist, and the Democrats wrong to support, Roman Catholic demands that public funds be used for parochial schools. The Ohio supreme court had recently upheld the Cincinnati school board's ban on hymn singing and the elimination of the reading of the Bible from the school curriculum. Based on that ruling, Hayes thought Catholics had no complaint about public schools. "We want to bring the children of Protestants, Cath[olics], Jews & Unbelievers together in the common School room." But while making his defense of public schools, which he believed

Lucy and Rutherford B. Hayes on their front porch of their Spiegel Grove estate in Fremont, Ohio. When Lucy died of a stroke in 1889 at the age of fifty-seven, Hayes commented that "the soul" had left their cherished home. He followed her in death less than four years later. Rutherford B. Hayes Presidential Center.

were the panacea for all social ills, he also knew he was appealing to Protestant prejudice against Catholics, which as a freethinker he did not share.

Once more Hayes triumphed by a narrow margin in a hard-fought campaign, and, looking beyond the governorship, at least ten Ohio papers announced they were backing him for the 1876 Republican presidential nomination. He recognized that his appeal was "on the score of availability," and he decided to "let availability do the work." Hayes did little to win the prize beyond securing a united Ohio delegation to the Republican national convention, which was held at Cincinnati's Exposition Hall, and taking care not to offend his five rivals for the nomination.

Fortunately for Hayes, his rivals were flawed. The front runner, Congressman James G. Blaine of Maine, apparently used his leverage as Speaker of the House in 1871 to sell some worthless railroad bonds to Tom Scott of the Union Pacific Railroad for $64,000. Senator Oliver P. Morton of Indiana was in poor health, too radical for moderates in the party, and too close to the Grant administration for reformers. Senator Roscoe Conkling of New York was even more closely identified with Grant and was too much of a spoilsman. On the other hand, the reformers' favorite, Secretary of the Treasury Benjamin H. Bristow of Kentucky, was hated by Grant and the machine politicians for exposing the Whiskey Ring of revenue officials who had robbed the treasury of millions in excise taxes and had ties to Grant's private secretary, Gen. Orville E. Babcock. And finally, John F. Hartranft, the favorite son of staunchly Republican Pennsylvania, was not needed as a candidate to carry his state.

Hayes was an ideal compromise candidate. He was a Union veteran who could identify Republicans once again with idealistic patriotism rather than political corruption and economic depression. As a congressman and governor he had struggled valiantly for equal rights, and he staunchly supported sound money. He was reform minded, yet he had remained loyal to Grant in 1872. Although forthright in his beliefs, he was by nature a conciliator who worked for party harmony. Finally, Ohio was a pivotal state for a Republican victory, and Hayes had carried it in three close gubernatorial elections. Availability did the work; his virtues triumphed over his rivals' flaws, and on the seventh ballot the Republican Party nominated Hayes for the presidency of the United States. The convention selected William A. Wheeler of New York as his running mate, strengthening the ticket in that crucial state.

Hayes was in for another tough political battle in 1876. The Democrats nominated for president the reform governor of New York, Samuel J. Tilden, a gifted political organizer, and filled out the ticket with Thomas A. Hendricks of Indiana. As was the custom in that era, neither Hayes nor Tilden participated actively in the campaign beyond writing formal acceptances of their nominations, which were in effect position papers. Tilden stressed his commitment to reform, frugality in government, and specie-backed hard money. Hayes affirmed his faith in nonsectarian public schools and his desire to resume specie payments for greenbacks, as scheduled, in January 1879. This action would return the United States to the gold standard. To arrest the drift of reformers away from the Republican party, Hayes called for the elimination of the spoils system and promised not to seek a second term, lest patronage be used to secure his reelection. He also pledged to promote honest and capable local government in the South when the constitutional rights of all citizens, black and white, were respected.

During the campaign Hayes shrewdly said nothing publicly beyond his published letter. Privately, he wrote encouragingly to his friends, but, despite moderate views, he warned his campaign biographer, William Dean Howells, to "be careful not to commit me on religion, temperance, or free-trade. Silence is the only safety." Nor would Hayes be provoked by Democratic accusations. "On general principles," he told Ohio congressman James A. Garfield, "I think explanations and defenses are bad things."

Theoretically, the Republican National Committee directed the Hayes presidential campaign. Its chairman was Zachariah Chandler, Grant's secretary of the interior and a spoilsman who ignored Hayes while cheerfully extorting "voluntary contributions" from civil servants to finance the campaign. Nevertheless, Chandler and his committee had limited resources, did not concentrate sufficiently on carrying doubtful states, and were ineffectual. Late-nineteenth-century political parties—lagging behind the organizational trend in American society toward consolidation and control at the top—were decentralized, and national committees were loose-knit superstructures with little power. State political machines and local party organizations, whose primary concerns were not national, provided dynamic leadership in presidential as well as other campaigns. Except for Ohio's party apparatus, Hayes was even more removed from state committees than he was from the Republican National Committee. If he had controlled his own campaign, he would have stressed that a Democratic victory would give "*the Rebels* control of the federal government," but that was what most Republican campaigners were doing.

On election day Hayes thought Tilden probably would win because the Democrats would resort to bribes and repeat voting in the North and "violence and intimidation" in the South. Unofficial returns seemed to confirm his analysis and Hayes went to bed that evening convinced that he had lost. He lamented that with a Democrat in the White House blacks in the South would suffer increased discrimination and violence because the Fourteenth and Fifteenth Amendments would not be enforced. In a few days, however, he concluded that he had won the election.

In fact, the 1876 presidential election was so corrupt that it is impossible to determine who would have won in an honest election. The Republicans used postelection frauds to counter preelection and election day violence and intimidation—aimed at black voters in the South—by the Democrats. Unofficial tallies of all votes cast—legal and illegal—gave Tilden a lead of a quarter of a million over Hayes and apparently more than the 185 electoral votes needed to win. But diehard Republicans claimed that on the basis of legal votes Hayes had carried South Carolina, Florida, and Louisiana, and with their electoral votes had beaten Tilden 185 to 184. The official votes of those three states, as determined by state returning boards dominated by Republicans (who were not above throwing out legitimate Democratic votes) were awarded to Hayes. Extralegal Democratic governments in those same states, however, also claimed victory and submitted electoral votes favoring Tilden. Hayes was always convinced that he deserved the disputed states. Indeed Hayes believed that if the election had been fair, he would have carried additional Southern states and a preponderance of the popular vote as well.

The federal Constitution requires that the presiding officer of the Senate (at that time Thomas W. Ferry, a Michigan Republican) count the electoral votes received from the states, in the presence of both houses of Congress. The Constitution, however, is silent on how a dispute over conflicting returns from a state is to be resolved. Ardent Hayes supporters argued that Ferry alone should decide which votes from South Carolina, Florida, and Louisiana to count, but many Republicans thought that view was extreme. All Democrats believed that a joint session of Congress should decide what electoral votes to count. Although they controlled neither the presidency nor the Senate, the Democrats controlled the House of Representatives and with it a majority in a joint session of Congress. Out of this impasse came the Electoral Commission Act (1877), which intended to allow seven Republicans, seven Democrats, and an independent—Supreme Court Justice David Davis—to decide which electoral votes to count. Davis, however, declined to serve on the commission, after he was elected senator from Illinois by Democrats who, in a monumental miscalculation, thought they were buying his support for Tilden. With no other independent on the U.S. Supreme Court, Justice Joseph P. Bradley, a Republican, took Davis's place. By an eight to seven margin, the commission awarded the disputed electoral votes to Hayes, giving him 185 and the presidency by one vote.

Frustrated and infuriated, Democrats delayed the count with a filibuster that both threatened to prevent Hayes's inauguration and aimed at salvaging concessions from Republicans. Democrats in Florida had already, on January 1, achieved "home rule" (in effect a white-supremacy state government after the state supreme court revised the official vote cast in 1876). They wanted to achieve home rule in Louisiana and South Carolina, too, by the removal of federal troops sustaining their Republican-led state governments. In addition, a minority of Southern Democrats wanted to secure federal support for constructing the Texas & Pacific Railroad. Claiming to represent enough Democrats to allow the count to be completed on schedule if they got home rule and the railroad, negotiators met with Republicans close to Hayes. He did not think the Southern negotiators were reliable, and although his friends "bargained," they did not concede anything beyond Hayes's acceptance-letter assurance that he would withdraw the troops when the Fourteenth and Fifteenth Amendments were obeyed.

Had there been no negotiations and no lobby seeking a land grant for the Texas & Pacific Railroad, the count would have been completed on time. Most Democrats, especially Speaker of the House Samuel J. Randall of Pennsylvania, realized that if their party plunged the nation into chaos on March 4, presidential inauguration day, it would be severely damaged in the eyes of Northerners, which might then provoke a new wave of Reconstruction legislation. Even so, fifty-seven diehard filibusterers, controlled by neither negotiators nor by lobbyists, prolonged the struggle. March 1–2, in one of the longest and stormiest sessions of the House, they offered various dilatory motions, which Randall refused to entertain, and he finally forced the completion of the count. At 4:10 A.M. on March 2, 1877, Ferry, guarded by four men with revolvers, announced that Rutherford B. Hayes, by a margin of one electoral vote, was the next president of the United States.

Hayes, on board a train bound for Washington, awoke to the news of his election at Marysville, Pennsylvania.

Hayes entered the White House with the poorest mandate in history. Approximately half of the American electorate and a majority of the House of Representatives were Democrats who thought he was elected by fraud. In addition, the Republicans, while united in the electoral crisis, were riven with factions: reformers versus spoilsmen, friends of Grant versus followers of James G. Blaine, those who would continue to support Southern Republican state governments versus those who would abandon them to home rule, those who supported hard-money versus those who supported soft money. Apart from the Ohio delegation, President Hayes had few congressional friends, and his cabinet selections, which could not satisfy everyone, made enemies of many powerful party leaders. Not only did he fail to include in his cabinet any of his rivals for the presidency or their minions, he horrified many members of his party by appointing Carl Schurz, a Liberal Republican reformer who had bolted the party in 1872; William M. Evarts, Roscoe Conkling's archenemy in New York; and David M. Key, a former Confederate from Tennessee, whom Hayes hoped would help attract Southern support for his administration.

Hayes's inaugural address reaffirmed his nomination letter of acceptance; the South would have home rule if it would accept the whole Constitution and respect the civil rights of all its citizens. Hayes, however, anticipated a new conciliatory Southern policy when he called for "a union depending not upon the constraint of force, but upon the loving devotion of a free people." He gave scant comfort to the Texas & Pacific Railroad lobby, merely suggesting the South deserved the considerate care of the federal government, limited by the Constitution and by economic prudence. As the foundation of prosperity, Hayes had more faith in the schoolhouse than in the railroad and called for supplemental federal support to enable all states to support free public schools for all their children. Hayes also called for a "thorough, radical, and complete" reform of the civil service and eschewed partisanship by reminding himself "that he serves his party best who serves the country best." He blamed the depression in commerce and industry, which had gripped the country since the Panic of 1873, on the fluctuating value of greenbacks—fiat money not backed by gold—and looked toward the scheduled redemption in 1879 of greenbacks with gold, which would put the United States back on the gold standard. "The only safe paper currency," he believed, "is one which rests on coin basis and is at all times promptly convertible into coin."

On taking office, Hayes faced a huge administrative task. He had to fill approximately a thousand offices that required senatorial confirmation. Loathe to make hasty appointments, he filled vacant positions but gained time for a careful consideration of other appointments by allowing incumbents to remain on the job until they were either reappointed or replaced. Hayes also faced a knotty Southern problem, but fashioning a Southern policy could not be postponed. Extralegal Democratic governments controlled virtually all of South Carolina and Louisiana, challenging the legitimate Republican governments, which existed only because federal troops protected them. With the exception of the few square miles surrounding statehouses in Columbia and New Orleans, Reconstruction had ended before Hayes entered the White House. Hayes had to decide whether or not to reinforce or to evacuate these remaining Republican "beachheads." Their position was precarious, but their legitimacy was based on the actions of Republican-controlled state election returning boards, as was Hayes election to the presidency.

Although they were legitimate, it was impossible for Hayes to continue to prop up these Republican governments. Restoring authority would require more troops and a long-term occupation of these Southern states. The U.S. Army, reduced since the Civil War to 25,000 men, was scattered, and the Democratic House of Representatives refused to appropriate funds for it beyond June 30, 1877, if the army continued to support Reconstruction governments. For Hayes to send South Carolina and Louisiana sufficient troops (which were not available at the time), he would have to rely on public opinion to force appropriations from Congress. The public, however, appeared unwilling to sustain further military occupation of the South. Many moderate Republicans (including Hayes) thought that military occupation exacerbated racial problems, polarized politics along the color line, and failed to help either blacks or the Southern Republican party. Voters indicated a growing disillusion with radical Reconstruction of the former Confederate states. With the country in a severe depression, people were more concerned about their own economic problems than with the fate of black and white Republicans in the South. A workable military option did not exist for Hayes.

The question really confronting Hayes was not whether the troops should be withdrawn, but when. Faced with a no-win situation, he tried to salvage something from it and used the tenuous presence of troops as a bargaining chip. Before withdrawing any of them, he wanted guarantees from the de facto Democratic governments in South Carolina and Louisiana that the Fourteenth and Fifteenth amendments would be obeyed. Upon receiving unequivocal promises that the civil, political, and educational rights of all citizens would be respected, as well as hints of Democratic defections to the Republican party, Hayes withdrew the troops. He was guardedly optimistic that the Southerners would keep their promises, but he added, "Time will tell."

Time did tell: the promises were not kept, and Democrats remained loyal to their party. They realized that Hayes gave them nothing beyond what the political temper of the country forced him to. Still, Hayes hoped he had gained something by the withdrawal of the troops. He did not perceive how pervasive racism was and assumed that educated and cultivated men (like himself) in the South would keep promises and deal fairly with blacks. He was angered when the promises were broken and had twenty-two South Carolinians arrested after the congressional elections of 1878 for intimidating voters, but legal maneuvers and all-white juries prevented convictions. Yet Hayes insisted that his Southern policy was working. He did so in part because the politician in him refused to admit that his policy had failed, but also because he was a patient reformer who believed he had taken the necessary first steps in solving a difficult problem. He had faith that progress in race relations would come not from military occupation but over time in small increments through education that would result in the enforcement of the laws by civil tribunals.

Hayes's moderation and patience were also apparent in his approach to civil service reform that was less than "radical" and displeased many. His stand against nepotism annoyed Grant (who had appointed numerous relatives). His refusal to appoint his own brother-in-law, Dr. Joseph Webb, as surgeon general of the Marine Hospital Service—a position for which he was well qualified—estranged Webb and caused Lucy heartache. Because civil servants to a large extent ran political campaigns and were assessed to finance them, reformers were pleased and spoilsmen outraged when Hayes, on June 22, 1877, forbade political assessments of civil servants and their participation in the electoral process. But John Sherman, who used Treasury Department patronage in his attempt to win the 1880 Republican presidential nomination, distressed reformers when he did not prevent violations of the spirit of the president's order.

Hayes's civil service policy enhanced the power of the president at the expense of Congress. When he attempted to fire Chester Arthur, who as collector of the port of New York headed its customhouse (the country's largest and most complex office), because he did not favor reform, Arthur's patron, Senator Roscoe Conkling, objected. He and his spoils-minded Republican colleagues temporarily prevented the removal and upheld "senatorial courtesy," the right of senators to control federal appointments in their states. Hayes ultimately triumphed over senatorial courtesy, and by the end of his administration senators and congressmen could suggest but not dictate appointments. Arthur was removed from the New York Customhouse, and at Hayes's insistence it became a showcase for reform. Hayes also ordered, but did not demand, that other major post offices and customhouses adopt civil service rules. With Hayes attempting only what he considered possible, reformers complained that he did not go far enough, and spoilsmen howled that he was destroying party organization. But Hayes had left the organization sufficiently intact to win the election of 1880. The reformed New York Customhouse proved the practicality of the merit system and made possible the passage of the 1883 Pendleton Civil Service Reform Act, which established a federal civil service based on competitive examinations rather than spoils. That act led to a greater stress in elections on issues, which presidents were better able to define, than on spoils, which congressionally dominated state and local party organizations depended upon.

Hayes traveled more than any previous president—to New England, to the South, and to the West Coast in a two-month journey. He spoke at Civil War–veteran reunions, at state fairs, and state capitals, at schools—including a government American Indian school in Oregon—and colleges. Rather than campaign for candidates on his trips, he gave minispeeches at nearly every whistle stop to rally support for issues close to his heart: equal rights for all citizens, universal public education, and the gold standard.

Hayes not only clipped the powers of Republican senators but also, from 1879 to 1881, prevented the Democratic Congress from destroying his veto power. With a majority in both houses of Congress, the Democrats added to appropriations bills riders that would repeal election laws designed to enforce the Fourteenth and Fifteenth amendments. These laws aimed to protect black voters in the South and to prevent ballot box stuffing in Northern cities. Eager to preserve laws that would advance equal rights and anxious to preserve the president's constitutional power to approve or reject bills, Hayes vetoed the appropriations bills and almost gleefully accepted the Democratic threat to shut down the government. In veto after veto he rallied Republicans in Congress and the nation to his side and forced the Democratic leadership to back down. By adding to and preserving presidential powers and publicizing issues, Hayes was a forerunner of modern presidents who stressed leadership.

Although his contemporaries gave Hayes high marks for his presidency, historians a hundred years later have been less favorable. They enjoy quoting Henry Adams's dismissal of Hayes in 1876 as "a third-rate nonentity" but fail to note that by 1880 Adams lauded him for conducting "a most successful administration." Modern critics, calling him "an inept politician," stress that Hayes abandoned Southern Republicans, was a lukewarm civil service reformer, championed the gold standard, promoted the acculturation of American Indians, broke the Great Railway Strike of 1877, negotiated the treaty that for generations ended Chinese immigration into the United States, and invited derision of himself and his wife—whom they, not contemporaries, called "Lemonade Lucy"—for banning liquor from the White House.

These criticisms are unfair or untrue and fail to appreciate either his genuine successes, such as with civil-service reform, or his limited options in areas such as Southern policy or Chinese immigration. Hayes vetoed the Chinese Exclusion bill of 1878, but recognizing the temper of Californians, especially following the anti-Chinese riots in San Francisco, negotiated a treaty that allowed restrictions but did not prevent all Chinese immigration. Congress later went beyond the spirit of that treaty by suspending indefinitely the immigration of Chinese laborers to the United States.

Hayes's unswerving monetary orthodoxy worked well in his administration—which was marked by a stunning business revival, an increase in foreign trade, and a drop in interest rates that accompanied the resumption of specie payments in January 1879. Prior to that business revival, the severe depression following the Panic of 1873 had led to widespread unemployment and, among those lucky enough to keep their jobs, wage cuts and increased workloads.

When Hayes took office in 1877, the conditions for a violent confrontation between capital and labor were present and required little to set off a chain reaction. That same year, presidents of four trunk-line railroads linking the East and Midwest agreed to cut employees' wages again by 10 percent and to increase the size of trains; work stoppages in major cities quickly spread from Baltimore to St. Louis. Strikers were soon joined by mobs of unemployed men and boys bent on rioting and looting. In Pittsburgh fifteen to twenty-five people died when the mob routed the Pennsylvania National Guard and then went on to destroy 104 locomotives and 2,152 freight cars belonging to the Pennsylvania Railroad. Hayes was neither friendly to railroads nor hostile to labor, nor did he end the Great Strike. Despite the begging of Tom Scott, president of the Pennsylvania Railroad, Hayes would not allow troops to operate trains. He also refused to use obstruction of the U.S. mail as a pretext for intervention. Hayes dispatched the few army detachments at his disposal to keep peace, and only when requested by state and local authorities. The army was universally respected and did not fire on the strikers.

Hayes ultimately arrived at an Indian policy that was humane but paternalistic. By the end of his term, he realized that uprooting American Indians was "wrong" and embraced four ideas that would bring Indians into the American mainstream. First, young Indians of both sexes should receive industrial and general education to both support and protect themselves. Second, Indians should gain title to land as individuals but with the proviso that it be nontransferable for a period of years, to protect them from scheming whites. Third, Indians should receive fair compensation for lands not needed for individual allotments, the amount to be invested for their benefit. Fourth, after securing education and land, Indians should become citizens of the United States. The development of economic self-sufficiency, the ultimate elimination of reservations, and full participation in the political system would transform them from American Indians into Indian Americans. In 1887, six years after Hayes left office, his ideas on land and citizenship for Indians would be incorporated in the Dawes General Allotment (Severalty) Act.

Hayes's position on alcoholic beverages has been widely misunderstood. It was calculated to keep both topers and teetotalers in the Republican party. Prior to becoming president, Hayes drank moderately outside the home, but following his first presidential state dinner, where drinks were served, Hayes decided to set an example by not drinking himself and banning liquor from the White House. He did not, however, favor Prohibition. Hayes's ban illustrates his prowess, rather than ineptness, as a politician. His symbolic temperance stand (which, contrary to popular belief, was his decision not Lucy's) was a shrewd political move and not merely a moral gesture. The highly visible act of having water flow like champagne at state dinners and receptions (as Secretary of State William M. Evarts quipped) kept temperance-minded Republicans from bolting to the new Prohibitionist party. Together, "wet" and "dry" Republicans handily won the election of 1880, with James A. Garfield defeating Winfield Scott Hancock, but after Hayes's successors served liquor at White House functions, defections to the Prohibitionist party cost the Republicans the election of 1884, as Democrat Grover Cleveland beat Republican James G. Blaine.

Hayes, a professional politician, succeeded by appearing to be above the political fray, but that clever ploy gave rise to the misleading notion that he was unskilled. He was aware that as a moderate reformer, a pragmatic idealist, and a gentle partisan, he was a more available and attractive candidate than the overtly political James G. Blaines and Roscoe Conklings of his day. Influencing historians of our day but not voters of their own era, these politicians viewed Hayes's style of politics with contempt. Hayes had his proverbial good luck—surviving frontline action, winning close elections, benefiting from an economic recovery—but his shrewd behavior abetted fortune. In 1877 the country was divided, distracted, and depressed, but when Hayes left office in 1881, he observed with pride that the country was united, harmonious, and prosperous. He had found the Republican party discordant, disheartened, and weak, but he left it strong, confident, and victorious. Mark Twain, in fact, concluded that Hayes's presidency, in "its quiet & unostentatious, but real & substantial greatness, would steadily rise into higher & higher prominence, as time & distance give it a right perspective, until at last it would stand out against the horizon of history in its true proportions."

In retirement at Spiegel Grove, Hayes resolved to "promote the welfare and the happiness of his family, his town, his State, and his country." He remained to the end of his life deeply committed to the principle of equal rights. No retired president, with the exception of Jimmy Carter, has worked as hard as Hayes for social justice. Believing that the United States' government and laws could be no better than its people, he labored constantly to broaden educational opportunities for all underprivileged children. He was the major dispenser of monies for two private educational funds dedicated to helping black and white children in the South and campaigned in and out of season for federal subsidies for children of all races in impoverished school districts. Universal education, he believed, would combat poverty, ignorance, and prejudice and would prove that his Southern policy—persuasion in place of the bayonet—was the only real solution to Southern problems.

Hayes's faith in education was closely related to his interest in prison reform and in reducing crime. As a defense attorney, he had worked to keep clients from the gallows, and as governor he had been generous in commuting death sentences and in issuing pardons. In retirement, while president of the National Prison Reform Association, he opposed capital punishment. Hayes was convinced that criminals could be reformed by education and that crime was primarily the product of poverty and desperation and could be reduced by a more equable distribution of wealth.

In the last decade of his life, Hayes came to believe that the disparity of wealth—pitting industrial "kings" against laboring men—was the greatest problem facing the nation. He dismissed social Darwinism by observing that unregulated competition led not to the survival of the fittest but to the triumph of the most predatory corporations. He favored federal regulation of railroads and industry. To bring about a more equal society, Hayes also favored confiscatory inheritance taxes. And he continued to consider education a solution. Believing that if financial moguls and political leaders experienced the toil of manual labor, laws and policies would improve capital and labor relations and consequently ease class tensions, Hayes favored universal industrial education. He was a precursor to the early-twentieth-century Progressive reformers. In a moment of reflection on his life, Hayes concluded, "I am a radical in thought (and principle) and a conservative in method (and conduct.)"

Lucy Webb Hayes died in 1889 and, although Spiegel Grove was still lovely, Hayes discovered that "the soul" had left it. He found comfort in the writings of Ralph Waldo Emerson, continued to work for social justice and education, enjoyed the company of friends and young people, and, with his unorthodox Christianity, had no fear of death. Indeed, upon viewing Lucy's grave in the snow on January 8, 1893, Hayes wrote, "My feeling was one of longing to be quietly resting in a grave by her side." Less than a fortnight later he joined her. On January 17, 1893, a few days after a severe attack of angina pectoris, Rutherford Hayes died at Spiegel Grove. Three days later, a large number of mourners, including President-elect Grover Cleveland

and Ohio governor William McKinley, attended the short and simple service at Spiegel Grove. They then followed the casket, borne by men of the 23d Ohio Volunteer Infantry, to the grave where Hayes was buried next to Lucy with the salute from guns and the playing of taps.

Further Reading

Hayes's papers, beautifully organized, are at the Rutherford B. Hayes Presidential Center in Fremont, Ohio. His diary and a portion of his correspondence have been edited by Charles Richard Williams in *The Diary and Letters of Rutherford Birchard Hayes: Nineteenth President of the United States*, 5 vols. (Columbus: Ohio State Archaeological and Historical Society, 1922–26). The diary of the presidential years has been meticulously reproduced by T. Harry Williams in *Hayes: The Diary of a President, 1875–1881: Covering the Disputed Election, the End of Reconstruction, and the Beginning of Civil Service* (New York: David McKay, 1964). Letters relating to Hayes's chief postpresidential interest are in Louis D. Rubin Jr., *Teach the Freeman: The Correspondence of Rutherford B. Hayes and the Slater Fund for Negro Education, 1881–1993*, 2 vols. (Baton Rouge: Louisiana State Univ. Press, 1959). Charles Richard Williams also wrote an appreciative *Life of Rutherford Birchard Hayes: Nineteenth President of the United States*, 2 vols. (Columbus: Ohio State Archaeological and Historical Society, 1914). Harry Barnard's *Rutherford B. Hayes and His America* (Indianapolis: Bobbs-Merrill, 1954) is strong on Hayes's early years. The most recent full-scale study of Hayes's life is Ari Hoogenboom, *Rutherford B. Hayes: Warrior and President* (Lawrence: Univ. Press of Kansas, 1995). For works on the Hayes administration, see Kenneth E. Davidson, *The Presidency of Rutherford B. Hayes* (Westport, Conn.: Greenwood Press, 1972), and Ari Hoogenboom, *The Presidency of Rutherford B. Hayes* (Lawrence: Univ. Press of Kansas, 1988). Hayes's distinguished Civil War career is covered in detail in T. Harry Williams, *Hayes of the Twenty-third: The Civil War Volunteer Officer* (New York: Alfred A. Knopf, 1965), and briefly in Ari Hoogenboom, *Rutherford B. Hayes: "One of the Good Colonels"* (Abilene, Tex.: McWhiney Foundation Press, 1999). For information on Hayes's family life, see Emily Apt Geer, *First Lady: The Life of Lucy Webb Hayes* (Kent and Fremont, Ohio: Kent State Univ. Press and Rutherford B. Hayes Presidential Center, 1984).

James A. Garfield

Twentieth President of the United States, 1881

JOHN B. SHAW

Much has been written of James A. Garfield's rise "from a log cabin to the White House." President Rutherford B. Hayes, nearing the end of his term in the White House in 1880, advised stressing Garfield's rapid ascent from poverty to prominence as a self-made man. "Let it be thoroughly presented," he said at the start of Garfield's campaign for the American presidency that year. And "thoroughly presented" it was; his extraordinary rise to national fame was written about in campaign biographies and newspapers and displayed on posters and even in cartoons.

It is an impressive story. Born in 1831 in Orange, Cuyahoga County, Ohio, he was the fourth child of Eliza Garfield and her husband Abram, a dirt farmer in the wilderness of the Western Reserve who cleared the trees from his property and built his log cabin. James, the last American president to be born in a log cabin, lost his father when he was two. Brought up by his doting but impoverished mother, Garfield worked hard on farms around the area as a young boy, haying, chopping wood, and boiling salts. At sixteen he found employment on the Ohio and Erie Canal as a canal boy, prodding the horses that pulled the boats through the water. A year later he enrolled at a Methodist academy in Chester, Ohio, and subsequently he attended the Hiram Eclectic Institute, a school newly founded in 1850 by the Disciples of Christ. James rose to the top of his class and, by virtue of his keen intellect and phenomenal memory, soon was teaching his fellow students as well as learning, his interest being in classical studies. At twenty-three, still basically a country boy with an almost obsessive ambition, Garfield made the boat, train, and wagon journey to Williams College in Massachusetts. After translating Latin and Greek texts and solving a few mathematical problems, he gained admission to the junior class. Rising again, this time to be in two years the outstanding student of the college and the favorite of its president, Mark Hopkins, he graduated in 1856 and returned home to be an educator.

James Garfield was twenty-five years old when he arrived back in Ohio and began teaching at Hiram. A year later, in May 1857, he became the school's principal. It was while at Hiram, as the nation lurched onward toward a catastrophic sectional crisis, that his involvement in civic affairs began. Republicans in 1859 selected Garfield, articulate and bright, as the most effective candidate from Summit and Portage Counties to represent the district as state senator. Garfield won by more than 1,400 votes in his first electoral effort and, in January 1860, took his seat in Columbus as a state senator.

How could this schoolmaster, James Garfield, come to be selected as the best possible political candidate from his district? His ability as a compelling orator certainly helped Garfield to become known in the Western Reserve; also, his riveting preaching in the Disciples of Christ church contributed to his prominence.

But most important, Garfield had achieved unusual popularity throughout the district because of his debates with William Denton, a sophisticated and experienced English spiritualist, a debunker of the Genesis account of creation. For some time Denton, an atheist, had been traveling through the Western Reserve debating Christian ministers, shocking the conservative farmers and simple settlers with his account of the incredible antiquity of certain fossil remains. Just a year before the publication of Darwin's *Origin of Species,* Denton brought a new geology with which he hoped to tear down cherished biblical creation truths. He expected to brush aside the young Garfield with ease. But Garfield had studied the issues deeply, including all the recent geological and zoological literature, so that he could answer Denton in his own terms. Five debates in Chagrin Falls, Ohio, brought together huge, highly partisan audiences. The young James Garfield had seven hundred to a thousand "fans" on his side for each of the five nights. He wrote a friend, "For the last two days and evenings, it was a fierce hand to hand fight. . . . In almost every encounter I felt the iron of his strength bend in my grasp." His resounding triumph extended throughout northeastern Ohio, and he acquired a reputation as a keen debater and an eloquent speaker.

And so on January 1, 1860, Garfield took his seat in the Ohio legislature. The youngest member, he was eager but unseasoned; in fact, until he began his tenure as senator, he had had little interest in politics. A description of him in those days tells of his good-humored, attractive gawkiness: "He was full of animal spirits. . . . He was a tall, strong man, but dreadfully awkward. . . . He was left-handed, too, and that made him seem all the clumsier. But he was most powerful and very quick. . . . He had a peculiar way of shaking hands, too, giving a twist to your arm and drawing you right up to him. This sympathetic manner has helped him to advancement." In Columbus, Garfield, so exuberantly physical, learned from his roommate, Jacob Dolson Cox, to control his boyish spirits and to rule his excited outbursts. "Big and strong," wrote Cox, "he was apt to show his liking for a friend when walking with him by grasping him with a hug that would almost make his ribs crack, and his hearty roar over a bit of fun . . . would be emphasized by a grip like a vise upon your arm."

Impatient for quick recognition and to enhance his reputation, Garfield spoke to nearly every issue. He argued against an economy measure touching libraries, but without success; he spoke against a bill taxing dogs, again without success; and he opposed a bill that guaranteed that no more raids against sister states would originate in Ohio. This last item had to do with Ohioan John Brown's raid at Harpers Ferry, Virginia, on October 16, 1859. Brown and eighteen followers secretly entered Harpers Ferry and captured the federal arsenal, seizing weapons, which he planned to give to slaves and consequently ignite a widespread insurrection. The plan failed. U.S. Marines stormed the arsenal and captured Brown, who was put on trial for murder and treason. Found guilty, John Brown was taken to the gallows on December 2, 1959, and hanged. Garfield had strong but ambivalent feelings about the raid, leading him to oppose the state senate bill. One can see from his diary entry on the day of Brown's execution how conflicted Garfield's feelings were:

A dark day for our country. John Brown is to be hung at Charleston, Virginia. I have no language to express the conflict of emotion in my heart. I do not justify his acts. By no means. But I do accord him, and I think every man must, honesty of purpose and sincerity of heart. When I reflect upon his devoted Christian character, his love of freedom, his sufferings in Kansas, the humane purpose of his heart in going to Virginia, his frankness on the trial, his coolness and undisturbed serenity when the terrible sentence was pronounced, his terse, manly, eloquent speech, so full of soul and heroism:—when I remember all this, it seems as though God's warning angel would sound through that infatuated assembly the words of a patriot of better days, the words, "I tremble for my country when I reflect that God is just, and His justice will not always slumber." Slavery, be damned! Brave man, old hero, Farewell. Your death shall be the dawn of a better day.

In the summer of 1860 the nation prepared to elect a new president. Garfield, now reputed to be one of the Republicans' most effective stump speakers, made more than fifty political speeches on behalf of Abraham Lincoln, the Republican presidential candidate. A Cleveland reporter wrote of Garfield's platform style that he "clothes his ideas in such clear and unambiguous language that they are at all times readily comprehended." And William Bascom, in whose Columbus home Garfield was living, observed: "No man in my recollection has sprung so suddenly into favor as an orator."

Lincoln won the presidency that November, and the Republican ticket again easily prevailed in Garfield's district 6,672 to 3,998. A month later South Carolina seceded from the federal union, and soon other states followed. "The Rebellion," as it was called in Ohio, took center stage in the Ohio legislature in January 1861. Along with Cox, James Monroe, and William Bascom, Garfield joined a group of resolute Republicans sworn never to compromise with the South. He also understood that intractable behavior would end in crisis: "I do not see any way, outside a miracle of God, which can avoid civil war, with all its attendant horrors. Peaceable dissolution is utterly impossible. Indeed, I cannot say I would wish it possible. To make the concessions demanded by the South would be hypocritical and sinful; they would neither be obeyed, nor respected."

Garfield's stand on the issue of secession and war was his chief contribution to this, his second, session of the Ohio legislature. The national situation grew darker when the Confederate attack on Fort Sumter brought President Lincoln's proclamation calling for the various Northern states to provide 75,000 volunteers to crush the rebellion. Garfield enthusiastically supported emergency measures calling for a million dollar state loan to raise and equip a state militia. In the summer of 1861, Garfield and John Sherman, just appointed U.S. senator by the Ohio legislature and brother of Gen. William Tecumseh Sherman, spoke again and again to huge crowds. They urged young men and boys to sign up for Ohio's 7th Regiment of Volunteers. By this time James Garfield, too, pondered enlisting.

As he contemplated joining the military during the autumn of 1861, Garfield had been married for three years, and his first child had been born. The marriage was a cause of great distress to Garfield. In later years it would become the essential foundation upon which his life's happiness and success were based, but now, in 1861, the relationship was charged with distrust, anxiety, and guilt.

In 1856, before his marriage, when Garfield had returned from Williams College with his bachelor's degree, he found himself in a perplexing dilemma. His secret engagement of two years before to Lucretia Rudolph, a Hiram girl, compelled him to treat her as his "promised." At the same time he had become enamored of Rebecca Selleck, a woman he had met in Massachusetts. Lucretia, greatly disappointed in how things were turning out, left Hiram for Cleveland, where she taught school. She continued occasionally to see Garfield and to correspond with him whenever he wrote her. "I could never be your wife," she told him, "unless every feeling of your heart seconded the decisions of reason. Perhaps I ask too much, but, James, to be an unloved wife, O heavens, I could not endure it."

But Crete (Garfield's nickname for her) did indeed have to "endure it." In 1858, after Garfield became principal of the Hiram Eclectic Institute, he felt he had to do something about this long-standing relationship. He proposed marriage in April, and the two were married the following November. Lucretia, much in love with him, allowed herself to be drawn into the marriage, knowing full well "our marriage," as she wrote, "is based upon the cold stern word *duty*." She expected she and James were in for difficult times.

Restless and unhappy at the Hiram Eclectic Institute and dissatisfied with his marriage, Garfield had been only too eager to take on the public life of a senator in Columbus in 1860. Now he saw the military, too, as a way of avoiding domestic strife. Thus, although his convictions about the crucial principles of saving the union and fighting against slavery were certainly genuine, even deeply felt, still mixed with those finer motives was the pressing temptation to be away from an uncomfortable home situation.

In August 1861 Garfield entered the army as a lieutenant colonel in the 42d Ohio Volunteer Infantry. The inexperienced new officer did what a scholar and teacher would do. To prepare himself he embarked upon "research" in the field of military strategy. Along with his friend Dolson Cox, Garfield read biographies: one of Napoleon Bonaparte and the other of the Duke of Wellington. He did not, however, read the standard works studied at the U.S. Military Academy. Nevertheless, he came to believe that "total war" could only mean the annihilation of Confederate armies, not merely capturing Southern territory and cities. "I have flung myself and all my plans," he wrote a friend, "into the scale of the war; the struggle and the questionings are all over and I am busy and cheerful in the work of tearing down the old fabric of my proposed life and removing the rubbish for the erection of a new structure." He used blocks to represent companies, officers, and noncommissioned officers in order to practice infantry tactics while sitting in his quarters. As for the problems of discipline, drill, training, and tactics, he had only his school teaching experience to fall back on. He took command of a thousand young men, many of them Hiram boys he had recruited for his regiment, and, like the affectionate and effective teacher he was, he drew close to his men, knew them by name, enjoying great popularity among them. But the new colonel also learned that at times he must be "hard and almost unfeeling."

During the fall of 1861, the 42d Ohio bivouacked at Camp Chase, just north of Columbus. Their quarters and equipment were hopelessly inadequate and makeshift, and Garfield worked unceasingly to provide blankets "and other comforts for the boys." It was not until the end of November that they had even rifles, but by then they were ready to move out. After the war, in the regiment's official history, Garfield was much praised for his leadership, even at this early point:

> The influence of General Garfield upon the Forty-second Regiment was unbounded. As colonel not less than as Professor and Principal of a collegiate school, he evinced a rare and extraordinary power in controlling, interesting and inspiring young men. It was due largely to his enthusiastic efforts that the regiment was made up of some of the best material that Ohio had sent into the field. The careful, laborious education, the discipline, the quickening of individual self-respect that the regiment underwent at his hands while in camp Chase were never lost upon its men. Long after he had gone to other duties the recollection of his words was a source of inspiration.

In early December the regiment was ordered into eastern Kentucky to block the slow progress northward by Gen. Humphrey Marshall, who commanded about three thousand Confederates. Garfield himself, now a full colonel, still far from being a seasoned soldier, reported to Gen. Don Carlos Buell's Army of the Ohio's headquarters in Louisville. Giving him a brigade, including the Ohio 40th and 42d, and parts of two Kentucky regiments and two cavalry squadrons, General Buell entrusted the management of the expedition entirely to the discretion of Colonel Garfield.

By December 23, Garfield and a part of his brigade were at Louisa, Kentucky, ready to begin their advance southward to intercept Marshall's forces. Fortunately for Garfield, Marshall, a politician and a public man, had come into Kentucky to issue proclamations, invite recruits, and seize supplies, not to fight. According to one biographer, "he was at a loss as to the next step," as he faced Garfield's men. Had he been a different sort of leader, situated as he was on the high ground, and had his troops been seasoned fighters, Marshall might have wrought disaster on the inexperienced Garfield brigade as it made its way up the valley.

On January 10, 1862, the Battle of Middle Creek took place. It was a day-long skirmish, neither side clearly triumphant and neither side particularly hurt. From the hills on one side of the valley, Marshall's Confederates fired down on the attacking elements of the 42d Ohio, holding them to the low ground. Again and again the men of the 42d charged up the hill only to be repulsed when they approached the top. As the afternoon drew to a close, one more fresh column of the 42d happily appeared and splashed across the icy creek, to the shouts and cheers of their fighting friends, and as darkness overtook them, they all charged up the hill. The Confederates, however, withdrew from the hilltop and disappeared into the night. Both commanders reported victory, grossly inflating enemy losses, while shamelessly reducing their own. Officially, total federal casualties were twenty-one wounded and three dead, and Confederate losses totaled ten killed and fourteen wounded. Marshall retreated from the valley and soon withdrew his troops from Kentucky. Garfield claimed a victory.

For Garfield the success of the Battle of Middle Creek strengthened his reputation. Afterward, he would figure even more prominently in the consciousness of Ohioans. After the Federal army's debacle at Bull Run the previous summer, the Northern newspapers and people looked for hopeful signs wherever they could find them. Here was a victory. After all, Gen. Humphrey Marshall had retreated from Kentucky. Still, one must ask if Garfield was not exceedingly fortunate in his first martial endeavor; rather than massing his forces before Marshall, he had split them when he sent Cranor and his 40th Ohio to the rear of Marshall, not the tactic of an experienced commander. Luckily, Cranor decided against following his orders to move toward Marshall's rear and took it upon himself to rejoin Garfield in the Sandy Valley before the battle. Luckily, too, Marshall did not attack. And still more luck: the shells from Marshall's four guns, falling thickly amongst the attacking boys of the 42d Ohio, proved to be duds. Otherwise, the attack up the hillsides would have been quickly repelled, probably with heavy casualties. "It was a very rash and imprudent affair on my part," Garfield commented much later. "If I had been an officer of more experience, I probably should not have made the attack. As it was, having gone into the army with the notion that fighting was our business, I didn't know any better."

The outstanding qualities of Garfield's leadership, however, were well demonstrated after the Battle of Middle Creek. In the wintry weeks of February and March, he had to face serious difficulties of command, unconnected to the fighting. First, a problem arose with the shipment of supplies from Catlettsburg up the river. The Sandy River having risen above flood stage and the river captains having refused to risk their supply boats in the turbulent waters, Garfield himself took command of a steamboat loaded with provisions and personally sailed it up the swollen river to relieve his cheering men. The flood itself required quick thinking on Garfield's part: "I have never seen the fearfulness of water before. I detailed two men to take our stores further up the bank and secure them. We commenced early in the evening and worked till after midnight. I was conquered for the first time. In one hour the water rose twelve feet." And then, as the flood receded, sickness took over. Hundreds of soldiers fell ill and were taken to Ashland on the Ohio. Many died before they could reach home. Recalling particular men he had persuaded to enlist, who now were dying, Garfield felt special pangs of remorse. "I declare to you," he wrote his wife, "there are fathers and mothers in Ohio that I hardly know how I can ever endure to meet."

General Buell's commendation of Garfield was not far from the mark when he mentioned Garfield's "highest qualities of a soldier—fortitude, perseverance, and courage." Governor Dennison signed his promotion to brigadier general on March 19, the rank having taken effect on the preceding January 10.

Garfield's participation as a field commander all but ended with the Battle of Middle Creek. With his promotion to general, he was put in command of the 20th Brigade, Sixth Division, Army of the Ohio, and ordered to follow General Buell on to Pittsburg Landing on the Tennessee River, where Buell's forces would join with those of Gen. Ulysses S. Grant in the invasion of Mississippi. Garfield left his beloved 42d behind in Louisville under another commander. "I mourn like a bereaved lover for my dear old 42nd. In the midst of this great army I am alone." By the time his brigade reached Pittsburg Landing, the Battle of Shiloh was in the mopping up stages. Grant and Buell had already beaten Albert Sidney Johnston's Confederates, who withdrew twenty miles southward to Corinth, Mississippi, and Garfield had little to do. He was put in charge of rebuilding railways, posting guards, and digging trenches.

As the spring gave way to summer the army continued inactive, and Garfield grew restless and discouraged. "I begin to feel I am losing great opportunities for growth," he wrote to his friend Rhodes. "When I do get time for thought, I find myself looking back to what I have acquired as food for reflection, rather than looking around me at what I am now grasping." Depressed and irate over the failure of Gen. Henry Halleck, commanding the western department, to attack the Confederates at Corinth, Garfield fell ill with malaria and severe dysentery, a sickness to which he was particularly susceptible. When during these weeks of inactivity Garfield was sounded by friends at home as to whether or not he would allow his name to be put forward for nomination as representative to the U.S. Congress, he said he was willing. During the heat of the summer his health grew worse, so that in late July 1862, frail, his skin yellowed and sallow, his weight down more than forty pounds, he had to take a furlough to return home for recuperation. He reached Hiram on August 6.

In order to avoid his many friends in the Hiram area, he and his wife, Lucretia, and their child secluded themselves on a farm near Warren for about a month. On September 2 he was nominated as the Republican candidate for congress. Once his health had improved, he left for Washington to await his new assignment in the army and to watch the political results of the 1862 congressional election.

Those days in Washington throughout the autumn and into January 1863 were exceedingly frustrating for Garfield. He longed for action, distinction, a command of any kind. But the days were not wasted ones. His friendship with Ohioan Salmon P. Chase, the secretary of the Treasury, became a relationship of crucial value to Garfield. Under Chase's tutelage Garfield learned much about finance, which was to become one of his central interests. During the table talks held at the Chase mansion, often attended by Secretary of War Edwin Stanton, Garfield was also coaxed into altering his convictions about Lincoln, now seeing him as "weak and timid." About a "treasonous" George McClellan, commander of the Army of the Potomac, Chase told Garfield, "McClellan can never be a soldier; has no dash, no boldness in him and is the curse of our army." And he went on, "It is a disgraceful thing that an Administration whose every member has no confidence in a general yet have not enough spunk to turn him out." Thus, Garfield's low opinions of both the commander in chief and his commanding general were formed.

In these outspoken radical opinions Garfield revealed his tendency to lead, as they say, with his heart, not his intellect. He tended to accept uncritically the ideas and opinions of those men he happened to like. He had been unduly influenced by the sour complainings of both Chase and Stanton. Later, after forming a deeply trusting friendship with Gen. Irvin McDowell, he injudiciously took to heart all of the general's excuses for his failure of command at the Second Battle of Bull Run in August 1862, where he directed John Pope's largest corps during that federal defeat.

The fall of 1862 brought only one compensation to Garfield; he was elected to a seat in the House of Representatives for the Ohio 19th District. But he would not begin his tenure until December 1863. In the meantime, he waited impatiently for an assignment. Finally, it came. He was ordered to report to Gen. William Rosecrans's Army of the Cumberland at Murfreesboro, in east-central Tennessee. Rosecrans immediately took to Garfield. The two men discussed war, government, and, especially, religion. "I find him a man of very decided and muscular thoughts," Garfield decided. "I do not think him a great man, in the sense of being a comprehensive and profound thinker, but for sharp, clear sense, ready, decisive judgment and bold self-reliant action he is certainly very admirable and hence an effective general." That was Garfield's early opinion of his commanding officer; he would revise this view later in the year. On his part, Rosecrans wrote of Garfield: "The more I saw of him, the better I liked him, and finally I gave him his choice of a brigade or to become chief of staff." Somewhat perplexed by the offer of chief of staff under Rosecrans, Garfield worried that it might be seen in public eyes as a step down. "By taking that position," he wrote, "I should make a large investment in Gen. Rosecrans, and will it be wise to risk so much stock in that market?" In the end he decided to accept the offer.

In the early days of spring, as he came to know and admire Rosecrans, Garfield's spirits soared. Here was a general who would not delay but would assault the enemy, who knew he was fighting a total war. Garfield could hardly wait for action. But the days passed, and the long months crept by: spring grew into summer, and summer drew on toward fall. Still, there was no action. Lincoln and Halleck, now general in chief, continuously urged Rosecrans to push on to Chattanooga, before the weakened enemy recovered from major defeats at Gettysburg and Vicksburg that July. Surprisingly, Rosecrans kept procrastinating, insisting on more cavalry, or more troops, before attacking. His seventeen general officers, to Garfield's disgust, agreed that delay was the better part of valor. Garfield, bewildered as to why an advance should not be mounted before the rains set in, wrote a memorandum debating the general officers' conclusions of delay, presumptuously setting his own opinions against theirs. He also wrote numerous complaints to friends in Hiram and to officials in Washington, critical of Rosecrans for not taking the initiative while opportunities prevailed.

Finally the federal armies in the Western Theater moved. Ambrose Burnside entered Knoxville on September 3. Rosecrans's troops occupied Chattanooga six days later, then advanced into northern Georgia in pursuit of the Confederates. The Battle of Chickamauga commenced during the third week of September, and Rosecrans's forces were now engaged in what would become the bloodiest battle in the West. Garfield's participation has remained an enigma for all these years. At the end of the first day, September 19, the federal forces had held their lines intact. As Garfield wrote in one of his dispatches to General Granger, "We have repulsed them at nearly every point today though they have attacked with superior numbers."

On the second day, when Bragg's Confederates renewed their attack, Rosecrans initiated a series of changes along his line of defense, moving divisions out of position on the right to bolster sections on the hard-pressed left, where the fighting was most intense. In so doing he mistakenly thought a gap had opened between two of his divisions. He sent another division to fill it, thus opening a real gap. By chance, this opening occurred at the same moment Gen. James Longstreet's veterans of the Army of Northern Virginia began an attack in the very area being emptied of defensive troops. Eight brigades poured through the opening, spreading panic among the Union soldiers. Rosecrans, his headquarters overrun, himself retreated, bewildered by the event. Fortunately, Gen. George Thomas, taking what was left of the army, held his line in a last ditch stand. Garfield, who had ridden with Rosecrans to the rear, toward Chattanooga, hearing the fighting still in progress over by Thomas's line, guessed that Thomas might have held. He attempted to urge Rosecrans to return to the field. Failing in this, he rode back to where Thomas battled. Thus, Garfield was the one officer of the defeated right wing of Rosecrans's army to return to the left wing, still intact thanks to General Thomas. What he thought he could accomplish in this action is hard to say. His campaign biographers referred to this ride back into action as crucial to the success of the battle: "It was a perilous ride," one campaign biography asserted: "almost alone he pushed on over the obstructed road . . . found the heroic Thomas encircled by fire, but still firm, told him of the disaster on the right and explained how he could withdraw his right wing and fix it upon a new line to meet Longstreet's column. . . . The movement was made just on time. . . . As night closed in upon the heroic army of the Cumberland, Generals Garfield and Granger, on foot and enveloped in smoke, directed the loading and pointing of Napoleon [artillery] guns." Alan Peskin, Garfield's most recent and more objective and judicious biographer, writes in a different vein: "Whatever did happen on that famous ride, its practical results were negligible. Thomas was perfectly capable of holding firm without Garfield's assistance. Garfield had really undertaken the ride for his private satisfaction. By leaving Rosecrans he had disassociated himself from the taint of defeat." That is, perhaps, cynical. But we recall Garfield's statement about making "a large investment in General Rosecrans" and his asking "will it be wise to risk so much stock in that market?" At any event, contemporary historians of the Civil War in recounting the details of the Battle of Chickamauga, do not mention Garfield at all.

As he traveled to Washington that November to carry Rosecrans's official report of the battle to the War Department and to take his seat in the Congress, Garfield stopped in Ohio long enough to tell of his dramatic ride. Newspapers and his friends and followers from Ohio were soon singing Garfield's praises. Whereas Thomas became known as "the Rock of Chickamauga" for his leadership, Garfield was, at least in Ohio, "the hero of Chickamauga."

Perhaps the final word as to Garfield's contribution to the war in the west should be spoken by Gen. J. D. Cox, a friend of Garfield's, it's true, but certainly also an objective commentator: "No one has questioned that Garfield's influence in his staff position was a good one, assisting his chief in maturing a wise plan of campaign, aiding in bringing the organization of the army to greater efficiency, systematizing the routine of so complicated a machine, and finally in advocating action early and decisive. No candid person can deny that Garfield's presence at the headquarters of the Army of the Cumberland was valuable. . . . The campaign of 1863 owed much to him." And so Garfield's military experience came to an end. For a green and completely untrained civilian-soldier, one must admire his quick self-education, courage, and confidence.

On December 5, 1863, Garfield, resigning his commission, took his seat as a member of the House of Representatives for the 19th District of Ohio. At age thirty-two, he was its youngest member. In looks and outward demeanor he hadn't changed a lot since his days as an Ohio legislator: still handsome, tall, warm, and hearty. He had the same robust exuberance and zestful enthusiasm in his response to others, the same ability to inspire faith in himself—"the spontaneous shining forth of light which was in the man"—that had characterized him two years before. Two descriptions of Garfield in ordinary poses will show something of his personality. First, a local friend, Charles Henry's wife, Sophie or Sopha (he called her "Soph") recalls a campaign picnic: "After Mr. Garfield spoke, I had a splendid dinner and supper ready for him. . . . When the feasting was over, under the maples in front of the house, General Garfield, Mr. Rhodes, and Charlie reclined upon the grassy slope through the warm autumn afternoon. They smoked and plied each other with school boy raillery and uproarious jest, until now and again they rolled over and over upon the ground and stirred the very trees with their Olympian laughter." The Ohio novelist William Dean Howells presents a different aspect of Garfield's character. He and his father, a newspaper publisher, knew Garfield well. As a young man, Howells visited Garfield one summer evening in Hiram:

> As we were sitting with the Garfield family on the veranda that over-looked their lawn I was beginning to speak of the famous poets I knew when Garfield stopped me with "just a minute." He ran down the grassy space, first to one fence and then to the other at the sides, and waved a wild arm of invitation to the neighbors who were also sitting in their back porches. "He's telling about Holmes, and Longfellow, and Lowell, and Whittier!" and at his bidding dim forms began to mount the fences and follow him up to his veranda. "Now go on," he called to me, when we were all seated, and I went on, while the whippoorwills whirred and whistled round, and the hours drew toward midnight. The neighbors must have been professors in the Eclectic Institute of Hiram where Garfield himself had once taught the ancient languages and literature; and I do not see how a sweeter homage could have been paid to the great renowns I was chanting so eagerly; and I still think it a pity my poets could not have somehow eavesdropped on that beautiful devotion.

As a legislator during his nine terms in Congress, Garfield had many strengths. James G. Blaine from Maine, who entered the House at the same time as Garfield, had said of any new congressmen: "What a man gains in the House, he gains by sheer force of his own character, and if he loses and falls back he must expect no mercy and will receive no sympathy." Garfield accepted such a principle, knowing the "sheer force" not of his character so much as of his intellectual faculties would bring him eminence sooner or later. He stated his philosophy of representing his district in an open letter to his constituents in April 1864: "I believe a representative should get all the light on every matter of public importance that his position enables him to and then speak and vote in such a manner as will, in his judgment, en-hance the best interests of his constituents and the whole country. If the constituency, in reviewing the action of their representative, find him deficient in ability, judgment or integrity, they have always the remedy of choosing another in his place." He spoke well. In fact, he was probably the most effective speaker in the House. In the early days his orations often contained quotations from Greek and Latin literature or from Shakespeare, Tennyson, or Milton. They were carefully organized, clear, and, like the other members' speeches, long. In later years, Garfield learned to speak without the adornments of his learning, but with simple force and clarity. Sometimes the press quoted his pithy comments. For example, in discussing finances, he said in 1865, "The man who destroys the finances of a nation ruins it as thoroughly as he who destroys its army." That comment was often repeated. He turned to a more argumentative effect with greater emphasis on persuasion than on declamation. Whitelaw Reid, a friend and fellow Ohioan, once gently took him to task for speaking too many times during his first term: he told him that eventually the House would grow weary of his "polished periods" and begin to think he was "too fond of talking." Garfield himself in 1868 told his old friend Mark Hopkins, president of Williams College, that in those early years he had made the mistake of speaking too much. "During the last two years I have been trying to atone" for so much talking, he said.

He had a generous grasp of public affairs, and he was a hard worker with an incurable intellectual curiosity. His contemporary biographer, John Ridpath, tells the story of one of his first assignments in Congress: to investigate a request having to do with the use of chloroform in the military hospitals, which had come to the House Military Affairs Committee. Not knowing what to do about the request, the chairman gave the petition to Garfield, "expecting not to hear of it again." At the next meeting of the committee, however, Garfield "had a scientific and thoroughly written report ready, exhausting the whole subject."

Because he could organize his thoughts so rapidly, with such a ready supply of allusions at his command, Speaker Schuyler Colfax selected Garfield to present to the House the memorial note honoring Lincoln. Colfax made this request at 11:30 on the morning of April 14, 1866, the first anniversary of Lincoln's assassination. He asked Garfield to move adjournment and make an address at noon. Not a great admirer of Lincoln, as we've seen, still Garfield was able to compose in thirty minutes an eloquent, yet honest and sincere speech to the House. He spoke more forcefully of the nation's recent sacrifices than of the character of Abraham Lincoln. Calling him simply "a great man," he let Tennyson's words praise his character, quoting from memory an appropriate passage from "In Memoriam."

If an effective politician is one who schemes by devious means for party or personal ends, Garfield was not one. For one thing, he was too much a scholar. He had a reflective mind. He looked at issues from all sides; he believed in reconciliation after strife, not in retaliation but in unity. He did not "deal blows," as his fellow congressman James Blaine put it. He was not partisan enough. His first vote was against his party and the administration. This was ironic because Lincoln had asked him personally to give up his commission in the army and to take his seat in Congress so as to support the administration and the Republicans. Garfield's good friend Chase, who was in Lincoln's cabinet, admonished him to support the party, but Garfield could not agree. He kept his independent voting habits throughout his congressional career. His decisions would be based on abstract intellectual and moral principles, not on political expediency. The *Nation* wrote of him in 1880: "Mr. Garfield is one of the few Republican statesmen of the day who is a real orator and whose speeches one cannot easily sketch before he delivers them—that is, he is not a party hack and has personal opinions and utters them."

At times Garfield could become radical in his opinions. The question of Negro suffrage is a case in point. In a speech on July 4 in Ravenna, Ohio, he spoke words many of his constituents would have deplored. He declared that Negroes must have the vote as a means of protecting their rights. "I am fully persuaded," he said, "that some degree of intelligence and culture should be required as a qualification for suffrage, but let it apply to all alike. Let us not commit ourselves to the senseless and absurd dogma that the color of the skin shall be the basis for suffrage, the talisman of liberty." At about this time Garfield wrote his friend Burke Hinsdale in Hiram: "I am trying to do two things viz: be a radical and not a fool, which, if I am to judge by the exhibitions around me, is a matter of no small difficulty."

Also, for one in the political arena, Garfield was thin-skinned. Ohio's President Hayes said of him that he "could not face a frowning world." Take the case of the Credit Mobilier scandal. Major stockholders in the Union Pacific Railway formed the Credit Mobilier, a construction company that received loans and land grants from Congress. Certain executives of the company shamefully skimmed off many dollars of the company's assets from the government, and in order to forestall an investigation by Congress, a few influential congressmen received stock in the company, along with dividends. Garfield was unable to bring himself to admit his fellow congressman Oakes Ames had taken him in. He stated he had "never subscribed for a single share of the stock" and that he "never received or saw a share of it." This was probably not true, as revealed by the committee investigating the scheme. By saying the $329 dividend from the company had been a personal loan from Oakes Ames, not a payment, Garfield tried to evade the charges. In the end, though Garfield was never accused of dishonesty, this slightly tarnished his reputation. "The shadow of the cursed thing [will] cling to my name for many years," he wrote in his diary.

During the mid-1860s the Garfield marriage had come into its own. The first stage in this change in the relationship began with the quiet, tender weeks of September 1862, when, recovering from his bout with malaria, Garfield had been on leave from the army. He and Lucretia and their daughter isolated themselves at a retreat near Warren, Ohio. The couple became closer emotionally, as Garfield wrote in a letter to his wife as he traveled back to Washington: "The fragrance of the alabaster box, so long sealed, has been broken at last." Then, in December a year later, the tragic death of their three-year-old daughter, so idolized by both of them, brought them closer together. "We have come to be so much nearer and dearer to each other," Lucretia wrote. A new intimacy had sprung up. But perhaps the most important step in the establishment of their strong marriage was the successful outcome of a domestic crisis in June 1864. Garfield had apparently developed a "lawless passion" for a twenty-year-old widow named Lucia Gilbert Calhoun. When the affair began to attract attention, Garfield confessed his waywardness and asked Lucretia for forgiveness. He vowed never again to deceive her. She quietly and firmly informed him that if he would break off the affair entirely, she could see it in her heart to pardon him. He went to the widow and explained the situation, which she accepted, evidently, for she soon married a New York lawyer.

The results of this crisis were that Garfield felt more deeply beholden to Lucretia than ever before; and Lucretia, now seeing flaws in the character of the man she had so idealized, could love him more realistically for the person he was. Their marriage became close and intense. "You cannot be so much relieved at heart and mind as I am," Garfield wrote, "and I now say with a fuller, broader, and deeper meaning than ever before that there is between our hearts and lives neither substance nor shadow of sorrow, except that we are separated even for a day." He now began to have Lucretia and their growing family reside with him in Washington. When their first home was built in Washington in 1869, Lucretia felt she was "more a bride than I did eleven years ago . . . now much more your wedded wife taken to your hearth and heart." The marriage had begun again. From that point on, her role in Garfield's political life became fundamental to its success. He wrote to her in 1880, just before setting off for the Republican Convention in Chicago, which would nominate him for the presidency: "I am sure you have never yet realized how entirely this family are centered in you. If I were to try, I am sure I could not analyze the processes by which you have gained such an ascendancy over us all, but the power is none the less real." Harry Truman once said, "When a man gets the right kind of wife, his career is made." Garfield got "the right kind of wife," and he came to know it!

Garfield's accomplishments during his eight terms in Congress were considerable. In questions of finance, his chief interest, his influence dominated the House. Fiscally conservative to the core, Garfield worked for a sound money system, often against the interests of his constituents. He considered monetary policy "the issue of all issues." His early interest in this matter grew from his many discussions with Secretary of the Treasury Salmon P. Chase, his old friend from Ohio. He read widely in economic treatises, studying the history of finance in other nations and taking copious notes. His first great speech on financial reform took place on May 15, 1868. "I had the undivided attention of the best minds in the House," he wrote. He said that his friend Robert Schenck told him, "It would make me a greater reputation than all I had ever done in Congress before." Over the years Garfield was perfectly consistent in his conviction that a sound currency had to be based on a gold standard. The greenbacks issued by the Treasury during the war must be reduced as quickly as possible and paid back in coin. He wrote articles, gave addresses, and carried on debates, always stressing this fiscally conservative position.

On the tariff question he was not so rigid. In fact, his position, badgered as he was by his constituents, especially those in the iron industry, was ambiguous, even paradoxical. His convoluted view is seen in his two waffling political statements: "I am for a protection which leads to ultimate free trade. I am for that free trade which can be only achieved through protection." In the end, and before his election to the presidency, he was viewed as a "thoroughly practical protectionist."

One of Garfield's major contributions had to do with the census. From May until July 1869, Garfield, heading a committee on the census, spent long hours studying the methods and philosophy of census taking. One of the members of the committee wrote that the experience of working with Garfield, despite the heat, was one of "the most valuable and agreeable" of his career in Congress. A thoroughly "modern" man, Garfield believed in the value of statistics. "I have a passion for figures," he said, "when

James A. Garfield, the last American president to be born in a log cabin, rose from obscure poverty in Ohio's Western Reserve to national renown and eight terms in Congress using the inspiring story of his determined self-made manhood. He was the second U.S. president to be assassinated, in 1881. Library of Congress.

they have a scientific significance." He believed that real information is the beginning of change and hoped to apply modern techniques of information gathering to the matter of the census. Though his census bill passed the House that year, it was killed in the Senate. The painstaking work of the summer had been in vain, but in later years Garfield's principles for census taking were brought to bear on other census bills.

In 1866 A. G. Riddle, a Cleveland lawyer and later congressman, wrote: "You are now recognized both in Congress and in the field as one of the most valuable as well as promising men of these times." Eight years later, the Garfield name was indeed known throughout the nation. He had served as chairman of the prestigious Appropriations Committee and would have become Speaker of the House in the session of Congress beginning in 1876, had the Republicans not lost the House. He was seen as "an oratorical giant," and he had an intellectual courtesy and candor, appreciated by most. His particular gifts, his admirers said, were patience, thoroughness, conciliation and readiness to debate.

Garfield's political campaign of 1874 had been the stormiest of his life. He even feared he might lose the district. He had "enjoyed the discipline of success for many years," he wrote; now he would "pass through the discipline of misfortune." But though his popularity on the Western Reserve had definitely diminished and the opposition was determined, and though, as he told a friend, he had been "nibbled and kicked at by a little-souled set of men who would besmirch one whom they cannot hope to overthrow," he won once again, proving that in the Reserve he was nearly unbeatable. At about this time, too, he turned down the opportunity to have the governorship of Ohio: he thought there was not enough salary in it.

For some years he had been toying with the idea of retiring from public life, and in 1874, after the election, he thought the time had come to do so. In 1859 Garfield had entered his name as one intending to study law with a law office in Cleveland. He had then studied it assiduously on his own until 1861, when he passed the law examinations in Columbus. Later, in 1866, he had participated in a famous case before the Supreme Court, helping his side to win. During his years in the Army—serving on occasional court-martial cases—and while in the Congress, he had developed unusual talents and had much enjoyment in pleading his cases. He thought he would remain in the House throughout the congressional term ending in 1876 and then join a Cleveland law firm he had been negotiating with. He believed he could support his wife and five children more generously by practicing law than by remaining in public service.

It is not easy to retire from public life. Calvin Coolidge wrote in his autobiography that "the political mind is the product of men in public life who have been twice spoiled. They have been spoiled with praise and they have been spoiled with abuse. With them nothing is natural, everything is artificial. A few rare souls escape these influences and maintain a vision and a judgment that are unimpaired." Perhaps Garfield was one of these "few rare souls." He wrote his wife in October 1874: "I have carried out fully the programme I proposed last year. 1st to defeat my enemies (which was done last fall) and 2nd To demonstrate to them that I can do it again (which I have done this fall). It now remains to show people that I can lay down an important office for the sake of myself and my family." Garfield was now at the peak of his influence. He had risen, in the words of Alan Peskin, to the "status of an institution." Thus, when in 1876 pressures mounted, not just from friends but also from President-elect Rutherford B. Hayes, for Garfield to continue in his public work, he ultimately decided not to retire. This decision cost him his life.

Following the elections of 1874 and of 1876 Garfield continued as the leader of the Republicans in the House. Friends who believed him a viable presidential candidate often flattered him. He himself thought the presidency might be within his grasp. His wife had written him as early as 1875:

It seems to me there is very little now to tempt a man to go into the contest for the presidency. If it could be possible for any one to so tower above all others in true manliness and statesmanship that the people should demand him for their head such as one might accept the place with some gratification. It may be only a wife's fancy for the man she truly loves, and knows worthy of honor, but I have a very deep feeling that if there is such as one in the world you are that one, and I somehow feel that both the real and the accidental occurrences of your life . . . are all, in a quiet way, singling you out from the wrestling, struggling throng.

Garfield replied, saying simply, "I agree with you that shoving for the place is not a very safe means to secure it. I, at least, have been successful in keeping the maggot out of my brain."

Two events in late 1879 and 1880 prepared the way for the actions of the Republican convention in Chicago of June 1880. Before the end of his first term; Hayes had announced that he would not be running for a second term; and Garfield made a deal with Ohio's former senator John Sherman. He agreed to support Sherman for president, if Sherman would do the same for him in his bid to be selected as senator from Ohio. With

Sherman's backing, then, the Ohio legislature enthusiastically selected Garfield for the Senate. Not wishing to attend the convention at all, Garfield nevertheless felt obligated to go in order to nominate Sherman. With Hayes out, the Republican convention had three contenders for the highest office: former president Grant, supported by the Stalwarts and led by Roscoe Conkling; Senator Blaine, a longtime enemy of Conkling, who was running not just out of personal ambition but also to stop a third term by Grant; and John Sherman. Neither the Grant forces nor the Blaine supporters could muster enough votes to win the nomination. Nor could Garfield turn his Ohio delegation votes over to Blaine until Sherman told him to. Thirty-five ballots were necessary to break up the deadlock. Garfield's name more and more frequently was mentioned, until Wisconsin started the landslide that rushed him into the nomination. Mary Clemmer, a newspaper reporter, described the scene: "Other names seemed to sail out of sight, like thistledown in the wind, till one (how glowing and living it was) was caught by the galleries and shout after shout arose with the accumulative force of ascending breakers, till the vast amphitheatre was deluged with sounding and resounding acclaim. And he? There he stood, strong, Saxon, debonair, yet trembling like an aspen. It seemed too much, this sudden storm of applause and enthusiasm for him, the new idol." Lucretia Garfield was not so enthusiastic. She had written her husband that she did not want him to have the nomination "merely because no one else could get it." Garfield himself was stunned. "I don't know whether I am glad or not," he said. Garfield's old Hiram friend Corydon Fuller reported later that Garfield told him, "he did not deny he should have hoped at some future time to receive [the nomination], after he had become better prepared to execute its great duties; but as it had come unsought, he should accept it, and if elected, do the best he could."

Always one to compromise and reconcile, Garfield hoped to placate the frustrated Conkling-Grant faction by having a Conkling associate for his vice president. Thus Chester A. Arthur, one of the Stalwarts, became his running mate. Winfield Scott Hancock of Pennsylvania, his Democratic opponent, was an enormously popular Civil War general who had been severely wounded at Gettysburg. But for Garfield, there were his nine congressional elections, his record on the tariff, his own Civil War record, and his admirable life's story. He had a distinct advantage over Hancock. The main problem he had to face during his campaign, as well after his election, was to conciliate Conkling and his New York Stalwarts. In a meeting in New York in August 1880, Garfield agreed to consult with Conkling over patronage appointments for the State of New York; without that agreement, Conkling and Grant refused to participate in the Republican campaign. When they finally did so, neither would do more than mention Garfield's name. Garfield did win the election, but by only 40,000 popular votes. Still, the country expected much of him. The *Nation* wrote that there was no department in government of which he could not take charge. "He would have nothing to learn from any man in public life."

In preparing for his inaugural address Garfield read all the preceding inaugural addresses and then made a clear, forceful, sometimes eloquent — and long — oration. He emphasized the "triumph of liberty and law" after the War and the end of slavery, "the most important political change . . . since the adoption of the Constitution," and said about the former slaves: "They shall enjoy the full and equal protection of the Constitution and the laws." He disappointed many of his supporters by saying little about civil service reform, something his predecessor, Hayes, and other reformers had felt to be of great importance.

Garfield began his presidency by inciting the ire of Conkling when he made Blaine his secretary of state; Conkling took particular exception to this appointment of his old enemy because he thought Blaine now would be in a position to influence President Garfield in all his major decisions. Beset and thwarted by the animosity of the Conkling faction — Conkling was known as a "good hater" — appalled by the Star Route postal scandal (a legacy of the Grant administration) and plagued by the insistent demands of office seekers typical of the spoils system, Garfield found little gratification in office. From the moment he was nominated, through his election, and up until the day he was shot, Garfield was attempting to deal justly with Conkling, not cave in to the domineering Blaine, and, at the same time, make dozens of appointments, taking into account the fair geographical and political balancing of his party's demands. He had little opportunity to demonstrate competence or backbone in his executive function. Whether by luck or cunning, he did manage to defeat his implacable antagonist, Conkling, and his lieutenant, Thomas Platt; and he did make clear his independence from Blaine. But there were no crises against which to measure his resolve or wisdom, other than the postal scandal; rumors in Washington were rampant about that situation, which Hayes had not cleaned up. Five days after his inauguration, Garfield asked his newly appointed postmaster general, Thomas James, to "get cracking on this disgrace." "Put the plow into the beam, and after that . . . subsoil it," he ordered. When the gross extent of the scandal was discovered, James thought it so widespread that it might even harm the Republican chances in the next senatorial election. "Go ahead," Garfield told him, "regardless of where or whom you hit. I direct you not only to probe this ulcer to the bottom, but to cut it out." Garfield lived long enough to learn that the Secretary of the National Republican Committee, Stephen W. Dorsey, who had helped him in his campaign, was up to his ears in the matter. By June 29 enough evidence had accrued for Garfield to ask that the guilty ones be indicted. His conduct in the Star Route case, according to Postmaster James, "was honorable and courageous in a high degree and was inspired by a lofty sense of the duties of his office."

Though brief, Garfield's tenure in office provided two other indications, apart from his energetic handling of the Star Route affair, suggesting that he might have been a strong president. First, he encouraged Secretary of State Blaine to be firm and clear in his Latin American policy. For a number of years Garfield had taken special interest in Latin America, calling for closer diplomatic ties. "They are our neighbors and our friends," he said in 1876, anticipating similar statements from more recent presidents. Also, with Garfield's initiative, Blaine saw important trade benefits accruing to the United States in carrying out an activist policy in Latin America. Blaine, following Garfield's general principles, made strong assertions of neutrality for Panama, after the United States had built an isthmian railway and before the French DeLesseps canal scheme. Garfield also fully understood the country's potential as a two-ocean power.

The other strength hinted at during the few weeks of his administration had to do with finances. Already it has been remarked that the economy was one of Garfield's chief interests. A clear accomplishment for Garfield was the successful refunding of the national debt, achieved under the leadership of Garfield's secretary of the Treasury, William Windom. These three initiatives, Garfield's vigorous response to the Star Route affair, his Latin American policy, and his financial acumen in refunding the national debt, are mere straws in the wind, it is true. But they encourage one to think he would have done well during his term of office, with or without crises to rise to.

On May 4, in the midst of these decisions and during the thick of political infighting with the Stalwarts, Lucretia, Garfield's beloved wife, fell seriously ill with what was probably malaria. For her recovery, Garfield sent her to the Jersey shore, where she remained throughout June. They exchanged daily telegrams. She was to meet Garfield on July 2 to go east for his twenty-fifth Williams College reunion. Charles Guiteau, an unbalanced man who had thought he was largely responsible for Garfield's election and was disappointed not to receive a preferential appointment, had been stalking Garfield for some time. At the Baltimore and Potomac depot in Washington, D.C., he found his chance. He walked up behind the departing Garfield and fired two bullets into his back. Then he said, "I did it and will go to jail for it. Arthur is President and I am a Stalwart."

Garfield lay dying throughout the summer, sometimes able to conduct business, such as signing documents, but mostly painfully incapacitated, while his family and the nation waited anxiously, hoping and praying for his recovery. But he grew gradually weaker, dying on September 19, 1881??, at Elberon, near Long Branch, New Jersey. It was the anniversary of the Battle of Chickamauga. Once in the 1870s he had written to his wife that he hoped they might die together, that he could not bear to live "one day in the empty world without you." Sadly, Lucretia would have to live some thirty-seven years without him. She died in 1918.

Charles Guiteau was tried in January 1882 and sent to the gallows on June 21. He died singing hymns.

Garfield's biographer T. C. Smith wrote this about his renowned subject: "That there is a place in our American public life—and an honored place—for men who lead without rancor, persuade rather than order and care less for their own personal success than for the fate of measures, is abundantly shown by the rank accorded to such men as Franklin and Jay among the earlier statesmen, and Lincoln among Garfield's contemporaries. And even though the premature ending of his life prevented Garfield from attaining to their stature in our history, it is with them that he is to be grouped as a worthy representative of their type of political temper and action." Garfield himself felt that his life had been "a series of accidents, mostly of a favorable character." And it is true, he was very lucky— in his marriage, in battle, in politics, and in winning the nomination for the presidency. Still, Garfield had much more than luck. In the first place, he had charm: "He took people by storm," it was said; he made friends and kept them. His wife recalled in 1916 that "none of his pictures suggest at all the way his face lit up in conversation." His portraits invariably suggest a "settled or fixed" expression, not showing how responsive his face was. His personality was widely social, open, eager. To all "he turned an attentive gaze and a ready ear, and offered a hearty handgrasp, with a kindly charm of manner that stands out in everything written or said about him, as distinguishing him from all other men." His inexorable rise from obscurity in Ohio's Western Reserve to national renown in Washington, as Hayes said, was the inspiring story of a determined, self-made man, a man who read widely, studied long and hard, had insatiable curiosity, could speak forcefully, and was driven by a relentless ambition to achieve the best. His critics, although admiring his accomplishments, nevertheless found him too ready to compromise, too trusting in assessing others' motivations; too eager to bring bitter factions to peaceable unity; he lacked "ego," they said; he was "soft"; and he was not, in the contemporary term, tough minded. Perhaps such a man should never have let himself be found among bitterly warring factions nor should he have attempted to conciliate and compromise once he became the president of the United States. Ambition should have been made of sterner stuff.

Garfield's body lay in the rotunda of the Capitol on September 21 and 22; more than 70,000 mourners passed by. Then, by a slow, black-draped train, the body was carried along the familiar road from Washington to Cleveland, a route so often traversed by Garfield in the sixties and seventies. Again, huge crowds stood quietly watching as the train passed by, while bells tolled in villages and cities. The casket was placed on a grand pavilion in Cleveland's Public Square, a hundred feet in height, with a twenty-four-foot angel standing on a gilt globe. Here more than 150,000 people passed by. Then, on September 26, a four-mile-long procession began the slow progress eastward up Euclid Avenue to Lakeview Cemetery five miles away. Garfield was laid to rest to the singing of his favorite hymn, "Ho! Reapers of Life's Harvest":

> Mount up the heights of wisdom
> And crush each error low;
> Keep back no words of knowledge
> That human hearts should know.
> Be faithful to thy mission,
> In service of thy Lord;
> And then the golden chaplet
> Shall be thy just award.

Further Reading

At the time of Garfield's death, a number of campaign biographies reappeared, having added accounts of his assassination and death. These biographies emphasized his rapid rise from poverty-beset beginnings to eminence as a Civil War general and then national recognition as a leading United States congressman. Typically, the campaign biographies are generally unreliable, even though they were written while Garfield still lived.

The first truly authentic biography, however, did not appear until 1925. This is the two-volume work by the distinguished historian of Williams College, Theodore Clarke Smith, *The Life and Letters of James Abram Garfield* (New Haven, Conn.: Yale Univ. Press). The biography is a detailed and mainly accurate account of Garfield's life, generously illustrated by quotations from letters and documents. Smith was given permission to peruse the many personal letters and official documents carefully preserved by Mrs. Garfield. His biography may be characterized by "the fullness of the narrative." An undoubted admirer of Garfield and his family, Smith could hardly be called an objective biographer, nor, according to present-day historians, did he always make accurate use of his sources.

By 1964 the Garfield family had turned over to the Library of Congress all of these personal and public records, which then became available to historians. But an "authentic" biography had to wait until 1978—as the hundredth anniversary of Garfield's inauguration approached—before not just one, but two fine works appeared. The first is *The Garfield Orbit,* by Margaret Leech and Harry J. Brown (New York: Harper and Row, 1978), a book aimed more at the general reader than at the student of history. Unfortunately, Leech died before completing her manuscript. Professor Harry Brown, a Garfield scholar from Michigan State University, then served as both editor of her unfinished eight chapters and writer of the two concluding chapters and epilogue. Leech, with keen insight, is particularly interesting in her assessment of Garfield's personal life, the early days of his marriage, and his unusually close relationships with the friends of his youth.

The other work published in 1978 is what might be called the standard life of Garfield, Alan Peskin's simply titled *Garfield* (Kent, Ohio: Kent State Univ. Press), now in a second edition. This is a clear, objective life of the twentieth president. It is well written, sometimes even wittily so, in a forceful, interesting style. In fact, Peskin's lively narrative becomes downright exciting when he describes the dramatic moments of the Republican convention in 1880. It is a book for both the general reader and the student of history. It serves now as *the* Garfield biography.

Finally, most recently, John Shaw, retired professor from Hiram College, has edited about a quarter of the 1,200 personal letters exchanged between Garfield and his wife, *Crete and James* (East Lansing: Michigan State Univ. Press, 1994).

Benjamin Harrison

Twenty-third President of the United States, 1889–1893

G E O R G E   W .   G E I B

*O*ne day in the summer of 1856, a group of enthusiastic Republican supporters of their party's first presidential nominee, John C. Frémont, paraded through the streets of Indianapolis. They were looking for stump speakers who would join them in endorsing their candidate, and their attention fell upon a blonde, twenty-three-year-old lawyer who had recently opened a practice in the city. Entering Benjamin Harrison's office, the leaders picked him off his feet, carried him before a waiting crowd, and introduced him as William Henry Harrison's grandson. Benjamin took a moment to compose himself and then proudly announced, "I want it understood that I am the grandson of nobody. I believe that every man should stand on his own merits."

Benjamin Harrison has ever since been identified with Indiana. Yet the young man who defined himself on the stump that morning bore the stamp of his Ohio heritage. Born near Cincinnati on August 20, 1833, he was the second son of John Scott Harrison and Elizabeth Irwin Harrison. Their six-hundred-acre family farm, named The Point for its site on a sharp bend of the Ohio River, was a portion of the North Bend estate first created by John Cleves Symmes and later passed to his daughter Anna and her husband William Henry Harrison. Through the Symmes family line Benjamin was linked to the formative history of southwest Ohio. Through the Harrison family line he was linked both to the earliest days of the Northwest Territory and the state of Ohio through his grandfather William Henry, and to the American Revolution and the Virginia dynasty, as his great-grandfather Benjamin had been a signer of the Declaration of Independence.

Benjamin's father was an indifferent farmer who was often hard-pressed for money, a respected politician who was often chosen for local offices on the Whig ticket, and a caring parent who always placed special emphasis upon his children's education. Benjamin remembered his years at The Point as a time of play, hunting, chores, illnesses, and visits to his grandfather and the family library at North Bend. Benjamin remembered the dominant feature of his youth as his family's strong stress on education that he encountered at the series of schools to which his family sent him.

Because the Harrisons lived too far from any town to send their nine children to regular schools, John Scott Harrison built a one-room log schoolhouse on his farm. First educated at that school, Benjamin may have been most heavily influenced by his preparatory school years. At fourteen he entered Cary's Academy, later the Farmer's College, near Cincinnati, where he encountered Dr. Robert Hamilton Bishop. Bishop, one of the West's best early educators, was a wonderfully innovative instructor who enjoyed capturing the attention of young boys by drawing them into "equivalents," studies that substituted political discourse for the classical curriculum. Often using the published papers of Congress and congressmen, Bishop sought to develop both analysis and discourse while stressing a severe, classical presentation style. All of those skills were evident in Benjamin when he moved on to Miami University in Oxford, Ohio, at age seventeen.

Bishop probably also contributed to the strong interest in the Presbyterian Church that Benjamin had first encountered with his parents, who were devout Presbyterians. In an era when religious faith strongly influenced and was closely tied to personal behavior, Harrison was soon caught up in the quests for personal sacrifice and reformation that much of American Protestantism espoused. At the academy he attended regular services, kept a diary of personal experiences, delivered temperance lectures, and communicated his spiritual revelations with family and friends. For the remainder of his life he would place a high premium on church membership, his faith and Christian philanthropy, and the inner dictates of conscience.

Harrison took these traits as well to Miami, a small college with only a half dozen instructors, 250 students, and a traditional curriculum. Benjamin's preparation at Farmer's College qualified him to enter in the junior class; his talents soon defined him as one of the top students. Like many similar schools of the era, Miami's strength lay in its student societies, and particularly its literary and debating groups. Benjamin found the school congenial, especially after being accepted into the recently formed Phi Delta Theta fraternity and the Union Literary Society, a club whose members were interested in writing and debating. He was already exhibiting a tendency to engage in lengthy bursts of work. He graduated in 1852, third in his class, with a reputation as a good extemporaneous speaker, a serious student of ideas, and a sociable cigar smoker. His commencement speech was on "the Poor of England."

He also graduated as a young man very much in love and secretly engaged to be married. The object of his affection was Caroline Scott, the daughter of the Reverend John W. Scott, a Presbyterian minister and a professor of chemistry and physics at Farmer's College. Reverend Scott would soon become the founder of the nearby Oxford Female Institute. Benjamin and Caroline were married on October 20, 1853, at her home. At her request, her father performed the wedding. Benjamin had just turned twenty, Caroline, twenty-one.

Harrison's verbal skills pointed naturally to a career in which they could be used to best advantage. While at Miami he had been strongly drawn to the ministry, especially after attending a series of "revivals" held on campus and conducted by a famous Presbyterian minister, the Reverend Dr. Joseph Claybaugh. His marital considerations probably contributed to his decision to forego the ministry and pursue the law. His father's many political connections yielded an invitation for Benjamin to study in the legal offices of Bellamy Storer, a former Whig congressman, in Cincinnati. There the younger Harrison again proved himself an avid reader and hard worker. He completed his apprenticeship in less than two years and was admitted to the Ohio bar in early 1854. Well-connected and well-educated, he was ready to make his mark on the world.

He chose to leave Ohio to do so. On the surface it is an odd decision; his family ties and those of his new wife were there. He had a number of friends, especially from Miami University, in the Cincinnati area. His father had recently been elected Whig congressman from the district, and his father's network of connections offered the potential for both legal and political advancement in Ohio. Harrison himself later explained the move in much the way he addressed the Frémont crowd in Indianapolis, as an assertion of independence and a desire to succeed upon his personal talents. Later biographers are quick to remind us, however, that Benjamin's Indianapolis cousin, William Sheets, played a major role by promising to introduce Benjamin and Carrie to Sheets's large circle of political and

business acquaintances in a city that was less than 150 miles away from
The Point. The young couple moved in the spring of 1854. Harrison was
not yet twenty-one.

The next six years of his life were probably Harrison's greatest period of
trial. His wife's health, often endangered by overwork and stress, suffered
considerably during two difficult pregnancies as son Russell was born in
1854 and daughter Mary (Mamie) in 1858. He repeatedly sent his wife
back to family in Ohio for rest and treatment. The family's debts mounted.
Harrison's legal business, in the absence of immediate community reputation, was slow to take hold. Friends began to urge him to consider relo-
cating to a more congenial environment, but the youth who had already
met many personal challenges in the past with hard work and personal
resolve asserted himself. He found friends who would lend him money
under favorable terms. Most important, he began to establish himself as a
successful lawyer.

Harrison's legal success flowed from four main sources. First, he successfully applied himself to time-consuming branches of the law, such as
debt collection, that began to generate income. Second, he sought out
opportunities to showcase his extemporaneous courtroom speaker's skills,
particularly in criminal cases. Third, he formed a fortunate partnership in
1855 with William Wallace, son of a former governor, which allowed him
to service an established client base. And fourth, he began to attract attention to himself through politics.

Harrison had moved to Indianapolis at almost the same time as the passage of the Kansas-Nebraska Act (1854). It said that the settlers themselves,
not the national government, should settle the question of slavery in the
new states that were being carved out the western federal territories. The
act horrified many Northerners and set in motion the collapse of the Whig
party and a significant realignment of regional voting patterns. During the
turbulent second half of the 1850s, as the nation lurched toward civil war,
Harrison's father gravitated from the imploding Whig party to the American party alternative. The elder Harrison represented his Cincinnati district
in Congress until 1857, and his son closely followed his father's career from
Indianapolis, as well as the many bitter national debates. The younger
Harrison, as his interest in things political grew, did not simply copy or
mimic his father's positions. He emerged from a period of reflection and
self-examination to endorse the position that the extension of slavery into
the western federal territories was both politically and morally wrong. In
1855, Harrison supported a local anti-Nebraska coalition called the People's

party, and then he followed them into affiliation with the emerging Republicans. This put a severe strain on the relationship between Harrison and his father, who thought the Republicans' position on slavery too extreme.

From then forward, Harrison's public career was tied to that new party. His friend and partner, Will Wallace, encouraged Harrison to help campaign for John C. Frémont in 1856. Harrison endorsed local and state candidates too, ran successfully for the office of city attorney of Indianapolis in 1858, and won a hard-fought nomination from the 1860 Republican state convention for reporter of the supreme court of Indiana. Harrison's Supreme Court Reporter election victory assured his financial situation; in lieu of salary, state law allowed him to print and sell the reports of the court and to maintain a private law practice. Sensing an assured client base, he soon founded his own Indianapolis law firm, Harrison and Fishback, together with rising young attorney William Pinkney Fishback. He had established himself as a rising star of Hoosier law and politics in six difficult years. John Scott Harrison sent a special message of congratulations to his son on his victory but added that he hoped the Republican candidate for president, Abraham Lincoln, would not win. Lincoln did win, the Deep South seceded from the Union of American states, and the country slid toward armed conflict.

As the Civil War erupted in the spring of 1861, one might have expected Harrison to move quickly from the statehouse to the campground. Instead, he waited for more than a year before tendering his services to the Federal army. Most biographers attribute this to his desire to serve in the office to which the voters had just elected him, the familial problems that accompanied Carrie's third pregnancy and a stillborn child, and his continued and related quest for financial solvency with a wife and two small children to support. He surely feared the financial consequences of the loss of his elected office.

Harrison, who carefully followed the war's news during its first year, volunteered in July 1862, during a curious interview with his fellow Republican officeholder, Governor Oliver P. Morton. Convinced of the merit of the Union cause, Morton was energetic in raising, equipping, and financially supporting Hoosier troops. Union successes became personal victories to Morton; Union defeats became personal challenges to be reversed.

In that spirit, Harrison stood with Morton at a State House window on July 9, 1862, as the governor bemoaned the unwillingness of civilian workers to enlist in the Union forces. Responding to the appeal, Harrison offered to put his oratorical talents to work on a new recruiting drive. Morton apparently offered to exempt his political ally from service, but

Harrison's blood was up and he announced resolutely that he would join the men he raised. Morton agreed, appointing Harrison a lieutenant and promising a colonel's commission as a reward for successfully raising the regiment. Harrison went to work at once with all his intense energy. A flag went up outside Harrison's law office, a fifer joined his payroll, a tearful meeting with his wife secured family support, and patriotic notices appeared on the streets of Indianapolis for a mass citizen meeting on Saturday, July 12. Those of military age were urged to consider enlisting, those too old to serve were urged to contribute sums to pay enlistment bonuses. Morton chaired the meeting, Harrison gave the principal address, and more than eighty young men answered the call. Similar activities throughout Marion County and in nearby areas yielded nine other companies, and on August 8, 1862, Harrison became colonel of the new 70th Indiana Regiment. State Democrats vigorously attacked him for holding two lucrative offices (state officer and army officer), removed him from office in court proceedings in November 1862, and denied him the proceeds to which he was entitled for editing the court reports. Harrison had arranged that the income from the sale of the reports would go to Carrie to help support her and the family in his absence.

His service in the war would become one of the central features of Harrison's political resume, and his experiences would become a key feature of his political rhetoric. The initial experience of the 70th Indiana was primarily a progression of camps and garrison assignments. Apart from one skirmish at Russellville, Kentucky, the regiment spent its first year and half protecting fortifications and rail lines near Louisville, Bowling Green, and Nashville in the western theater. The lawyer who had succeeded by hard work, long hours, and personal discipline used the same traits to study military manuals and to instill discipline in his command. It may have bored and frustrated him and his men, but it produced one of the best trained regiments in the army. Then, early in 1864, the western Federal army was reorganized, and the 70th Indiana found itself part of Maj. Gen. Joseph Hooker's new 20th Corps assigned to eastern Tennessee. The 70th marched to join the army massing under Maj. Gen. William T. Sherman for the Atlanta campaign, from which Harrison would emerge as a highly respected field commander.

His first battle, at Resaca, Georgia, on May 14–15, 1864, saw him lead assaults against parallel lines of enemy entrenchments and capture several pieces of artillery. Harrison's next battles took place at New Hope Church on May 26–28 and Golgotha Church on June 15. At the latter battle he also doubled for a time as regimental surgeon. His clear orders, his personal courage, and his attention to his men's welfare demonstrated his skill as a commander and assured a warm welcome at every postwar reunion of the regiment.

It also won him command of the three-regiment brigade of which the 70th Indiana was a part. With them he continued the march toward the perimeter of Atlanta, eventually arriving at Peach Tree Creek on July 20. There his forces were held back by a divisional commander who failed to anticipate an enemy attack. Suddenly a Rebel force advanced toward a gap in the Union line, and without orders Harrison rode to his neighboring brigade commander, John Coburn, and asked him to support an advance. Coburn agreed, and Harrison led the men forward. It was the kind of personal leadership that soldiers admired. It also gained the recommendation from his corps commander, Joseph Hooker, that officially made Harrison a brevet brigadier general in February 1865.

The fall of Atlanta on September 3, 1864, permitted Harrison his first furlough since enlisting, during which he returned to Indianapolis to join the 1864 election campaign. There he spoke at rallies for President Lincoln and was again elected clerk of the Supreme Court. The furlough prevented him from returning in time to join Sherman's forces in the "march to the sea" but not from serving in other areas in the last months of the war. That December Confederates under John Bell Hood launched an attack on Nashville, Tennessee, in a final desperate effort to draw Sherman away from Georgia. Harrison first assumed command of a provisional brigade in Chattanooga, marching it to Nashville in time to fight in George H. Thomas's victory over Hood. Harrison then journeyed east to rejoin Sherman's army, which was now in South Carolina, although a bout of scarlet fever and numerous transportation difficulties left him only a few weeks to command his brigade before the war's end.

Before the soldiers went home, a grand review of the federal armies took place in Washington, D.C., on May 23–24, 1865. On May 24, General Harrison, following behind General Sherman, led his brigade down Pennsylvania Avenue along the grand parade route before thousands of cheering spectators. On June 8 he was mustered out.

The war affected Harrison in many ways. It gave him heroic status in the electorate in Indiana and the Republican press and earned him the nickname "General," which friends increasingly used as the years passed. It made military reunions and patriotic observances important parts of his public calendar, and it surely explains his later passion for Flag Day. It affected his health, too, particularly with a periodic hand infection that led him to wear the soft gloves that later caused critics to lampoon him as the "kid glove candidate." Above all, though, it confirmed his strong emphasis on the importance of personal character in the face of adversity.

The war also confirmed and strengthened his strongly partisan view of public affairs. Having fought in a terribly bloody conflict in which his foes were mainly Southern Democrats, Harrison, like his wartime ally Governor Morton, came to suspect conspiracy and disloyalty in nearly everything the opposition party might do. Voted out from his state office in 1862 by Democrats for partisan reasons and frequently criticized in the Democratic press, Harrison came to equate opposition to himself and his party with opposition both to the war itself and to the party that saved the Union. He accepted that the label of "Copperhead"—a silent, covert, and deadly snake—given to Northern Democrats during the war years, was a fitting one. The court-martial conviction of the Lincoln assassination conspirators in Washington, which occurred while Harrison was in that city for the Grand Review in 1865, only confirmed his dark vision of his Democratic opponents.

When Harrison resumed his law practice, he welcomed the opportunity to participate in the most visible and partisan trial held in postwar Indiana. The case was the culmination of the Indiana treason trials and issues stemming from the ex parte *Milligan* Supreme Court decision. Briefly summarized, Lambdin Milligan of Indiana was an active Peace, or "Copperhead," Democrat, charged with organizing a series of secret political societies under such names as the Knights of the Golden Circle and the Sons of Liberty. Within those groups, it was charged, he had planned organized opposition to the Federal Civil War effort. After provost marshals uncovered hiding places containing weapons, they arrested several prominent members of the Sons of Liberty, including Milligan. Charged with "conspiracy, affording aid and comfort to the rebels, inciting insurrection, [and] disloyal practices," Milligan was tried at Indianapolis by a military court, convicted, and sentenced to death. Before he was to be executed, the sentence was changed to hard labor in prison. Appeals eventually led to review by the U.S. Supreme Court, which in 1866 invalidated the conviction and released Milligan. The court's argument, which denied military jurisdiction in non-war zones where civilian courts were functioning, became a landmark decision.

As a result of the 1866 decision, Milligan appeared in court to demand damages of $100,000 from the members of the military tribunal. Starting in state court in 1868, Thomas Hendricks, Indiana's leading Democrat, argued for Milligan. When the case was transferred to federal court three years later, Harrison was appointed by President Grant to represent the U.S. government. The jurors were treated to one of the great debates in Indiana legal history. Hendricks built his case around the illegality of the military court and the personal harm done to Milligan, whose health had been destroyed as a result of his imprisonment. Harrison centered his on the compelling need of the United States to sustain the war effort, and his clients' (the members of the tribunal) adherence to their military duties; he did not believe in letting bygones be bygones. In his summation, referring to General Hovey's war wounds, Harrison "waved the bloody shirt" and exhorted, "Yonder, on the bloody sides of Kenesaw, he gave an arm, almost a life, for the country which he, and these his comrades, loved so well. While he lay upon the field, bleeding, almost dying, here in Grand Council in the State of Indiana Milligan and his associates were plotting treason; and now they seek to rob him of the little savings from the office which a grateful country, and a President who honors his valor, have conferred upon him, in order to enrich the traitors." Each side would claim vindication when the jury ruled for Milligan but awarded him token damages of only five dollars.

Harrison's willingness to accept high profile political cases also involved him in one of the key scandals of the era, the Whiskey Ring, which was a group of federal excise agents who accepted bribes from distillers seeking to avoid high taxes. One of the accused agents was Hiram Brownlee, son of a prominent Marion County, Indiana, family, accused of taking a five-hundred-dollar bribe in Evansville. Harrison agreed to defend Brownlee before Judge Walter Q. Gresham, a fellow Republican. The government's case rested primarily on the testimony of the briber, John Bingham, who had turned state's evidence. The centerpiece of Bingham's testimony was his description of Brownlee accepting the bribe while dressing for a wedding and wearing white kid gloves. Harrison focused upon that detail, and won his case by producing witnesses that Brownlee arrived barehanded at the wedding. It added a second dimension to later charges that Harrison was a "kid glove candidate"; it also profoundly annoyed Judge Gresham, who became convinced that Harrison, a vigorous temperance advocate, was hypocritical during this liquor-related case.

In the language of his era, Harrison exemplified the "genteel" tradition of an upper-middle-class Protestant who sought a refined and moral community directed by purposeful citizens. Soon after moving to Indiana, he joined the First Presbyterian Church in Indianapolis, attended services whenever possible, regularly taught Sunday school for young men, and observed the Sabbath strictly. He held himself to a high code of personal conduct and even refused, until the 1870s, to allow his children to take dancing lessons. He often gave his money to family members and community causes as quickly as he earned it. As an army officer he conducted regular mealtime prayers and avoided many social occasions that he deemed frivolous. He condemned alcohol abuse, and raised no objection when, in 1874, his political party adopted a platform condemning all alcohol sales. In private relations he sought out the company of like-minded people.

This strong focus upon church and family lent a continuing ambivalence as Harrison contemplated reviving his political career. He clearly enjoyed campaigning, where his speaking skills only improved with practice. He obviously felt deeply about many of the issues of the time, and wanted to promote the Republican party's solutions. He had personal ambitions that were often couched in his respect for his father's service in Congress. Yet he often seemed unwilling to take the steps necessary to convert his considerable talents and credentials into nomination and election to office. Part of the problem was obviously concern for his wife and children. Carrie continued to encounter periodic bouts of ill health; diagnoses often referred to overwork, and doctors had little to prescribe except long vacations, which often took the Harrisons for weeks at a time to resorts along the Ohio shore of Lake Erie. Then, as their children matured, other problems arose. Their son Russell, after graduating from Lafayette College and working at the Philadelphia Mint, moved west to seek his fortune, eventually marrying into a prominent Nebraska family and starting a mining and ranching career in Montana. To Harrison's alarm, Russell also showed a penchant for speculation, and a willingness to involve his father's political associates in the risky ventures. Letters of admonition from his father were fairly frequent.

Part of Harrison's ambivalence may also have been the deep, growing rifts within the Indiana Republican Party. Beyond their support for preserving the Union in the recent war, it was often difficult to tell where the Republicans were headed. In the 1870s, barely twenty years old, the party remained a coalition of disparate elements. Some were former Whigs, concerned with economic issues such as tariffs, sound money, stable banks, internal improvements, and industrialization. Others were former Democrats, concerned with personal freedoms, agricultural issues, and less government control over citizen's lives. Some, like Harrison, had strong moral outlooks that manifested themselves in plans for improvement of both the self and the state. Others were political pragmatists, willing to make the needed concessions, especially on patronage, that would motivate party workers and rally wavering supporters.

Indiana possessed a vital political life, marked by frequent elections for many local offices, aggressive political newspapers in most county seats, and a culture of participation that made rallies, picnics, and bonfires a significant portion of the community calendar. This political life also reflected a population mix that gave each party a good chance of success. In Harrison's time, Indiana was balanced between the major parties, and Democrats rarely polled less than 49 percent or more than 51 percent for governor. Many offices changed hands regularly in response to small changes in opinion or voter turnout.

Harrison encountered the reality of Indiana politics when he ran for governor in 1876. He had first tested the waters in the 1872 Republican state nominating convention. But a wealth of other candidates, hostility from some of his own Indianapolis supporters, and an apparent unwillingness to "work the crowd" at the convention hotels doomed his chances for the nomination. Worse still, a growing rift with Oliver P. Morton had put him at a disadvantage among many party regulars.

Harrison initially remained out of the race for Indiana's governor, but a scandal forced the Republican nominee to withdraw only two months before the election, and Harrison accepted the State Committee's desperate call to campaign for the office. His opponent was James D. Williams, one of those colorful rural Democrats who periodically surfaced in Hoosier affairs. Fond of campaigning in locally made workmen's denim clothing that gained him the nickname "Blue Jeans," the folksy Williams proved an entertaining and humorous stump speaker. Harrison did his best, but lost the race by a few thousand votes. Historians have tried to decide what, if anything, Harrison did to suffer his first general election defeat. Some have blamed the loss on national affairs, especially the scandals surrounding U. S. Grant's administration and the Panic of 1873. Others have suggested that Harrison's late entry in the race, while having to replace a scandal-tinged predecessor, was central to his failure. The machinations of Morton against Harrison and the derogatory "kid-glove candidate" remarks of his opponent all are cited too. But Harrison's party contemporaries were fairly well agreed that he was hurt most by the bone-dry temperance platform Indiana Republicans had reaffirmed in their spring convention, which angered enough Irish and German voters to assure defeat.

Defeat in his first general election did not end Harrison's political aspirations. He began an aggressive series of speeches and meetings across Indiana and extended his interests to neighboring states. In this he may have been motivated in part by concerns raised by a national railway strike in 1877. Always a champion of public order, Harrison took an active role in organizing a citizen militia in Indianapolis. He was helped by a good working relationship with Rutherford B. Hayes, which had developed the previous year when Harrison backed Hayes for the presidency. President Hayes eventually appointed Harrison to a commission concerned with Ohio River improvements. He used his appointment as a forum to stress his ideas of national economic improvement.

In 1880, Harrison played a skillful and successful game as the leader of the Indiana delegation to the Republican National Convention. Hayes had refused to seek a second term, and so the convention became a battleground among James Blaine of Maine, John Sherman of Ohio, and former president Grant for the nomination. Initially Harrison supported Blaine, but when thirty-three votes failed to produce a nominee, he induced the Indiana delegation to be one of the early states to swing their support in the deadlocked convention to James A. Garfield of Ohio. That move propelled the delegates in Garfield's direction and on the next ballot he received the Republican nomination for president.

That summer and autumn Harrison worked diligently for both national and state Republican candidates. He, for the first time, divided Indiana's cities and counties into small precincts, then appointed committees to identify and mobilize GOP voters in each. Garfield proved a popular choice in the fall election, carrying Indiana on his way to victory. Harrison gained his reward a few weeks later when the new Republican majorities in the Indiana legislature sent him to the U.S. Senate.

His six years in the Senate, from 1881 to 1887, projected Harrison onto the national stage. They familiarized him with national issues, introduced him to political power brokers, and eventually made him a serious presidential contender rather than just a regional favorite son. He defined himself most clearly on three political issues: the protective tariff, civil service reform, and enforcement of the Fifteenth Amendment. On each he walked a fine line between principle and partisanship, striving to base his position on the merits of arguments while recognizing the advantages to his party implicit in his positions.

The protective tariff was a traditional Republican position, vigorously attacked in the 1880s, on the grounds that it contributed to an unnecessary surplus while simultaneously discouraging foreign trade. Appointments for civil servants based on merit and competitive examinations were the centerpiece of much political reform in that era, especially after President Garfield was gunned down by Charles Guiteau, who had failed to secure a federal job through the spoils system. Reformers demanded merit appointments as an alternative to the aggressive spoilsmanship that often failed to look beyond party loyalty. Protection of black voting under the Fifteenth Amendment took on special immediacy as state after state in the South instituted massive disenfranchisement and racial segregation.

Senator Harrison's positions emerged quickly. He favored the principle of protection, while being willing to consider adjustments that encouraged trade. He favored appointing qualified individuals to office but thought that political commitments would not disqualify a candidate from a civil service appointment. In January 1883 Harrison voted for the Pendleton Act, which said that ability, not political loyalty, would be the basis for federal employment. He strongly opposed disenfranchisement of the very people for whom the Civil War ultimately had been fought.

In 1884 his party lost the presidency to Grover Cleveland, the governor of New York. Almost at once Harrison emerged as Cleveland's key Senate critic, attacking him upon the central issue of spoilsmanship. He built an elaborate legal brief detailing hundreds of removals of postal workers and other government employees for no apparent reason except the political greed of the Democratic party. Harrison also staunchly supported legislation that aided Union veterans, and he opposed the president's veto of veterans' pension bills that would have increased benefits. Harrison's attacks against Cleveland impressed many listeners because of his matured abilities, but they failed to carry sufficient Indiana legislators. In 1886 Democrat David Turpie's narrow victory denied Harrison a second Senate term. Even so, many Republicans saw him as Cleveland's most effective critic. The stage was set for Benjamin Harrison's bid for the White House in 1888.

Harrison's public record, on the surface, does not seem the stuff of which presidencies are made. He had never held a major executive office. He came from a state with only a moderate number of electoral votes. He had served just a single term in the U.S. Senate, where his most important piece of legislation was an unsuccessful bill to grant statehood to the Dakotas. If Harrison were to challenge Cleveland in 1888, his Democratic opponents certainly would make much of such a record. But balanced against such weaknesses were the dynamics of the late-nineteenth-century electoral process, and there Harrison looked much more attractive.

It is common to describe the years after the Civil War as a period of intense two-party competition. That was certainly the fact at the national level, where the major parties were fairly evenly balanced. Similar competition, however, was much less apparent within many of the states. Most often, one party dominated local and state politics within specific regions.

Democrats were equated with rebels and the Southern Confederacy, Republicans with Lincoln and the preservation of the Federal Union, and Northerners and Southerners were incited to vote against their old foe. Many are familiar with the "Solid South" that the Democrats created in state and local political affairs after the collapse of Reconstruction; a similar pattern existed in many Northern states, where voters might return an occasional Democrat congressman but seldom abandoned the Republicans at the statewide level.

Only two areas offered real competition at the state level. One was New York, where the Democratic strength in New York City was closely matched by Republican power upstate. The other area was the lower Midwest, where a very few percentage points often separated winners from losers; this was especially true of Indiana. The national conventions of both parties often responded to this dynamic by naming their presidential and vice presidential candidates from these areas. In 1884, the Democrats had done just this, nominating a ticket of Grover Cleveland of New York and Thomas Hendricks of Indiana. Consequently, the Democrats carried those two contested states, and thereby narrowly won their first presidential election since 1856, when the nation stood on the edge of the Civil War.

The knowledge that such states were often won or lost by 1 or 2 percent of the vote encouraged both parties to develop campaign practices that could win or lose the few independents who were out there. These voters were the era's classic joke about the mugwump, who sat on the fence with his mug on one side and his wump on the other. It was also an era when campaign managers often considered it their job to raise and spend money to gain the support of "floaters" and other questionable voters who considered a vote to be something too precious to sell cheaply. Reformers regularly protested against the more blatant practices of the time, but the practices continued to flourish wherever anxious politicians thought such tactics worked.

Harrison fit well within this political matrix. He was personally popular in Indiana, a favorite of Republican audiences. His active campaigns in 1880 and 1886 assured that he would take a disciplined and battle-tested cadre of Republican party workers into the races with him. The death of Vice President Thomas Hendricks late in 1885 denied the Democrats a Hoosier figure of comparable stature on their ticket. Even Harrison's lack of major executive office and consequent lack of significant appointive powers was an advantage when disaffected patronage seekers could be relied on to attack those (one thinks of the Garfield assassination) who had not rewarded their efforts.

Harrison had other personal advantages. A war hero, he was acceptable to Union veterans—who could be mobilized through groups such as the Grand Army of the Republic, the Union veterans' lobbying and fraternal organization. He was especially attractive to many Northern veterans—in contrast with Grover Cleveland, who had purchased a substitute so as to avoid the Civil War draft. Harrison's stands on issues such as the protective tariff put him within the mainstream of Republican economic policy, whereas his vigorous attacks on Cleveland convinced many that the former general would carry the political fight to the enemy "just as he carried the fight at Peach Tree Creek." In fact, Harrison's removal from the Senate was an assurance that he would cast no embarrassing votes as the presidential campaign progressed. Although we know he was reluctant to invoke family ties, his lineage as the grandson of an American president and great-grandson of a signer of the Declaration of Independence gave him a legitimization with many voters. It's well to recall, however, that his opponents counterattacked with perhaps the most famous Democratic campaign song of the era (to the tune of "Grandfather's Clock"), which started:

> His grandfather's hat is too big for his head,
> But Ben tries it on just the same.
> It fits him too quick, which has oft times been said
> With regard to his grandfather's fame.
> It was bought long ago, and it makes a pretty show,
> In this jolly hard cider campaign.
> But it don't fit, even a little bit,
> On Benjamin Harrison's brain.

None of the favorable factors guaranteed his nomination. The dominant presence in the Republican party was still the 1884 standard bearer, James G. Blaine, who enjoyed a very strong following. Other contenders included John Sherman of Ohio, William Allison of Iowa, and several favorite sons. Harrison himself initially began to show the preelection ambivalence that he had manifested over the governorship a decade before. But step by step, the hurdles were overcome. Blaine began to issue a series of statements that indicated hesitation about running and eventually took his name out of consideration. Most of the favorite sons, such as Chauncey DePew of New York, concluded Harrison was the most electable, or the least objectionable, of the frontrunners.

Most important, Harrison found two fine campaign managers in his friends Eugene Hay and Louis Michener. They quickly assumed the responsibility of making the actual party and delegate contacts, serving as protective conduits to Harrison. They stressed that the 1888 election would be largely decided in the states of New York and Indiana and that their man was electable in both. It took eight ballots at a hot, humid Chicago convention to make Benjamin Harrison the seventh man to win the Republican nomination for president. The convention then teamed him with Levi Morton, a New York banker with brief but highly respected terms of service in Congress and as ambassador to France, as his vice-presidential running mate.

Harrison proceeded to run a nearly flawless "front porch" campaign. He lived in a spacious Second Empire home that he had erected on North Delaware Street in Indianapolis a decade before. The home did not as yet have a wrap-around porch; it did, however, have a front stoop from which Harrison spoke to nearly a hundred visiting delegations as well as to groups of admiring neighbors. A local marching club, the Harrison Marching Club (today the Columbia Club), escorted delegations the mile and half from downtown Union Station day after day to hear Harrison deliver carefully outlined remarks on current events.

The crowds saw a fifty-five year old man, the average age of presidential aspirants at that time. Barely five feet seven inches tall, he was just above the height of the republic's shortest president, James Madison. Often called Little Ben, Harrison possessed a stout frame and a tendency to carry extra weight. The blond hair of Harrison's youth had aged to light brown, and he wore it short. He continued to wear the full beard that he had grown many years earlier. Always impeccably dressed in his favorite turn-down collars and speaking in a tenor voice that carried although it was soft, he projected an image of authority. Nearly 300,000 people heard him in person that autumn.

Because delegations were scheduled in advance, Harrison could be ready with prepared outlines. And as they could be slated every day except Sunday, his managers could keep up an almost daily flow of press releases, which allowed Harrison to develop his issues and to respond to challenges as they arose. Initially, he and other party members made the decision to focus on the tariff. In his most recent state of the union address on October 6, 1887, Cleveland had taken a surprisingly strong stand against protection; Harrison saw an opening and began developing a moderate protectionist position. He focused on the competition from cheap foreign labor and its threat to the American worker and the American wage. His goal was obviously to portray Cleveland's position as extreme, while making openings to organized labor.

Harrison was also aided by the services of noted writer Lew Wallace, a fellow Indiana Republican, who bent his literary talents to a widely circulated campaign biography, *Life of General Ben Harrison*. The author of *Ben Hur* built a word portrait heavy with Harrison's speeches and strong on his character. Widely used as a party speaker's guide, many workers undoubtedly reflected Wallace's conclusion. "General Harrison is now in the prime of life, clear in mind, vigorous of body. His character, both public and private, is absolutely stainless. He loves his family, his fellow-men, his country, and his God. Such a man cannot be inflated by success or embittered by disappointment. . . . He holds himself subject to the popular will."

As predicted, the election was decided in New York and Indiana. In the former state, Harrison's pro-labor stance effectively neutralized attempts to portray him as the worker's foe. In the latter, in his careful front porch appearances he avoided mistakes almost until the end. Then, in one of more curious events of the campaign, he encountered the matter of the Dudley letter. William W. Dudley was a Harrison supporter from Indianapolis who became treasurer of the Republican National Committee in 1888. Late in the campaign a letter surfaced, purportedly discovered by a postal worker who mistakenly opened a circular to party leaders in Indiana. In the circular, over Dudley's signature, was a call to action that concluded, "Divide the floaters into blocks of five and put a trusted man with necessary funds in charge of these five and make him responsible that none get away and that all vote our ticket." Dudley disavowed the document, but Democrats delighted in presenting what they considered evidence of planned voting fraud.

Harrison was embarrassed but not destroyed. When the votes were cast, almost every state supported the same party as they had in 1884, with the exceptions of New York and Indiana. In the Empire State, Harrison won by a margin of 13,000 out of 1,300,000 total votes. In the Hoosier State, his margin was just over 2,000 out of 537,000. It was enough, and the results were even historic. For the first time since 1840, when his grandfather had defeated Martin Van Buren, an incumbent president was defeated in a general election. By an electoral college margin of 233 to 168, Benjamin Harrison was made the twenty-third president of the United States. The road that began in Ohio had led through Indiana to the White House.

New presidents often use their inaugural addresses to set the tone of their administration; Harrison delivered his lengthy text on Monday, March 4,

1889, standing bareheaded in a cold rain on the Capitol steps. He emphasized two main topics: the importance of religion in civil society and the manner of implementation of his party's platform. He made much of American political progress over the previous one hundred years, placing himself at the centennial of George Washington's first inauguration. Speaking with the voice of a good Presbyterian and Christian moralist, he invoked Almighty God, the "sweet offices of charity," temperance, virtue, and the other "influences of religion." From them he built a call for national unity, fair wages, honest ballots, and civic education. "Let us exalt patriotism and moderate our party contentions," he declared. Nowhere do we find the anecdotal, self-deprecating humor that was one of his rhetorical trademarks. Harrison was taking himself, or at least his office, very seriously.

He spoke of his priorities. In foreign affairs, he promised to support the Monroe Doctrine and to promote foreign trade. Regarding defense policy, he talked of an expanded navy with new bases ringing the Americas. He advocated statehood for four territories in the West, and he called for protection of suffrage for all citizens in the South. And concerning economic policy, he promised to avoid unneeded Treasury surpluses and to place tariffs within the context of economic growth and fair labor policies. His sharpest words were for trusts. "If our great corporations would more scrupulously observe their legal limitations and duties, they would have less cause to complain of the unlawful limitations of their rights or of violent interference with their operations." He spent more time talking about patronage than any other issue, promising to respect both the law and individuals' qualifications for office.

The presidency that followed has generally achieved indifferent ratings. Republican partisans, then and since, have given Harrison higher marks than Democrats. But all have agreed that, in the absence of either major scandals or breakthrough accomplishments, among America's chief executives he ranks somewhere nearer the midpoint than either extreme. What is missing in most of these assessments is a recognition that Harrison's overall "average performance" is composed of a striking mixture of extremes: solid successes and serious shortcomings.

It is often a useful device to see Harrison as a leader with one foot in the past and one in the future. The year 1890 saw the sordid action at Wounded Knee. Although no one knew it at the time, this was the last battle between the Indians and the U.S. Army. Much of the conflict resulted from the staggering migration of people, acquisition of territory, and settlement of the frontier since the founding of the country. Each year Americans filled in the frontier, until finally, during Harrison's presidency, the superintendent of the census for the United States declared that the frontier had ceased to exist. In a twist of irony, the announcement came in the same year as the tragedy at Wounded Knee. The same year saw the start of an era of trust-busting as Harrison signed the Sherman Anti-Trust Act of 1890.

Another important consideration is that his party suffered a devastating defeat for Congress in the 1890 autumn elections. Although the Senate was usually Republican in this era, the House was much more often Democratic. In 1888 Harrison had carried with him into Congress a paper-thin Republican majority, and the new Speaker, Thomas "Czar" Reed, had generally maintained party discipline. But in 1890 the GOP numbers plummeted from 175 to 88 seats, and the Democratic count soared from 161 to 235. Harrison was an able enough negotiator that he occasionally carried a bill or amendment in Congress during 1891 and 1892, the last two years of his presidency. However, his real legislative record is found in his first two years; it is there many modern analyses seek the roots of his problems.

Harrison was an active leader. He enjoyed holding informal meetings, employed the newly invented telephone, used his small staff to advantage in communicating his wishes, and often included cabinet members in his personal life. He also paid keen attention to the separation of executive and legislative powers and was reluctant to trumpet occasions when he had quietly been able to steer programs through the processes of government. Other active players in his administration, or their later biographers, have claimed credit for ideas, amendments, arrangements, or negotiations that we know Harrison helped develop. Perhaps the best conclusion to draw is that Harrison managed in the manner that he practiced law; he worked from an established set of principles, developed a proposed course of action, argued it vigorously when in public venues, and negotiated privately to advance his client's best interest.

Harrison and the GOP started on a strong political note by pushing for the statehood of territories in the new Northwest. The author of a Dakota bill while in the Senate, Harrison argued in his inaugural address that the populations of a number of western federal territories exceeded those of several of the original states at the time of the Constitution's ratification a century earlier. In November 1889 the president signed statehood bills for North and South Dakota, Washington, and Montana—followed within a year by Wyoming and Idaho. One political result of this was the addition of twelve new seats in the Senate and seven in Congress. In every initial election, the new states favored the Republicans, giving Harrison a safe party majority in the Senate and buttressing his shaky House support.

But debtors are also voters, and in the 1880s they had started to vote for candidates who advocated expansion of the money supply and inflation. The first popular solution had been to print more paper currency, greenbacks, as the growth of a third party greenback movement attested in several farming states. Late in the 1880s, however, the focus shifted to silver, which attracted two very different groups: debtors, often farmers, who had been seeking cheaper money for years, and silver miners, especially in the mountain states and territories, who were seeking a market for their metal. The former wanted more (and cheaper) money and saw silver coinage—especially unlimited amounts of it—as the goal. The latter sought a profit and saw a favorable government purchase ratio as the key. At a time when the commercial ratio of silver to gold (their relative market values) fluctuated between 20:1 and 30:1, the government's legal ratio of 16:1 looked very attractive. The two groups forged an alliance of convenience, offering more money for the debtor and more profit for the miner. It especially appealed in the West, newly strengthened by a dozen senators.

However, Harrison likely spoke for a majority of his party when he advocated sound money to those who feared that monetary expansion would trigger dangerous inflation. Harrison also probably reflected a majority view of his party when he worked with legislators who sought a compromise that would offer some limited relief without attacking the underlying gold standard. The result of protracted discussion in 1890 was the Sherman Silver Purchase Act. This committed the national government to purchase a fixed weight of the metal and pay for it in certificates, which might be redeemed in silver coin. As a compromise it fell short of "free silver," and in so doing annoyed the silver wing of the party, which became an undependable element within the GOP.

This undependability became apparent as the Republicans struggled with the tariff issue. Harrison was again in line with a majority of his party when he urged revisions that would afford protection where needed, avoid a government revenue surplus, and encourage negotiation of reciprocal foreign trade agreements. But, as the bill that became the McKinley Tariff worked its way through Congress, the devil appeared in many details. Legislators frequently sought to protect narrow district or state interests, and such products as sugar and tin plate became symbols to many of preferential deals. Harrison did win broad power to negotiate, but at a price of a complex and cumbersome piece of legislation that proved hard to explain or defend on the campaign trail.

The other major legislative arena in which one can detect Harrison's hand, as well as his problems, was that of black voting rights in the South.

Commentators have often noted that Harrison was the only American president elected without a popular vote plurality. Many observers fail to add that this was a direct result of the widespread disfranchisement of Southern black voters, the great majority of them Republicans, during the 1880s. It deeply troubled Harrison, both as politician and moral leader. As a politician he saw a one-party Democratic South being fortified. As a moral leader he saw hard-won rights being threatened and even openly denied to a race that had been U.S. citizens for only about two decades. As he said in his inaugural address, "The community that by concert, open or secret, among its citizens denies to a portion of its members their plain rights under the law has severed the only safe bond of social order and prosperity. The evil works from a bad center."

Harrison, having long professed a moral dislike for forced servitude, had joined the Republican party in a period when the expansion of slavery was a central divisive issue. The Republican response to disfranchisement was the introduction of a new voting rights act in 1890, sponsored by Henry Cabot Lodge of Massachusetts. The bill was carefully crafted to pass legal review, invoking the clear voting guarantees of the Fifteenth Amendment and limiting itself to disfranchisement in congressional elections. And it entitled those protesting improper state practices that denied voting rights to appeal to the federal courts for redress. Different in form from many of the acts of the Reconstruction era (1865–77), the bill still unleashed a firestorm of Democratic criticism. Although not an army measure, it was branded a "force bill" and eventually died in the rush to adjourn Congress in fall 1890.

None of his legislative activities helped Harrison with his concurrent inability to manage the federal patronage in ways both politically effective for his administration and personally acceptable to him. Harrison came to office in the wake of the 1883 Pendleton Act, for which he had voted. In 1888 his careful campaign speeches had reassured many genteel reformers that he believed merit, not politics, should determine most appointments. But upon taking office, Harrison still had nearly 2,000 significant government positions and many lesser offices (including nearly 50,000 postmasters of small, fourth class post offices) under his control.

On lesser appointments, Harrison followed modern management practice and delegated responsibility for screening and recommending candidates to others. The fourth-class postmasters he turned over to Deputy Postmaster General James Clarkson, who had previously worked for the Republican National Committee and who returned to that body to help manage the 1890 congressional campaign. Clarkson saw his job as a simple matter of removing active Democrats and naming active Republicans. He did so, with Harrison's ultimate approval, at about the same rate (changing a quarter of the total appointees) that Cleveland's administration had.

On more substantial appointments, Harrison felt he was personally responsible for the review and the final decision. He was elected in an era when presidential staffs were small and review of potential nominees was a common practice. His own strong sense of character caused him to believe he could recognize similar traits when he interviewed others. His Indiana experiences had convinced him that many elective officeholders were far more prone to recommend friends and supporters than to seriously consider an individual's fitness for a given position. Convinced that unfitness opened the door to failure, Harrison was eager to avoid the scandals of subordinates that had so damaged Grant.

Harrison's suspicion of politicians' recommendations was heightened by his ambivalent approach to party leaders. He knew he needed them, and as a practicing politician he was well aware that many states had at least one Republican boss who relied on patronage as a tool of leadership. In the 1888 Republican nominating convention, his managers had often worked closely with those men to move delegates into Harrison's column. As a former senator, he was also aware that a number of those bosses either sat in Congress or had considerable influence over those who did.

However, as a man of strong moral character with a high sense of the dignity of his office, he felt uncomfortable being beholden to such bosses. He had disapproved of more than one proposed deal as the 1888 convention proceeded, and he apparently felt that he had come to power having made only a minimal number of commitments. Some commentators have suggested that Harrison may have held in the back of his mind a desire to build a network of skilled appointees who would look to him, and not to the state leaders, in the coming months of his administration. It quickly became apparent that in his decisions a recommendation from a state Republican leader was more often a negative factor than a positive one.

The result was a long, uncomfortable, time-consuming activity of his presidency. Sitting in his office for an average of six hours a day for many long weeks, he personally interviewed hundreds of aspirants. Convinced that he should justify his decisions, he often outlined his reasons for refusing the request to the unhappy applicant, which consumed even more of his time. Tired, stressed, and probably annoyed by many of the presentations, he assumed a more and more stern demeanor, often standing during the interviews or drumming his fingers on the arm of his chair. Even those whom he eventually nominated often remembered their interviews with displeasure. Theodore Roosevelt, the future president from New York, whose national career Harrison set in motion by naming him to the Civil Service Commission, remembered the "little grey man" who "treated him with cold and hesitating disapproval." Soon people were saying that President Harrison could speak to a crowd of ten thousand and make every one leave his friend but could speak individually to each of the ten thousand and make every one leave his enemy.

Harrison brought the same approach to his cabinet selections too. With one exception—the party's 1884 presidential nominee, James G. Blaine, as secretary of state—Harrison filled the cabinet with a group whose distinguishing traits included their quiet competency, their membership in the Presbyterian Church, and their lack of ties to state political bosses. With such appointees, but without the support of many angry Republican leaders, Harrison would attempt to conduct his administration.

Such legislative and patronage concerns provide the context for evaluating Harrison's role in the 1890 Republican congressional defeats. Three main approaches have been proposed to evaluate him. The first of these argues that the 1890 vote was decided primarily on local issues and that Harrison's performance played little part. A second argues that the 1890 vote was partially a referendum on the legislative record and that Harrison and his legislative allies share some responsibility. A third argues that the withdrawal of effective party worker support was the key and that Harrison's patronage decisions were central. Each of these approaches deserves consideration.

The emphasis on local issues notes the resurgence of moralistic social issues in many areas in the late 1880s. Whether in mandated Sunday closings, liquor restrictions, curfews, or other expressions of mainstream Protestant piety, such blue laws drove away drinkers, recent immigrants, or other elements of the GOP coalition. Certainly such a problem had appeared for the Republicans in the 1870s in Indiana, as it might have in other states. If voters were annoyed, Harrison's moralistic side would only have confirmed their annoyance. But it seems odd that such a protest would occur simultaneously and unexpectedly in a number of states or that it would dissipate so quickly in the 1890s, when more normal voting patterns prevailed.

The emphasis on national legislation reflects the growing power of the press and the growing economic concerns of an America caught up in the industrial revolution. Fears of trusts, concerns with debt and money supply, and annoyance with changing schedules of tariff taxation were breeding varieties of popular protest that would yield the Populist disturbances of the 1890s. Anecdotal evidence suggests that several changes in prices, particularly for tin-plate goods, annoyed many homemakers and were blamed on the McKinley Tariff. Measures that make sense as compromises in Washington may have looked to voters like abuses. The main problem with this argument is that it offers a series of repeal remedies that could easily have been passed in a Democrat-dominated House in 1891 and 1892 and often were not.

That leaves the patronage issue. Harrison had not endeared himself to many state party leaders with his approach to appointments, and it is very tempting to see numbers of those grassroots workers taking a holiday to show their dissatisfaction. Certainly a number of members of the movement to remove Harrison at the 1892 convention read the evidence this way. The one drawback to this is that patronage workers generally were expected to intervene with the marginal, floating vote, and the GOP clearly lost by more than a block of five.

What may instead have happened is that the GOP encountered one of those occasional elections in which voters announce by their ballots that they are tired of hearing the old issues being articulated or debated yet again by political leaders. Often explained as a matter of younger age cohorts entering the electorate, it represents a particular kind of demand for change. By 1890 there was an obvious contender for the honor of "an issue whose time has passed," and it was the Civil War.

Most states set the age of twenty-one as the minimum for voting. This meant that no person under forty-six could have voted during the Civil War, no person under fifty-one could have voted in Lincoln's first election, and no person under fifty-seven could have voted in 1854, when the embryonic Republican Party was first on ballots. Yet military rhetoric and wartime issues—"waving the bloody shirt," "vote like you shot"—continued to take up a great deal of public discourse. Republicans were still nominating standard bearers, holding rallies, waging campaigns, and asking party captains to serve in the trenches. By their increasing demands for pensions, the Civil War veterans were themselves giving ample evidence of the same aging process.

Harrison, too, may have contributed to this generational uneasiness in several ways. He had a strong sense of history and viewed his presidency as an ongoing series of commemorations of past national achievement. In one tour in 1889, he retraced George Washington's route to the republic's first inauguration in New York City, making well-publicized speeches along the way. Harrison also continued to show a special fondness for patriotic observances. He promoted Flag Day as a national observance and frequently attended GAR (Grand Army of the Republic) reunions. Even the Henry Cabot Lodge voting rights act, with its echoes of Reconstruction, may have unintentionally served to reinforce the view that his administration looked backward.

Whatever the case, Harrison's party lost dramatically in 1890. Unable to gain much from the new House controlled by Democrats, the president shifted his emphasis to the executive arena as his term wound down. He had always sought a regular working relationship with his cabinet, in some ways anticipating modern practices. Harrison accepted the invitation of his postmaster general, John Wanamaker, to stay at a summer cottage near Cape May Point, New Jersey, and turn it into the summer White House. The houses and the hotel in Cape May where the cabinet and staff soon joined him are among the visible artifacts that survive of the Harrison presidency.

Of greater significance, Harrison became more and more involved in foreign policy. The United States was emerging from a period called "isolation" by some and "free security" by others into an era marked by the challenges posed by expanding industrial empires. As early as 1881, James G. Blaine, when serving as secretary of state under Garfield, had proposed the outlines of a United States response that Harrison would eventually adopt. As its centerpiece, this policy called for European noninterference in the affairs of the Western Hemisphere, in terms at least as old as those of James Monroe's 1823 Doctrine.

To promote hemispheric solidarity, Blaine and Harrison called for cooperation with the nations of Latin America through a series of Pan-American meetings and a number of bilateral trade agreements. They also cooperated with Navy Department proposals to expand and modernize the fleet, obtained coaling stations for the fleet in the Caribbean and Pacific, and developed plans for a transoceanic canal in Central America under U.S. control. Usually identified with Presidents William McKinley and Theodore Roosevelt, this agenda actually took long strides forward under President Harrison and Secretary Blaine.

To this day, it is uncertain which man provided the impetus after Harrison's election to the presidency in 1888. The original ideas clearly came from Blaine, who worked toward it in his early months under Harrison. But Blaine suffered an ever-increasing series of family and health problems, which incapacitated him for longer and longer periods prior to his formal resignation in 1892. As Blaine faded from the scene, Harrison took forceful command to ensure the program's continuation into 1893. Observers noted that Harrison did not like to negotiate: he liked to propose and then demand acceptance. He took the position that he had carefully considered the situation before making an offer, that he was speaking from the great economic strength of the United States, and that it was in the best interest of others to agree. To the surprise of many critics, this often worked, particularly with the numerous trade agreements he made in the Caribbean basin.

His approach was less successful with Chile. Although not a territorial imperialist (beyond a few naval bases and coaling stations), Harrison had a strong sense of American national power and regional interest; he did not like to see lesser powers interfere with the emergence of his designs, and he could adopt a belligerent spirit that many thought was more than mere bluff. During Harrison's administration, Chile underwent a revolution that involved the United States in disputed arms sales, the presence of refugees in the U.S. embassy in Santiago, and the deaths of two sailors in a riot in Valparaiso in October 1891. Harrison demanded apologies and solutions and, before the Chileans made the concessions demanded, was clearly considering war as an alternative. It was a "big stick" policy a decade before Teddy Roosevelt coined the term.

This stance was made possible in part by significant American naval rearmament under Harrison, who aggressively expanded the tentative naval construction initiatives of Chester Arthur's administration in the early 1880s. The naval program was a response to the dramatic transformation of other navies, such as those of the Germans and the British, in an era of rapid industrialization. Its key advocates included a number of younger naval officers who were convinced that national power and building the United States into a great world power required a first-class navy. Perhaps the most influential proponent was Adm. Alfred Thayer Mahan, who published his instrumental *Influence of Sea Power Upon History, 1660–1783* at this time. The new navalists were interested in steam power, modern gunnery, and armor plate, with enough ships and firepower that could defend the coasts of the Americas from any European fleet and make its presence felt globally.

Harrison liked the nationalism, the hemispheric implications, and the possibilities for the American economy offered by such a program—and he advocated it throughout his term. He was greatly helped by his secretary of the navy, Benjamin Franklin Tracy, an enthusiastic spokesman and efficient manager of the naval program. Here again Harrison played an active role, particularly after Tracy was severely injured in a house fire and the president administered artificial respiration to save his life. Together they sought appropriations for more and bigger warships, while Tracy successfully convinced steelmaker Andrew Carnegie to manufacture the necessary nickel-alloy steel armor. Of the ten modern ships that would later fight in the Spanish American War, seven were authorized in Harrison's term. He used his last months in office to promote, unsuccessfully, an annexation treaty with Hawaii, using the already familiar arguments of navalism.

Contemporaries considered Harrison a lame duck by 1892, the fourth year of his presidential term, particularly because he continued to run afoul of several key state bosses. Bitter conflicts with Senators Thomas Platt of New York and Matthew Quay of Pennsylvania stood out. The very sharpness of the antagonism, in fact, probably explains why Harrison sought a second term. Many of his inner circle believed that he was planning to step down at the end of his term, until he learned that Quay and others had begun to plan to replace him with the ailing James G. Blaine. The general who had refused to back away at Resaca and Peach Tree Creek reacted as expected.

Harrison announced in May 1892 that he would seek a second term and put the power of his office and his much-maligned patronage appointees to work. His managers promptly forged a coalition from the South, rich in delegates if poor in electoral votes, and the small states of the North. Blaine, close to death, proved a poor rallying point, and the dissidents were unable to shift enough support to William McKinley of Ohio to pose a threat. Harrison won on the first ballot. His victory over his critics may have been the only vote in 1892 that mattered to him; certainly he did little campaigning thereafter.

Some attribute his lack of campaign activity to his sense of the dignity of his office. It is more likely that the determining factor was the accumulation of problems in his official and personal family. A cloud of illness and injury seemed to hang over them, of which Blaine's illness and Tracy's house fire were only two examples. Worse, the first lady became sick again in the fall of 1892, this time with pulmonary tuberculosis. Harrison tried to maintain some semblance of a schedule of meetings, but clearly his attention was on his wife and not his opponent, again Grover Cleveland. On October 25, 1892, less than a month before the election, Caroline Scott Harrison died, devastating her husband of nearly forty years. Harrison was deep in personal grief when he learned that he had lost the presidency to Cleveland.

Returning to Indianapolis, Harrison assumed a number of roles, including that of elder statesman. In addition to editing various public papers, he wrote two books of commentary. *This Country of Ours* appeared in 1897; *Views of an Ex-President* came out in 1901. They show a man of pride and conviction, most pleased when his party returned triumphantly to power in 1896 with William McKinley's victory. *This Country* was essentially a civics textbook, in which Harrison presented an outline of the formal processes of national government in the context of the need for active citizen participation. Lauding patriotism and respect for the law, denouncing lynching and other denials of civil authority, and praising renewed patriotic ceremonies, he encouraged each reader to be alert to abuses, whether by government or by its enemies. Inviting others to evoke the patriotism he described in his recollection of the Atlanta campaign, his message was one of urgency and of renewal. *Views* was a collection of speeches given after 1892 on varied topics. In this book he used a variety of occasions to reaffirm his pride in the American experiment, his respect for the Founders, and his interests in piety and participation. Occasionally reverting to his partisan self, his most ringing sections were denunciations of the "free silver" movement in 1896, advocated by McKinley's Democratic presidential rival, William Jennings Bryan.

Harrison also returned to legal practice. He accepted selected cases, most notably representing Venezuela in its Guyana border dispute with Great Britain. He was also offered a professorship in law at the University of Chicago, but he turned it down. In 1896 he married Mary Lord Dimmick, the widowed niece of his first wife. Harrison was sixty-two; Mary was thirty-seven. A daughter, Elizabeth, was born the following year. (Many years later, Elizabeth would marry the grandson of her father's political ally and secretary of state, James G. Blaine.) Harrison's older children, Russell and Mamie, strongly opposed the marriage and subsequently distanced themselves from their father.

Over the next six years Benjamin, Mary, and Elizabeth Harrison lived happily in Indianapolis, as the former president practiced law, followed politics, and wrote his books. In March 1901, Benjamin Harrison fell ill with influenza, then rapidly had to battle a growing number of respiratory infections. He died of pneumonia on March 13, 1901, at the age of sixty-seven. Harrison's body lay in state in the Indiana statehouse, where thousands of mourners paid their last respects. Following a funeral service at the First Presbyterian Church, which he had joined when he first moved from Ohio to Indiana, he was buried next to Carrie in Crown Hill Cemetery.

Throughout his life Benjamin Harrison asked to be judged on his merits. He hoped others would recognize his morality, his energy, his bravery, and his patriotism. He wished they would accept his partisan stances in the way a jury accepts the arguments of a good trial attorney. He did not emphasize personal style and resisted public interest in his family and pri-

Elizabeth Harrison rests her head serenely on the shoulder of her father, Benjamin Harrison. A widower, in 1869, at sixty-two, Harrison married Mary Lord Dimmick, age thirty-seven. Elizabeth was born the following year. Benjamin Harrison Home, Indianapolis.

vate life. He helped to shape the politics of the Progressive Era and America through the issues and programs he championed in his presidency. By style and conviction a man of the Civil War era, he is simultaneously our first modern president.

Further Reading

The defining biography, Harry J. Sievers, *Benjamin Harrison*, vol. 1, *Hoosier Warrior* (Chicago: Henry Regnery, 1952), is excellent; vol. 2, *Hoosier Statesman* (New York: University Publishers, 1959), is adequate; vol. 3, *Hoosier President* (Indianapolis: Bobbs-Merrill Company, 1960) largely has been supplanted by the American Presidency series volume by Homer E. Socolofsky and Allan Spetter, *The Presidency of Benjamin Harrison* (Lawrence: Univ. Press of Kansas, 1987).

Allan Spetter, "The Historian (Albert T. Volwiler) and the Presidential Widow (Mrs. Benjamin Harrison): A Twenty Year Correspondence," *The Old Northwest* 16, no. 1 (fall 1992) tells a fascinating tale of the family's attempt to produce an earlier biography. Charles W. Calhoun, "Civil Religion and the Gilded Age Presidency: The Case of Benjamin Harrison," *Presidential Studies Quarterly* 23, no. 4 (fall 1993): 651–67, explores the value structures of Harrison and his era. Calhoun is the primary commentator on the 1999 C-Span television documentary "Benjamin Harrison," available through the C-Span Archives at Purdue University.

Harrison was a fine extemporaneous speaker, and his published speeches are entertaining reading. The best collection was prepared for his second presidential campaign, Charles Hedges, comp., *Speeches of Benjamin Harrison* (New York: United States Book Co., 1892). The campaign biography by Lew Wallace, *Life of General Ben Harrison* (Indianapolis: Union Book Co., 1888), is also a good read.

Several Web sites offer insights into Harrison. The President Benjamin Harrison Memorial Home is found at <www.presidentbenjaminharrison.org>.

This chapter is indebted to the numerous political historians who have invited us to consider the social and behavioral dimensions of late-nineteenth-century voting. Among the best are Melvyn Hammarberg, *The Indiana Voter: The Historical Dynamics of Party Allegiance during the 1870s* (Chicago: Univ. of Chicago Press, 1977); Charles S. Hyneman et al., *Voting in Indiana: A Century of Persistence and Change* (Bloomington: Indiana Univ. Press, 1979); and Paul Kleppner, *The Cross of Culture: A Social Analysis of Midwestern Politics, 1850–1900* (New York: Free Press, 1970).

PART III

*From Gilded Age to
Roaring Twenties*

The National Story

In the four decades following the Civil War, the United States was dramatically transformed from a rural, agrarian nation dotted with insular communities into a vastly different society. Immense commercial and industrial enterprises developed during those forty years. Entrepreneurs and capitalists amassed enormous personal fortunes. Sprawling metropolises replaced small towns. Millions of immigrants poured into the United States altering the face of society. These changes fostered among many Americans a deep pride in their modernizing country. Among other citizens the changes bred deep fears about the direction that the United States was taking as it headed toward the twentieth century. Nineteenth-century writer and lecturer Mark Twain was often acerbic in his critique of American society. In his novel *The Gilded Age* he lampooned this era as ostensibly attractive but actually deceptive in appearance—one too frequently tawdry below the shiny gold veneer.

The United States has always been a nation of immigrants, but between the Civil War and 1900 the number of people arriving on American shores increased dramatically. More than 14 million immigrants entered the United States in those decades. In 1882 more than 2,100 people arrived each day. The flood of immigrants was critical in meeting the need for more workers to fill jobs in expanding American industries. Most people came to America because of difficult conditions in their homelands and for the promise of opportunity in the United States. Employers went overseas to sign up people who would come to America and work in their factories and mines. Most immigrants, however, did not need to be recruited by anyone. People knew of the opportunities that the United States offered; some had received letters from relatives already living in America offering tantalizing details. With great expectations they resolved on their own to arrange transoceanic passage and to relocate.

Unlike those who had emigrated to America before the Civil War era, many of these "New Immigrants" came from Asia or southern and eastern Europe. This, in turn, stimulated a growing fear and often intense hatred of these immigrant groups among numerous more settled Americans. As more and more immigrants entered the United States, quite a few people worried that jobs would be taken away from American workers. Labor leaders argued that the immigrants were often willing to work for a lower wage than other American workers. Others believed that the New Immigrants were culturally so "different" that they could never become "good" acculturated and assimilated Americans. For these and other reasons, various organizations lobbied the federal government to restrict immigration. However, not all Americans were disturbed by the millions of people entering their country. Many applauded the sentiments of poet Emma Lazarus, whose words are written on the base of the Statue of Liberty, which was erected in the harbor of New York City in 1886:

> Give me your tired, your poor,
> Your huddled masses yearning to breathe free,
> The wretched refuse of your teeming shore,
> Send these, the homeless, tempest-tossed, to me:
> I left my lamp beside the golden door.

Ellis Island, also situated in New York harbor, was one of the principal ports of entry into the United States for immigrants. The sight of the Statue of Liberty greeted millions of newcomers upon their arrival.

Like immigration, urbanization also increased dramatically. In 1861, when Abraham Lincoln began his presidency, one in every five Americans lived in a city. Thirty-five years later, as William McKinley became chief executive, one out of three Americans were city dwellers. By 1920 and Warren G. Harding's presidential election victory, nearly half the nation's people were urbanites. The main reason for the spectacular growth of cities was the steady expansion of industry. Most newcomers settled in the cities, looking for work in industrial America, and they chose living quarters in the safety and familiarity of ethnic neighborhoods. Hundreds of thousands of Americans gave up the hard and often profitless life of farming and relocated to urban America. Cities grew so rapidly in the late nineteenth century that there was not enough time to plan or prepare for such enormous expansion. Burgeoning cities were unable to provide the services needed by their residents, and frequently they could not even meet the basic needs of inhabitants. Consequently, serious housing, sanitation, health, overcrowding, transportation, and crime problems were widespread.

Local politics in many municipal governments became hopelessly corrupt during this period. Powerful political machines led by individuals called bosses controlled the cities. They provided desperately needed services for city residents—ones that the ill-prepared city governments could not—in return for votes and favors. The people by and large appreciated the help of the bosses. Reformers consistently rebuked them. Politicians regularly danced at the end of the strings they pulled. Many bosses, such as William Marcy Tweed in New York City, George Cox in Cincinnati, and Abraham Ruef in San Francisco, became wealthy at the expense of the taxpayers. At the national level, although there were certainly conscientious Democrats and Republicans, the two major political parties for the most part provided little leadership for the country during this Gilded Age. Too often they demonstrated an overwhelming indifference to the needs and concerns of the majority of citizens. More and more Americans charged that democracy, rule by the people, had been replaced by plutocracy, rule by the wealthy—that representatives of industry and big business dominated American politics at all levels. The only significant reform made in this era was the beginning of a merit-based civil service to replace patronage and the spoils system.

As the late nineteenth century waned, Americans began to demand more government involvement and assistance in solving the serious problems plaguing citizens and society. Farmers led one major attempt, forming the People's Party of the U.S.A. in 1892, better known as the Populist party. In their first platform, the Populists asserted: "We meet in the midst of a nation brought to the verge of moral, political, and material ruin. Corruption dominates the ballot box. . . . The fruits of the toil of millions are boldly stolen to build up colossal fortunes for a few. . . . We have witnessed for more than a quarter of a century the struggles of the two great political parties for power and plunder." The party ran well in the presidential election of that year, and the Populists hoped that they might soon move from being a third party to one of the two dominant political parties in the country. That dream never materialized, especially after the Democratic party expropriated the Populists' ideas in the 1896 presidential contest. Nominating the same candidate for the presidency that year, Nebraskan William Jennings Bryan, the Populists and the Democrats went down to a resounding defeat at the hands of Republican William McKinley of Ohio. By 1900 the Populist party was dead, but demands for political and societal reform were not.

Two key traits characterize the American experience between McKinley's victory in 1896 and Warren G. Harding's election to the White House in 1920. One was the rise of the United States as a world power. The other was an immense national housecleaning movement led by reformers who called themselves "progressives."

Three beliefs dominated American foreign policy during the nineteenth century: manifest destiny, isolationism, and anti-imperialism. Manifest destiny asserted the right and the fate of the United States to spread from the Atlantic to the Pacific, a goal achieved by 1848 after war with Mexico. Isolationism reflected Americans' desire for the United States to remain, as far as possible, separate or isolated from involvement with other nations. An imperial nation is one that follows a policy of establishing colonies and building an empire. Because the United States was born from a colonial revolution against imperial Great Britain, Americans historically opposed the policy and practice of establishing colonies and maintaining an empire.

In the decades following the Civil War, however, a growing number of citizens wished that the United States would move away from the doctrine of isolationism and expand its influence overseas. These expansionists included farmers and industrialists who wanted to find new markets for their goods. Others wanted the United States to challenge the hegemony of Great Britain, France, and Germany, which then occupied the summit of the world political order. As industry boomed and Americans settled the last of the western frontier, government policy became increasingly expansionist. Between 1867 and 1898 the United States purchased Alaska from Tsarist Russia, annexed the Midway Islands in the central Pacific, and secured the Hawaiian islands as a territory of the United States. Additional land acquisitions would come as a result of war with Spain.

In 1895 revolution broke out on the Caribbean island of Cuba. Cuba was one of the last vestiges of the once-mighty and immense Spanish empire in the Americas. Determined to hold onto its colony, Spanish authorities confronted the revolutionaries with brutal resolve. In January 1898 the U.S. battleship USS *Maine*, under orders from President McKinley, steamed into Cuban waters with no specific military objective other than showing an American presence. On February 15 the *Maine* exploded at its anchorage, killing 266 sailors. Americans blamed Spain and demanded retribution through war; in April 1898 they got their wish. The United States fought a successful ten-week war against Spanish naval and ground forces over the spring and summer of 1898. As a result of the peace treaty, the United States acquired from Spain the Philippine Islands, Puerto Rico, and Guam. This "splendid little war" secured the United States an empire. Expansionists applauded. Other Americans expressed dismay that their country was abandoning its historic policy of anti-imperialism.

The United States entered the twentieth century with a new president, Theodore Roosevelt, an aggressive expansionist. Succeeding the assassinated William McKinley, he brought the United States into the twentieth century as a major world power. Roosevelt modernized the United States Navy, taking it from being the fifth-strongest navy in the world to the third, and he took the Panama Canal zone from Colombia. The president let the world know that the United States controlled the Western Hemisphere through the Roosevelt Corollary to the Monroe Doctrine, which declared that this hemisphere was America's sphere of influence and that it unilaterally reserved the right to intervene in the internal affairs of any country in it.

The Progressive movement paralleled in time the rise of the United States as a world power. The movement comprised a variety of groups that sought to find solutions to the distressing domestic problems turn-of-the-century America faced, caused directly or indirectly by the rapid industrialization of the United States. Men and women were stirred to action both by what they saw around them and by the work of journalists called muckrakers. These writers exposed the widespread corruption of the American political process, the necessity of increasing democracy in the United States, the abuses of big business, the abject poverty of workers, the desperate need for consumer protection laws, and the deleterious effects of liquor consumption on bodies and families.

The progressives challenged Americans to accept a greater degree of social responsibility and help lessen society's problems. During the first two decades of the twentieth century, they worked hard to bring about reforms in American life. Settlement houses were started to meet the needs of the residents of urban slums. They offered services to the poor, such as free medical clinics, visiting practical nurses, penny bath programs, hot lunches, playgrounds for children, and literacy classes. Other progressives tried to undercut the power of bosses and the political machines through such changes as direct primaries and the secret ballot. Reformers hoped to allow people to become more directly involved in the political process through the initiative and the referendum, which permitted citizens to approve or reject a law already passed by the state legislature, and by the recall, which allowed voters to decide if an elected official should remain in office.

Thomas Jefferson a century before had declared that "the government that governs least, governs best." The progressives hoped to change Americans' long-standing agreement with this assertion, maintaining that a big, strong, activist federal government should be embraced as an instrument for achieving human good rather than as a threat to basic liberties. Under the leadership of three progressive presidents, Roosevelt, Taft, and Wilson, the federal government passed laws to regulate business, protect labor, conserve natural resources and wilderness areas, and safeguard the public from shoddy and even dangerous products. During these presidencies, the progressives sought to make constitutional a federal personal income tax in the hopes of redistributing personal wealth in the United States. They also wanted greater democracy by amending the Constitution to provide for the popular election of U.S. senators and for national women's suffrage. They moreover desired to eliminate the myriad problems and dangers that liquor consumption caused by means of a federal prohibition amendment. They realized these objectives with the addition of the Sixteenth through Nineteenth Amendments to the United States Constitution during the Progressive era.

The progressives, however, ignored the needs of black Americans and accepted the nation's way of handling racial issues as appropriate. Consequently, the near-absolute segregation of the black and white races in the South by means of Jim Crow laws continued. President Wilson ordered the employees in many federal departments to be separated by race. Lynchings not only continued during this era but increased. Between 1900 and 1914 more than 1,100 blacks were lynched in the United States. Black leaders such as Booker T. Washington and W. E. B. DuBois tried to help members of their race achieve equality. Washington founded Tuskegee Institute in Alabama, hoping that blacks might secure advancement in society if better educated. DuBois helped found the NAACP (the National Association for the Advancement of Colored People) in 1909. An effective spokesman for the organization, he also served as the editor of the NAACP's magazine, *The Crisis*. Despite their efforts, blacks continued to suffer racial discrimination.

When Woodrow Wilson became president in 1913, he hoped to work primarily on domestic concerns. However, as problems mounted in Europe, foreign affairs became his chief concern. Hostility and unrest among the Great Powers had been growing in Europe since the late nineteenth century. As a result of a system of military alliances among these nations, the war that started in 1914 as a regional conflict in the Balkans between the Austrians and Serbs spread to most of Europe. Although frequently provoked, the United States managed to avoid military involvement in World War I for three years. When it finally declared war against Germany and its allies in the spring of 1917, the two key characteristics of the era merged: progressivism and the rise of the United States as a world power. Wilson proclaimed that the United States entered the war not to secure territory and riches but to use this opportunity as a "war to end all wars" and to have American might "make the world safe for democracy." In other words, the president launched the United States on an international progressive housecleaning crusade to establish a "new world order."

Millions of Americans contributed to the Allied victory in 1918 by aiding at home and serving in the armed forces overseas. The Treaty of Versailles, which ended World War I, was harsh on Germany and helped to destroy Wilson's dream for a "just and lasting peace." With hundreds of thousands of American veterans dead or wounded, Americans wondered whether the price paid for international progressivism and the move away from the traditional policy of isolationism had been too costly. After the war, optimism and hope in America about establishing a progressive new order at home or abroad waned. Many Americans wanted little to do with domestic reforms or international problems.

Warren G. Harding sounded the right note during the 1920 presidential campaign when he asked Americans if they wished a return to "normalcy." The nation responded favorably to his query, sending Harding in a landslide victory to Washington as the nation's twenty-ninth president. Americans, putting progressivism and internationalism behind them, soon became caught up in the "good times" of the Roaring Twenties: prosperity, consumerism, jazz, flappers, shorter hemlines, bootleg liquor, Al Capone, Duke Ellington, F. Scott Fitzgerald, and Babe Ruth.

William McKinley

Twenty-fifth President of the United States, 1897–1901

H. WAYNE MORGAN

On September 14, 1906, the fifth anniversary of President William McKinley's assassination, dignitaries and citizens in Columbus, Ohio, attended the dedication of an impressive monument in his honor. The structure formed an arc-shaped exedra, with a group of allegorical figures at one end representing Peace, a single figure at the other, Labor. In the center a statue of McKinley, posed as an orator, stood high above both the monument and the walkway leading into the state capitol building.

It was not easy to see this ending in his beginnings. He was born in Niles, Ohio, on January 29, 1843, the seventh of nine children of William McKinley Sr. and Nancy Allison McKinley. Their ancestors had left Scotland and northern Ireland in the eighteenth century and moved west with the expanding frontier lines of the new United States of America. The parents embodied the stereotype of the frugal, canny Scots-Irish, eager to succeed through hard work. William Sr. worked in iron foundries before becoming a modest businessman, and Nancy took charge of the home and children. The family were devout and active members of the Methodist Episcopal Church, with its strong emphasis on civic duty, sobriety, and reason, as well as personal fulfillment and salvation.

The young McKinley behaved much like other boys in frontier Ohio. Yet later commentators and family members noted that he also differed from his peers: he was active but also displayed a streak of reflection and thoughtful sobriety, and he was serious and responsible, but not earnest. Some of this demeanor resulted from his mother's close attention. She expected great things of him, preferably in the church, and combined a stern sense of discipline with affection and support. He was also a middle child in a large group of siblings, which enhanced his tendencies to harmonize issues and avoid conflict. There was nothing pretentious in this basic psychology, and he often later said that he enjoyed a simple upbringing. But from an early age he knew right from wrong and developed a sense of being special.

The family wanted the best available education for the children. Nancy McKinley later said: "I brought up all my children to understand that they must study and improve their minds." When McKinley was eleven years old, they moved to the nearby hamlet of Poland, Ohio. Its muddy streets and ragged edges melded into the environment, but it also boasted a well-known seminary, or high school. McKinley learned the basics of English, literature, and history there. He was bright and committed to study. Few young people attended college, but his sister Anna donated her modest savings, earned from teaching, to help him enroll in Allegheny College, in Meadville, Pennsylvania, in 1860.

Ill-health and poor finances forced him to leave Allegheny in the spring of 1860, yet he went with a good command of English, an ability to present his views, and a love of reading, which led to self-education. He had also gained human skills in class work, debates, and social settings. He was, as he often said later, a country boy, but with a view of something beyond the horizon.

McKinley returned home, taught at a rural school, then worked at the local post office, but his horizon grew as civil war approached in 1861. At Allegheny College and in the community, he had vigorously argued for the Union position. His personal response to the crisis involved both practicality and belief: the Union had developed as a nation, and slavery was wrong. "Politically, the McKinleys were staunch abolitionists," his mother recalled, "and William early imbibed very radical views regarding the enslavement of the colored race." He consulted with friends and family, then joined the 23d Ohio Volunteer Infantry Regiment in June 1861.

William McKinley fought in many engagements during the war. As a young private he first served in Western Virginia. He advanced to the rank of commissary sergeant, and in a famous incident during the deadly battle of Antietam in September 1862 he provided much-needed food and water to his men under heavy fire. In the latter part of the Civil War McKinley saw action at the battle of Winchester, in the Shenandoah Valley of Virginia. His comrades admired his reliability and calmness, yet he remained somewhat apart from them. He neither drank nor smoked and disliked the rough language around the campfire and bivouac. He was genial but serious, more noted for following the war in newspapers and reading books than for any reveling in or out of camp. McKinley was steadily promoted into staff positions and was a brevet major at the war's end. This title became his trademark in a long political career.

McKinley's service and his rank as major later helped him among the voters of Ohio and then the nation when he entered politics. He also had the support and friendship of Rutherford B. Hayes, one of his first superiors in the 23d OVI, and of other veterans who became politicians, such as James A. Garfield. McKinley matured during the war; ever observant of the life around him, he learned how to deal with people, both soldiers and leaders, and how to organize and conduct solutions to problems.

McKinley's service was as hard, dangerous, and uncomfortable as any other veteran's, yet he seldom referred to it after the war. He praised the soldiers who saved the Union and freed the slaves but did not discuss his own roles. He agreed with a comrade who said later: "Why, he did just what the rest of us did. Never shirked his duty. He was a good, square fellow." Sometimes a certain wryness crept into his speeches or conversation when the subject came up. "My comrades," he told a reunion of the 23d Ohio Volunteer Infantry in 1897, "the memories of war are sweeter than service in the war [laughter]. It is a good deal pleasanter and very much safer to fight our battles o'er as we are doing today than it was to fight them from '61 to '65." His service was a source of pride, a fund of nostalgia, but above all, an education.

McKinley's superiors suggested that he remain in the army, given his abilities as a staff officer. There were always dangers in the service, even in peacetime. The work would be routine and advancement slow. His father was opposed. Nancy McKinley always imagined her son as a bishop, but he felt no calling. William was already interested in politics, despite the family's objections to such a rough-and-tumble, probably sordid career. All in all, law seemed to be the surest road to success. He would move toward politics via a legal career. And if politics failed, he could always fall back on practice law.

As was the custom in legal education, he studied with a prominent attorney in Poland, Ohio, then attended the Albany (New York) Law School in 1866–1867. Friends there remembered his studious demeanor and quick mastery of the law. But he was not all work and was a genial companion at the theater and literary discussions. He avoided controversy, never complained, and smoothed the waters for other people. He remained naive and unsuspecting but quickly learned social skills and acquired new tastes.

McKinley was admitted to the bar at Warren, Ohio, in 1867, then moved to Canton, largely at the behest of his sister Anna, the principal of one of the city's grammar schools. He liked this substantial community, a crossroads for local farms and workshops, with services such as banking, medicine, and the law. It had good streets, rail connections, and a variety of stores. It looked as if it were going somewhere, and it bore the marks of what he thought was civilization. Canton was the seat of Stark County, and political discussions dominated the livery stable and courthouse. News of national affairs came via the telegraph and an active press. McKinley was a staunch Republican in an area that balanced between the major parties. Working and living in Canton he had ample opportunity to discuss and debate the reigning issues of the day, but the young attorney made no enemies during often intense discussions because of his affable personality. He had an introductory taste of politics when elected Stark County's prosecuting attorney for 1869–1871. His bid for reelection failed.

McKinley's private legal career continued to prosper, and he clearly had a future in Canton. He made the greatest progress in his personal life when he fell in love with Ida Saxton, probably the most visible belle in town. Her grandfather had founded the *Repository*, Canton's newspaper, which he edited for more than fifty years. Her father was a banker and a leading citizen. Ida was pretty, delicate, and stylish. She had a somewhat nervous disposition and could be alternately domineering and dependent. Yet this was a love match for them both, and they were married on January 25, 1871.

Their first daughter, Katherine, was born on December 25, 1871, and for the rest of his life, McKinley referred to Katie as his Christmas present. A second daughter, Ida, came on April 1, 1873. The McKinley household seemed to be developing on solid, traditional lines: loving parents, beautiful children, and a home with social graces. But the family's serenity did not last. Ida was a sickly infant and died on August 22, 1873, before she was six months old. Mrs. McKinley was distraught, and grief brought her instabilities to the fore. She was often deeply depressed, had migraines, and sometimes fainted or had "fits." She understandably overprotected Katie, for fear something would happen to her. Ida's protectiveness failed, and three-year-old Katie died of typhoid fever on June 25, 1875.

These tragedies profoundly affected the couple. Ida steadily retreated into invalidism. Some days she functioned well, and on others, she remained in a dark room, averse to sound or light, suffering a migraine or phlebitis. Doctors had no cures and only marginal treatments. Bromides and sedatives were the most effective remedies, but they simply calmed her. She clung to her husband, who became a devoted companion and nurse, reading every mood, sensing every change of feeling in her. She feared being separated from him, and he remained at her beck and call the rest of his life. The marriage settled into routines that were fairly common, at a time when there were few answers for nervousness or invalidism. She became dependent, and he became supportive and long-suffering. McKinley's feelings combined true love, pity for a woman ravaged in her youth, and the desire to maintain proprieties. In one sense this response solidified basic aspects of his personality for his political future. He was calm in almost any situation. He observed and listened carefully, tried to persuade rather than to insist, to suggest not command. In a very real sense his role as a husband after Ida's illness was a bridge between his private and public lives, creating an emotional whole.

Despite these tragedies, McKinley now opted to pursue a political career. He campaigned in 1875 for his old commander Rutherford B. Hayes, who was seeking an unprecedented third term as governor of Ohio. The Major became a popular figure on the hustings in Canton and its environs. He was attractive, with personal charm and physical dignity, though young. He was adept at shaking hands, patting children on the head, tasting homemade pies, and at all the other touches that were so important in humanizing politicians. Party loyalties divided the electorate closely and passionately. Voters were well informed, or at least had strong opinions. They responded best to anyone with whom they could identify as both a person and an embodiment of larger ideas. McKinley helped Hayes, who was now positioned for the Republican presidential nomination in 1876. McKinley won the contest for Congress in his district that latter year and served in the House of Representatives from 1877 to 1891, except for a brief period in 1885–1886 when he lost a disputed election.

William McKinley came to Congress as a moderate Republican. His appeal among constituents was diverse. His district included many workers who usually voted Democratic, yet they liked him because he espoused their interests. The Republican middle class of professionals, small-town movers and shakers, and big businessmen liked him because they saw him as a potential spokesman.

The decades after the Civil War witnessed the growth of the United States as the world's leading industrial power. McKinley appreciated how entrepreneurs and businessmen struggled to survive, let alone succeed, in the confused and aggressively competitive industrial revolution that was transforming the nation. He knew that small workshops, raw materials producers, or craftsmen faced stiff competition from each other, from the larger firms that were developing, and from imports. McKinley accepted this broad industrialism and its uncertain rates of success or failure. He never doubted that individual initiative and effort drove the economy, but he also believed that government should help develop the infrastructure and protect markets. It might appropriately even regulate some business activity. But individual effort developed the economy.

The tariff was the identifying issue of his political career in the House of Representatives, and he became an expert on it. The original tariff dated from 1789 and was designed both to raise revenue through import duties and to foster domestic enterprises in the new republic. By McKinley's time the tariff debate focused less on revenue than on whether and how the national government should use taxes on imported goods to protect American business from foreign competition. He believed the United States could be a unique, self-contained "home market," so rich in resources and in its people and their skills that it could be economically self-sufficient. He believed that protection was necessary and consistently tied it to producers, workers, and consumers, not just to business. He spoke more for small business and labor than for big business, which generally found protection marginal to its interests. And he raised the doctrine beyond materialism to a grand idea. Under it the disparate parts of the continental economy would compete to produce good jobs and fair prices. They in turn would foster national unity and domestic order.

McKinley entered the political culture of Washington in 1877 with ease. He was still youthful and dynamic in his mid-thirties but gave the impression of dignity beyond his years. He was always well dressed, usually in a black frock coat. He was easily approachable, and his charm and courtesy quickly became legendary. He remained temperate in his personal habits. He still did not drink, but he now smoked cigars and was familiar with the spittoon.

Congressmen did not have offices, so he maintained a cramped sitting-bedroom at the Ebbitt House for himself and Ida, with a small room across the hall where he received visitors and studied. He often left conferences to check on Ida's well-being. The McKinleys were not socially active, owing to her health, but both often helped their friends President and Mrs. Hayes in social affairs at the White House. As McKinley's fame and authority increased, theirs became a somewhat harried existence, and they tried to stay in Canton when Congress was not in session.

McKinley's salary was $5,000, and he had a modest income from rents and later from a legacy to Ida from her father. Yet money was a concern. He once advised a friend to avoid public office. "Before I went to Congress I had $10,000, and a practice worth $10,000 a year. Now I haven't either." He was not interested in money for himself but for Ida's security. Tempting opportunities sometimes came his way. Tom Scott of the Pennsylvania Railroad offered him $25,000 a year, but after surveying the situation he declined. Politics was always surprising: no one could tell what lay ahead for him. He also "had an idea that he was serving the country a little," and he liked his status and visibility.

That status came from his work in the House, where he quickly became well known. "Unlike most new members, McKinley did not rush madly into the wordy arena," one commentator noted. He did speak against an effort to reduce the tariff in 1878 and was a major Republican spokesman on this and other issues by the mid-1880s. He enjoyed debate in the House, and as one observer noted, "He was generally regarded as one of the members who had something to say, and who said it well, and when he had said it, stopped." He had mastered the history and politics of tariff protection and presented the economic case clearly and concisely. He quoted relevant statistics, was adept at the occasional literary allusion, and could silence an obstreperous colleague, generally with an appeal to facts. Through it all, he remained calm and courteous, essentially a problem-solver, wishing to move legislation he liked. He had many opponents but few personal enemies. Thomas B. Reed of Maine, noted for his commanding physical presence and sharp tongue, marveled at McKinley's ability to shrug off criticism or resist the temptation to skewer a colleague. "My opponents in Congress go at me tooth and nail," he said, "but they always apologize to William when they are going to call him names."

The press dubbed McKinley the "Napoleon of Protection," and cartoonists often depicted him wearing a uniform and cocked hat in the style of the late French emperor. He had his hands full being reelected from a district that the Democratic-controlled Ohio legislature often redrew in an attempt to eliminate him. Nevertheless, he survived nearly all challenges. He was a familiar figure on the national campaign circuit, speaking often for friends and taking a major role in presidential politics. He was highly visible in the national conventions of 1888 and 1892 that nominated Benjamin Harrison. By then a significant element of the party saw him as a new force in Republican affairs, one marked for presidential consideration.

McKinley's congressional career peaked in the session of 1889–1891 when he served as chair of the Ways and Means Committee, which managed tariff measures. After hectic and bitter debate, he produced one that bore his name, the McKinley Tariff of 1890. His tenure in the U.S. House of Representatives ended when he lost the 1890 election because of a ger-rymander to his congressional district and a backlash against Republicans in general because of rising consumer prices, which many people blamed on the tariff. He left Congress in 1891, undaunted in his belief in protection and sure that the issue would bear him to greater things.

McKinley's congressional career had laid the foundations for his national appeal. He was a recognized spokesman of both labor and capital in his ideal of economic development. He had dealt publicly with a major national and international issue in protection. He was an effective and popular speaker. He had traveled widely and saw how diverse the country was and how to unify his party's elements. He seemed young enough to be innovative, mature enough to be wise, and sensible enough to attract an array of voters.

McKinley could have waited until the next election in 1892 and tried to return to the House of Representatives, but he had gone about as far as he could in congressional politics. Returning to a comfortable law practice was possible, and he doubtless wanted some peace and quiet. Yet the call of politics was strong, and perhaps practicing law would seem tame after shepherding bills through the House, debating opponents, and campaigning for friends around the country. And there were opportunities in politics other than in the House, as the *Cleveland Leader* noted as soon as McKinley lost his congressional seat: "The result makes Major McKinley the next governor of Ohio, if he can by any means be prevailed upon to accept the Republican nomination next year."

McKinley accepted the Republican party's nomination in June and began campaigning in August. Even seasoned politicians and journalists were surprised at the public response to his tours of the state. Huge crowds greeted him in the cities, and most of the populations of small towns turned out to hear him expound the tariff's virtues. Voters wanted to see and hear him. More to the point, they liked him; he was one of them.

McKinley won by a respectable 20,000 votes. He took office in January 1892 with a Republican legislature and had considerable success in obtaining his agenda. He secured safety legislation for workers, especially in railroading. Another law passed during his tenure supported voluntary arbitration of labor disputes, which he had long championed in Congress. The legislature also enacted a corporate franchise tax. These measures addressed current concerns and were about as activist as the lawmakers would accept.

McKinley accepted renomination in June 1893, and this time Ohio voters gave him a victory margin of 80,000 votes. He and his supporters saw reelection as validation of his personal status among voters and as a major step toward the presidential nomination in 1896. But his second term was far different from the first. The country entered a deep depression in the spring of 1893, which affected Ohio's industries. A rash of strikes and labor turmoil in Ohio required the national guard to maintain order. McKinley had considerable support—which he retained during this time of troubles—among workers. He sympathized with all parties caught in the economic downturn, but his first duty as Ohio's chief executive was to maintain order. Associates remembered that he often stayed in his capitol office all night, reading and sending telegrams and directing national guard units around the state. McKinley knew that militiamen were often friends or relatives of strikers, and he urged arbitration, or at least reason and calmness, wherever possible. He headed fund drives to provide food and necessities to the unemployed. The depth of the depression was bleak, but the governor emerged unscathed, appearing sympathetic and helpful about hardship while enforcing the law fairly.

Hard times made Democrat Grover Cleveland's national administration bitterly unpopular. The Democrats as a party had reduced the tariff, which led to charges that they had intensified, if not caused, the depression. The Republicans had lost the national House in 1890 and in 1892, but in 1894 they seemed poised to recapture control and there was an unprecedented demand for McKinley to speak in the off-year congressional elections of that year. He responded, both to help Republican candidates and to begin his run for the presidential nomination in 1896. The statistics of the effort that followed were little short of amazing. He gave about four hundred speeches to two million people during the summer and fall of 1894, traveling 12,000 miles. He focused on the upper Midwest but appeared in almost every district where Republicans needed help. He had become an excellent stump speaker, speaking in a clear, pleasant mid-range voice, treating a few ideas, especially the need for protection, and avoiding grandiloquence. This made him seem both real and safe. The message was simple: it was time for change, time to stop talking about tariff reform, which upset business and led to hard times. He and the GOP would bring order and safety to national affairs. The effort worked. The Republicans recaptured the House, the Cleveland administration slid into torpor, and McKinley appeared to be the best-known political figure in the country.

McKinley was not surprised that he now seemed destined for the presidency. Over the years he had told several people of his long-standing strong belief in this outcome. By the summer of 1892, he told one acquaintance: "I shall in 1896 be nominated and elected to the presidency of the United States. I have never been in doubt since I was old enough to think intelligently that I should sometime be made president. Events are now shaping themselves in such a manner that my prediction will be fulfilled four years hence. These you may regard as the words of a fatalist, and I am not sure that I am not one." Perhaps he was right, but facts also mattered. As he later told a prominent newspaperman, he represented national interests and issues, came from a major state, and was a popular campaigner. "I cannot subscribe to the idea that accident or luck had very much to do with making me president of the United States." He might have added his skill at organization, avoiding personal controversy that could cost him intra-party support or popular votes, skill at keeping his name before the public, and choosing able subordinates.

Marcus Alonzo Hanna was the ablest and most necessary of these lieutenants. Born in 1837, making him slightly older than McKinley, Hanna had built successful enterprises in Great Lakes shipping, iron work, and other ventures based in the Cleveland area. He first met McKinley in the early 1870s when the latter successfully defended a group of miners charged with trespass in a strike. Hanna was impressed with McKinley, then gradually became aware of his developing role first in Ohio, then in national politics in the 1880s. Though Hanna was committed to the state's leading Republican, Senator John Sherman, he saw McKinley as the man of the future. Hanna was not personally interested in office, but he found politics fascinating and hoped to help make things go from the background.

In the years to come, political enemies, newspapermen, and cartoonists completely distorted their relationship. Democrats depicted McKinley as a puppet on Hanna's string, ignoring his lifetime of service in national politics. They turned Hanna into "Dollar Mark," covered with dollar signs as a master of indifferent capital, forgetting his good relations with his own workers and his frequent criticisms of other businessmen for being out of touch with the realities of a new economy. Although this was all predictable "politics," especially in 1896, it was also a characterization wide of the mark. Hanna was always the loyal subordinate. He was deferential and cooperative in McKinley's presence, yielding to his judgment and plans, fulfilling orders with care and dispatch. Everyone who worked closely with either man, while admiring their separate skills, agreed that they were not equals. They were, however, indispensable to each other, and together made one superb politician. In politics Hanna spent the same intense energy that had made him successful in business. He was a master organizer, attending to details, with a keen eye for efficient subordinates. He was a supreme realist about humankind and human institutions. McKinley was cautious in his sphere of politics; Hanna was often blunt in his. McKinley was adept at finding the right words and ideas in writing and speaking, whereas Hanna provided the necessary means.

The first step to capturing the nomination for McKinley was to secure the support of delegates to the various state conventions that would in turn instruct the delegations to the national convention. The process started for McKinley in the congressional elections of 1894, when he vividly illustrated his effectiveness on the stump, and collected favors from local leaders. Delegate selection began in earnest in 1895, when Hanna and McKinley started wooing those in southern states. There was no significant number of Republican voters in the region, but its state delegations were important in nominating a national candidate. Hanna arranged for potential delegates to meet McKinley in his winter home in Thomasville, Georgia. He also began to outline formal campaign organizations, select subordinates, and plan the final campaign. Hanna probably spent $100,000 of his own money in this effort, which laid a sound foundation for the state-by-state struggle in the rest of the country for the final presidential contest.

McKinley left the governorship of Ohio in January 1896 and devoted himself full-time to the process of securing instructed state delegations. He presided over a small but efficient staff in Canton and kept in touch with leaders via the telephone and telegraph. The most immediate problem was how to overcome the mixed lot of other GOP hopefuls for the nomination. Former president Benjamin Harrison was the most obvious possible challenger. From 1889 to 1893 he had headed an administration that produced landmark legislation such as the McKinley Tariff, the Sherman Silver Purchase Act, and the Sherman Anti-Trust Act. Despite this record, Republicans suffered defeat in the midterm elections of 1890 at the hands of a restless electorate that seemed generally dissatisfied with politicians and their answers to issues. Harrison was also personally unpopular with party leaders, who found him cold and inept in dealing with them and other individuals. The president had forced his renomination in 1892, then lost the general election to Grover Cleveland. Harrison was not very tempted in the spring of 1896 and declined to seek another nomination.

The East had two familiar aspirants: Levi P. Morton and Thomas B. Reed. Morton was governor of New York and had been vice president for Harrison. He supported the gold standard, an issue coming to the fore in the 1890s, and was the candidate of monetary safety. However, he represented the past and the influence of some party leaders rather than any current popular appeal. Reed of Maine was a noted congressmen and Speaker of the House in 1889–1891 and 1895–1899. He had the luxury of a safe congressional seat, which McKinley never knew, and freely indulged in trenchancy and sarcasm that made him feared rather than liked. Reed believed in protection and gold and was the choice of those who wanted an inflexible leader for traditional principles. He had no following outside of the Northeast. Senator William B. Allison of Iowa was a possible candidate in the West. He had an impressive congressional record, was moderate on the money question, and had important friends within the party leadership. He would be a logical compromise candidate but preferred congressional service and so was not available.

These were all honorable men who had paid their dues to the party and stood by their principles. In an ordinary year, any would be a viable candidate. They all seemed to be possible challengers to McKinley. Yet when measured against them, McKinley seemed refreshingly new, with broad popular appeal, and he was a seasoned and effective campaigner. In the face of rising public discontent and the continuing depression, McKinley seemed experienced and safe. He and his managers capitalized on all of this in a slogan that had great appeal: "The People Against the Bosses." One by one, the state conventions instructed delegations to back McKinley.

The national convention turned out to be a coronation rather than a contest. McKinley's operatives arrived in St. Louis early in June to find a sea of support for him, expressed in buttons, banners, hats, crockery, and other familiar political paraphernalia. Fate allowed Ohio to give him the necessary majority on the first ballot, and the rest was anticlimactic. New Jersey's Garrett A. Hobart was named for the vice presidency.

Only the problem of the party's stand on the money question darkened this triumph. Various schemes to expand the nation's money supply, through issuance of paper or silver coinage, appealed to staple producers in the West and South as a means of raising prices and reducing debts. Business elements in the East, and to some extent in the Midwest, feared that any divergence from "sound money," or gold-backed currency and coinage, would frighten businessmen and investors and further delay recovery. They favored a strong platform plank in favor of gold, as well as tariff protection. McKinley and Hanna devised a subtle strategy to neutralize the issue within the party. They allowed numerous important people to think that they had persuaded McKinley to accept a gold plank in the platform, when in fact he had done so well before the convention met. This allowed them to feel influential and guaranteed their support.

The Republicans expected an easy campaign, but to the surprise of political leaders in all parties, the Democratic convention met in Chicago in early July and nominated the little-known William Jennings Bryan of Nebraska for president. His "Cross of Gold" speech at the convention, arraying Haves against Have Nots, and the West and South against the East, was a sensation. In his powerful manifesto against the gold standard, he proclaimed. "You shall not press down upon the brow of labor this crown of thorns! You shall not crucify mankind upon a cross of gold!" There was a compelling logic in Bryan's selection. At thirty-six he seemed youthful and energetic in a political system that looked tired if not exhausted. He had served a Nebraska district in the national House from 1891 to 1895. Defeated in a bid for a Senate seat, Bryan retired from electoral politics to spread the word for free silver as a journalist and speaker. In 1896 he seemed to have at least a chance to marshal discontented voters everywhere.

Bryan further shook the political landscape when he decided to campaign throughout the country in a special train, both to contact voters and to dramatize his cause. This defied the convention that presidential candidates did not overtly seek the office, but relied on party organizations and a few statesmanlike appearances. This drama, allied with his appeals for free silver as a panacea for the country's ills, challenged Republican plans for McKinley. He could not seem above any divisive battle.

Hanna perceived the threat in Bryan's underdog role at once and urged his candidate to mount a vigorous challenge, as he had in other campaigns. "You've got to stump or we'll be defeated," he told McKinley, who pondered, then answered: "You know I have the greatest respect for your wishes, but I cannot take the stump against that man." Other callers echoed Hanna's concerns and advice, but they met McKinley's stubborn refusal to copy the opposition. A similar campaign would make him seem defensive, always answering Bryan rather than espousing his own and the party's ideas.

Events in Canton suggested an answer to the problem of how to wage the campaign. No sooner had the news of his nomination come over the telegraph than people rushed to McKinley's home on North Market Street. Fire bells rang, whistles blew, and brass bands materialized. For the rest of the day, trains brought well-wishers from neighboring towns, many hanging on the sides of crowded cars. The crowds demanded speeches from McKinley, and newsmen arranged interviews. By that evening, when the people had departed and the noise subsided, the yard was a wasteland of trampled grass, and most of the picket fence was gone as souvenirs.

William McKinley (*left*) conducted the famous Front Porch Campaign of 1896 from this home in Canton, Ohio. Hundreds of thousands of people came to greet him and hear his message. Here McKinley is joined in 1900 by his second vice president, Theodore Roosevelt, whom McKinley found a bit too young, nervous, and impulsive. Library of Congress.

As McKinley and his staff thought about a good public response to Bryan, they saw that if the candidate could not go to the people, they could come to him. This would allow McKinley to meet and address many different groups while remaining dignified and careful. Thus was born the "Front Porch Campaign," one of the most famous presidential campaigns in United States history.

Hanna established headquarters in New York City and in Chicago, where the Midwest would be the major battleground. He assembled talented staffs, who focused on trying to inform and convince voters that the country's economic recovery and stability depended on Republican victory. Millions of pamphlets extolled the virtues of protection and other issues in every language spoken in the United States. Every noted Republican who could speak anywhere had a full schedule, and the party supported local clubs and speakers.

Canton was the epicenter of the campaign between the first part of September and election day in November. Any group could apply to meet the candidate. They came in delegations whose appearance the staffs had arranged meticulously. A time was set, they received railroad tickets and full instructions about how to act and what to do once in Canton. McKinley, careful to avoid any embarrassments or comments that might require defense, required delegation leaders to visit him with their proposed remarks before coming to Canton. He listened to their brief texts, suggested changes, and cautioned them not to depart from the script.

At the appointed date and time, the group appeared at the Canton railroad station, disembarked, arranged its banners, and marched up Market Street. En route they passed returning groups who boarded a train and left town. Once it arrived, the delegation waited on what was left of the yard until McKinley opened the door, acknowledged their cheers, and attended to the leader's speech. He swore fealty to the candidate and party and promised to return home and work for victory. McKinley, of course, had read these remarks, but as one observer said, he listened carefully and looked as if he were a child encountering Santa Claus. When the spokesman finished, McKinley mounted a box or chair and spoke to the group briefly about the dangers of inflation that would follow free silver, the merits of protection, or the folly of experimenting in hard times. His responses were brief, simple, and focused on a few themes. They subsequently appeared as pamphlets and in monthly collections of his speeches, which went out to potential voters. When he finished, he invited the group to come across the porch, shake hands, and exit through the house for the trip home. About 500,000 people came to Canton in this manner, and McKinley often spoke to a dozen or more delegations every day. Meanwhile, across the country, the campaign depicted McKinley as the "Advance Agent of Prosperity" whose victory would restore prosperity and a "full dinner pail" for everyone.

This huge effort required money, which Hanna and his lieutenants raised from businesses, party organizations, and individuals. They spent about

$3.5 million, the largest sum for a presidential campaign to date. The Democrats were sure that the rich and corporations had provided a colossal slush fund to intimidate voters or to drown out Bryan's effort. They were right to find Hanna's fund-raising impressive and wrong to conclude that he had intimidated or purchased voters. Whereas McKinley spoke from his porch in Canton, Bryan spoke almost five hundred times from his train, at whistle stops, towns, and in large cities across the country. His press coverage was as intense as McKinley's. It was hard to imagine that anyone anywhere did not know what each candidate espoused. Theodore Roosevelt later complained that Hanna had advertised McKinley as if he were a patent medicine. This was true enough, but Bryan too had presented himself as if he were a commodity. This was the new order of politics, focused on imagery, name recognition, and the repetition of a few simple ideas. Both campaigns revealed the power of political advertising. Hanna had simply established an enviable pattern for the future.

Election day brought impressive results. McKinley became the first presidential candidate since U. S. Grant to receive a majority of the popular votes. He carried California, Oregon, and the great crescent of states from North Dakota through the Great Lakes and eastward to Maine, with just over 7.1 million popular votes and 271 electoral votes. Bryan won the always solidly Democratic South, as well as the plains and the mountain states, areas that favored free silver, with 6.5 million popular votes and 176 in the electoral college count. The Republicans took the industrial states that also had profitable diverse agriculture and carried both houses of Congress. McKinley won every urban area in the country, which testified to the party's identification with industrialism. Throughout the campaign, he had emphasized diversity and welcomed new voters into the party. The banners he saw from his front porch identified ethnic and occupational groups that would figure prominently in future successes. McKinley had laid the groundwork for more victories if his party could restore prosperity and govern successfully.

William McKinley became president on March 4, 1897, and immediately asked a special session of Congress to act on the Republican program. The first result was the Dingley Tariff, which contained higher average rates than the president probably wanted, but which allowed negotiations for a form of reciprocity that would modify tariff rates without harming domestic producers. McKinley also fulfilled the party platform's promise of 1896 to seek an international agreement on remonetizing silver while not threatening the de facto gold standard. Neither effort succeeded, but both were sincere and helped develop an activist image for the party on major issues. Although the Atlantic economy had weathered the sharp depression that began in 1893 and was poised for a cyclical upturn, the new administration's actions did end business uncertainties that had retarded recovery.

The new president brought fresh ideas and procedures to his work. First, he ended the negative siege mentality that marked the Cleveland administration. His natural charm and interest in people served him well as he welcomed visitors of all kinds. He dealt easily with visiting dignitaries, politicians, and groups. He was especially mindful of congressional opinion and often interrupted business to hear a member's complaints, requests, or occasional demands. He listened patiently and dispensed large quantities of what his staff called soothing syrup. He explained his position on appointments or pending legislation with care and courtesy, and made few enemies when he rejected a request. These touches in human relations came to McKinley naturally, but they helped smooth the path of legislation in Congress, and of politics in general. A new saying made the rounds in Washington about the current chief executive and his two predecessors: Harrison froze callers out, Cleveland kicked them out, and McKinley kissed them out.

McKinley and his able secretary, George B. Cortelyou, reorganized the White House office routine to improve efficiency and allow greater access to a wide range of people. Unlike Cleveland, McKinley did not view reporters as enemies but as agents who might help promote his policies. He established a "newspaper row" in the mansion with desks and telephones where reporters could observe daily business and write dispatches. They could not quote him without permission but could see many visitors. Cortelyou organized regular press briefings and provided press releases on events the president thought important. McKinley himself was famous for understanding public opinion. He read a few papers every day and relied on Cortelyou's summary of representative sheets. And he learned much from visiting politicians. Reporters also accompanied him in a special railroad car on his many trips, where he both spoke to large crowds and shook countless hands, while further gauging opinion. He now created news and avoided confrontation with the press. All of this made the man and the office seem open and human, with profound implications for the future, as the presidency expanded in both functions and popular expectations.

In the spring and early summer of 1897, while McKinley was busy establishing his administration and attending to economic legislation, a dangerous situation was intensifying in Cuba. The island, which Christopher Columbus had claimed for Spain in 1492, was the last significant vestige of Spain's New World empire. The Cubans had staged a destructive revolt between 1868 and 1878, which solved few basic issues and ended in a stalemate. They rose again in 1895, dedicated to independence more than ever. Their guerrilla warfare, aimed at making the Spanish seem helpless, depended on the hit-and-run attack against the Spanish military and on the machete and the firebrand to destroy Spanish property. The resulting destruction of most of the island's sugar plantation economy was bad enough. Suffering among civilians, in both the countryside and the towns, marked every step of this grim, remorseless combat, which neither the Spanish nor the Cubans seemed able to win.

McKinley inherited a Cuban policy that had stressed the need for Spain to pacify the island either through Spanish victory or Cuban autonomy. The Spanish insisted that the conflict was no concern of the United States. This was unrealistic. The island was only ninety miles from the U.S. mainland and had figured in American foreign policy almost since its beginning. Americans had substantial involvements there, and the island was economically dependent on the United States. Above all, the American public saw the conflict as one of freedom against an inhumane Spanish tyranny. Richard Olney, Cleveland's secretary of state, bluntly reminded Spain in 1896 that "the United States cannot contemplate with complacency another ten years of Cuban insurrection, with all its injurious and distressing incidents." The new president hoped to avoid intervention and in his inaugural address had disavowed overseas conflicts, insisting, "Arbitration is the true method of settlement of international as well as local or individual differences."

It was easier to say this than to secure a peaceful resolution of conflict. The Spanish seemed committed to retaining the island, whatever the cost. Prime Minister Cánovas del Castillo said in 1896 that Spain would fight to the last soldier and the last peseta. This attitude was incarnated in Gen. Valeriano Weyler, soon nicknamed "the Butcher," who set out to subdue the rebels with fire and the sword. Spanish leaders could not relinquish Cuba or yield to American demands without losing their status in world affairs. More importantly, defeat might easily translate into revolution at home. The Spanish regularly charged the American government with having a pro-Cuban bias, failing to interdict supplies to the rebels and keeping the insurrection alive with threats of intervention. To impatient Americans, in and out of public life, Spanish policy seemed based on obfuscation, deceit, and delay in the hope that something would turn up to save them.

Like Cleveland, McKinley rejected Spain's indictments but wanted to end the conflict. He would not grant the Cubans belligerent status, and the Navy made every effort to interdict illegal supplies and arms. The administration's view of the rebels was ambivalent; they had the better part of the argument because they sought freedom, yet they also defied laws against gun-running. Their junta in New York exaggerated most reports from Cuba, which agitated American public opinion and kept the issue alive in Congress and the press. They, like the Spanish, destroyed American property in Cuba. The rebels were a varied, often incompatible group representing most of the island's discontented elements, united only in their hatred of Spain. They wanted American aid as long as it led to their independence. They rejected the idea of autonomy within Spanish jurisdiction, even when it was the basis of McKinley's policy.

To American policy makers and interests, the rebels often resembled ungrateful relatives, full of demands but with no assets. Though tension with the rebels was not clear at first, time and events made policy makers suspicious of their abilities to cooperate in reconstructing the island or to restore confidence in Cuba's future if they achieved independence. A very real question shadowed the elegant diplomatic wrangling with Spain: Could the United States accept Cuban independence if it seemed likely to lead to more instability in the island?

McKinley had to devise a policy from these often conflicting emotions and interests. He was reticent about this, as always, and did not leave a record of his thinking. The party platform on which he ran in 1896 generally recognized American interests abroad and praised the Cubans' heroic struggle for liberty. Because Spain could not control the island or end the rebellion, the United States should "use its influence and good offices to restore peace and give independence to the island." He doubtless agreed with these generalities but said nothing about Cuba during the presidential campaign.

He began his presidency with a fair understanding of foreign interests that affected tariff reciprocity and a general desire to expand commerce. But like most presidents, he learned on the job. He could secure specific information about the island as he needed it. The State Department and various bureaus furnished him with information on Cuba's past and present and on diplomacy with Spain. He received regular reports from the U.S. ministry in Madrid and the consuls in Cuba. He read the newspapers, which impressed on him the fact that Cuba was a political as well as a diplomatic issue that he must solve. On the whole, McKinley was as well prepared as most presidents, with the added advantage of a highly developed sense of politics and public opinion and a genuine personal desire to end the suffering in Cuba.

McKinley employed one other source of information that was common among presidents: the personal agent. He asked an old political friend from Illinois, Judge William J. Calhoun, to tour Cuba and report on what he saw. Calhoun filed his report on June 22, 1897, confirming the president's worst fears: "I traveled by rail from Havana to Matanzas. The country outside of the military posts was practically depopulated. Every house had been burned, banana trees cut down, cane fields swept with the fire, and everything in the shape of food destroyed. It was as fair a landscape as mortal eye ever looked upon; but I did not see a house, man, woman or child, a horse, mule or cow, nor even a dog. I did not see a sign of life, except an occasional vulture or buzzard sailing through the air. The country was wrapped in the stillness of death and the silence of desolation." He doubted that Spain could either end the rebellion or make genuine autonomy work. Only American pressure, and possibly intervention, could solve the problem.

Calhoun's report and similar information from other sources laid the basis for McKinley's policy. He would press the Spanish to end reconcentration, aid the dispossessed, and abandon their destructive mode of warfare. They must also grant an armistice. During this truce all parties would assess their demands, and the subsequent negotiations would result in viable home rule or autonomy within Spanish jurisdiction. McKinley did not say so but must have assumed that autonomy would finally lead to independence. This approach reflected his own belief in compromise and in solving problems a step at a time. It was specific enough to appeal to all parties, he thought, and to produce some incremental results on which to build. It was also broad enough to survive unexpected events. It was a suitable approach for domestic affairs, and it might even work among international powers.

McKinley's policy, outwardly hopeful, was born in fatalism if not pessimism. The Spanish had been so intransigent in pursuing the war, and so prickly in protecting their pride, that no compromise solution seemed likely. Yet fall 1897 brought a few glimmers of hope. Conservative Prime Minister Cánovas was assassinated in August, and a new more liberal ministry soon decided to recall General Weyler and to proceed with autonomy. By November the government in Madrid had prepared the basic decrees that began the autonomy process.

McKinley proceeded along the road he had mapped, aware of the political risks in Congress, determined to make a defensible record, and hopeful of the chance of success. His December 6, 1897, annual message to Congress summarized the conflict and Cuba's importance to the United States.

He approved the Spanish initiatives, particularly of relieving Weyler and moving to end reconcentration. He reminded everyone, especially the Spanish, of options still remaining for the United States: recognizing Cuban independence, neutral intervention to impose a settlement, or intervention on one side. He rejected belligerent status for the rebels and disavowed annexation of the island. In the meantime, the conflict continued as politicians orated, diplomats talked, and American newspapers pontificated. The Cubans showed few signs of softening their demands for independence.

The new year opened with some guarded optimism about Cuba. Madrid proclaimed the basic autonomy decrees effective January 1, 1898, which seemed to start the preparations for Cuban self-rule within the Spanish Empire. Reactions were varied. The American press and other interests welcomed the idea but would wait upon events, fearing that Spain lacked the means to create true autonomy. The McKinley administration saw the plan as a first step and would continue to press for its speedy realization. Spanish patriots resented the American pressure behind the plan and continued to oppose Cuban independence. The Cuban rebels saw it as a sham. The worst and most ominous response, however, came from Havana, where antiautonomy elements attacked newspaper offices that displayed the decrees and caused significant disturbances. This shook the American administration's belief in Spain's ability to implement true autonomy.

Concern about the implications of these events had no sooner subsided than another crisis threatened McKinley's diplomacy. On the morning of February 9, 1898, the *New York Journal* published a front-page facsimile of a letter from Enrique Dupuy de Lôme, the Spanish minister in Washington, to a friend in Spain. In the course of analyzing the Cuban issue, Dupuy de Lôme characterized McKinley as "weak and a bidder for the admiration of the crowd, besides being a would-be politician who tries to leave a door open behind himself while keeping on good terms with the jingos of his party." This was offensive enough, but the administration focused on another paragraph concerning the pending negotiations for a trade treaty with Spain: "It would be very advantageous to take up, even if only for effect, the question of commercial relations, and to have a man of some importance sent hither in order that I may make use of him here to carry on a propaganda among the Senators and others in opposition to the junta and to try to win over the refugees."

The president never supposed that the Spanish had ever admired him, and he brushed off the personal element. The cynicism about the trade treaty, however, indicated a broader Spanish duplicity. One further point complicated the issue: the Cuban junta in the United States had used the letter stolen from the mails to inflame congressional and public opinion to support their independence, in opposition to McKinley's diplomacy. This may have been a moment when the administration concluded that the rebels were irresponsible and incapable of governing an independent Cuba.

Madrid recalled Dupuy de Lôme and the agitation subsided. It seemed that diplomacy could continue. Meanwhile, the battleship USS *Maine* arrived in Havana Harbor on January 25, its ostensible purpose to express goodwill, while a Spanish ship would do the same in an American harbor. The *Maine*'s presence also emphasized American interests in Cuba, which the local Spanish deeply resented. Its role in history was far larger. On the evening of February 15, 1898, the ship exploded and sank in the murky waters of Havana Harbor, claiming the lives of 258 American sailors.

President McKinley rose from bed to receive the news a few hours later and understood that the tragedy would greatly increase the pressure on him to intervene. Congress and the public doubtless would conclude that the resentful Spaniards sank the ship and that further diplomacy was pointless. The president resolutely opposed precipitate action and instead selected a commission of experts to examine the shipwreck and to assign blame if possible. "I shall never get into a war unless I am sure that God and man approve," he told friends. "I have been through one war; I have seen the dead piled up; and I do not want to see another."

As the *Maine* commission went about its work, yet another incident sharpened the debate. Senator Redfield Proctor, Republican of Vermont, had watched reporting of events in Cuba with a skeptical eye. He was noted for a calm demeanor, given to facts and reason rather than histrionics. Friends suggested that he visit Cuba and report his findings; he would speak for reason and would command respect. By late February he had agreed and left quietly for Cuba. While there he talked with diplomatic representatives, businessmen, relief workers, and common people. He stepped over dead bodies in the streets and alleys of towns he visited, saw starving and diseased prisoners in concentration camps, and viewed the physical destruction in the countryside. Proctor reported to the Senate on March 17, 1898. The hushed and attentive members heard him describe in an unemotional tone what he had seen, without appeals to passion. First, the war was a stalemate. Second, the Cubans distrusted Spain and would not accept autonomy. Third, despite their divisions, the Cubans might be capable of self-government. He left the final solution of the problem to McKinley and the public but emphasized that further fighting between Spaniards and Cubans would produce a human catastrophe greater than the one he had just seen.

Proctor's speech made a profound impression: the inhumane warfare made Cuba a legitimate American interest. All parties should seek some kind of compromise, and if that proved impossible, the American people would be justified in acting. In Madrid, the American minister Stewart Woodford emphasized this bluntly when talking with Spanish officials.

The *Maine* commission report reached McKinley on March 24. It held that an external force had caused the explosion but assigned no blame. Congress received the report on March 28, which produced a volatile debate as members, the public, and the press assumed Spanish responsibility. McKinley soothed tempers, delayed, pressed the Spanish one last time, and realized that the rest of the course pointed to intervention. At the last hour Madrid granted a suspension of hostilities. Some observers and later historians assumed that this meant Spanish capitulation. But policy makers in Washington saw the gesture as more delay, hedged with qualifications that would allow the Spanish to recover, then resume hostilities after the rainy season ended in October. The administration, now distrustful of any Spanish promises, shifted its basic demand from autonomy to Cuban independence, which Spain would not accept. McKinley believed that the conflict would cease only with Spain's removal from the Americas, which meant war.

The sensational press did not force McKinley into war. Indeed, he read little of it. On his orders, the White House staff omitted it from the daily press summaries. He was more likely to listen to a senator than to an editor. Public opinion moved McKinley, and that opinion and the politicians who represented it expressed reasonable beliefs and sincere aims. They could not accept an indefinite conflict in Cuba, and McKinley's final view that the conflict must stop reflected their feelings. Americans sympathized with the Cuban rebels and were appalled at the human and physical destruction of the island. They disliked and distrusted Spain as a residual imperial power. The business community finally accepted war to end uncertainty and doubt about Cuba.

On April 11 the president sent Congress a request for authority to intervene in Cuba. The long, uninspiring message recapitulated his diplomacy and justified neutral intervention on the grounds of humanitarianism, protection of American nationals and interests in the island, and the need to end the conflict to save Cuba for the present and future. He opposed recognizing the Cubans, who he now doubted could govern themselves, and favored independence only after the island was pacified and after a period of American tutelage. Fierce debates over Cuban independence wracked Congress, but the president kept firm control in the name of party unity and executive authority. The final resolution of April 20 contained the necessary authority for him to act, and the Teller Amendment disavowed any intention to remain in Cuba once the Cubans seemed ready for self-government. The Spanish broke relations, and the U.S. armed forces mobilized. McKinley asked for a war declaration on April 25, which Congress made retroactive to April 21.

Although the arrival of war relieved the tension, the president naturally was disappointed. After the war was over, McKinley referred, in his December 1898 annual message to Congress, to being "grieved and disappointed at this barren outcome of my sincere endeavors to reach a practicable solution." He told many people that with more time he could have avoided war, which was overly optimistic. At the end, the Cubans thought they were in sight of victory. The Spanish believed that they were at least undefeated and might win. The Americans saw an indefinite stalemate.

American attention focused on Cuba as the nation mobilized, but the war's first action occurred in the distant Asiatic theater. The Philippine archipelago was still part of the Spanish Empire in 1898. The president and navy had approved stationing Comdr. George Dewey's far-eastern fleet at neutral Hong Kong, poised to attack the Spanish squadron at Manila Bay when war came. On the evening of April 30 a fleet of six modern American warships approached the bay. A Spanish fleet of ten older vessels guarded Manila, the Philippine capital. At dawn on May 1, Dewey's fleet opened fire on the Spanish squadron, which Dewey destroyed by noon. He cut the cables to Hong Kong, but not before a message, which was relayed to Europe and then the United States, reported American victory. Commodore Dewey became an instant American hero.

McKinley immediately understood that an American presence in the Philippines was a consequence of the war. He authorized forming an army expedition to control Manila and its environs. The Filipinos, like the Cubans, were fighting to win their independence from Spain, and McKinley forbade American diplomatic and military officials to speak with anyone concerning the disposition of the islands. In doing so, he made perhaps the most fateful decision of the war in establishing an American presence in the Philippines not easily removed. His action also made retention of the islands seem logical and necessary.

Meanwhile, in June 1898 U.S. military action had begun in Cuba. About 17,000 American soldiers landed near Santiago in southeastern Cuba. To capture the city, the Americans had to defeat the Spanish forces on the hills overlooking Santiago. They did so on July 1, fighting major battles at the hilltop village of El Caney and at San Juan Hill. A naval victory in Santiago Bay on July 3 followed those triumphs. Two weeks later the Spanish commander in Cuba surrendered to the Americans. Shortly after that, American forces landed in Puerto Rico, another Spanish-controlled island in the Caribbean. The Spanish forces there surrendered without a battle.

McKinley was an effective and active commander in chief, determined to end the conflict in Cuba with minimal bloodshed. He controlled the prosecution of the war and had to think of the ramifications of victory. He intended to expel Spain from the Caribbean and establish a kind of American protectorate in Cuba prior to its self-rule.

The Philippine Islands were in a different category. They had not figured in the diplomatic negotiations that ended in war. Any decision about their disposition would affect the interests of the United States and of other powers, and the choices were not easy. What were America's long-term interests in the islands? America had intruded on the Filipinos as a result of the war. Was it responsible for their well-being? Could the president logically acquire only a naval base in Luzon, the principal island, without controlling the remainder of the confused archipelago? Could the United States recognize the chief rebel, Emilio Aguinaldo, and establish a protectorate over the Philippines while he tried to gain control of the islands? This was a responsibility without power, a new and uncomfortable idea for Americans. Could McKinley simply withdraw after a peace treaty, leaving the islands to Spain and continued warfare? The islands then would ultimately pass through purchase or conquest to another power, most likely Japan. Would the American people and government be comfortable with this Japanese expansion, especially because the United States had annexed the Hawaiian islands that summer, in part to prevent apparent Japanese influence there? The United States seemed poised for great power status. Could it play any future role in Asia without a presence there?

McKinley analyzed these scenarios during the summer as victory in Cuba materialized. As usual, he kept his own counsel but left clues as to his thinking. He did not disavow acquiring the islands. It also seemed most unlikely that he would abandon the military presence in Manila. In dealing with Spain about the armistice, he left the disposition of the islands to the peace commissioners who would meet in Paris in October. In so doing, he allowed public opinion favoring retention to develop. He deftly managed his cabinet and party leaders to support some kind of overseas expansion for a variety of reasons. And he listened to many visitors without indicating any final views. He was cautious, understanding the responsibilities as well as the prospects involved. But early in the process he wrote a private memorandum: "While we are conducting war and until its conclusion we must keep all we get; when the war is over we must keep what we want." Above all, he sounded the views of the American public, especially in an October speaking tour from Washington to an exposition in Omaha, Nebraska. Huge crowds greeted him at every stop. He did not talk about the Philippines specifically, but of duty, destiny, and patriotism. The public cheers gave him the answer he wanted. All options seemed fraught with unpredictable dangers except retention, which appeared logical, necessary, and suitable for the country's new status as a world power.

McKinley was a devout Christian, conscious of duty as well as interests. He turned to prayer, as he told a group of visiting clergymen in 1899 whose leader reported his comments in 1903. The president sought divine guidance, which finally came. The United States could not simply leave the islands to Spain, which would be "cowardly and dishonorable." Allowing them to fall to another power would be "bad business and discreditable." The Filipinos were divided and unready for self-rule, and "would soon have anarchy and misrule over there worse than Spain's was." Duty required that the United States acquire the islands, explained the president, and "educate the Filipinos, and uplift and Christianize them, and by God's grace do the very best we could by them, as our fellow men for whom Christ also died." This report was uncharacteristically dramatic for McKinley, but it did outline both the interests and the emotions that shaped his final decision. In the end, he did not doubt American ability to develop the islands, or that its people wanted and would benefit from American control. Both American and Philippine interests coincided, in his mind, and his idealism ruled. In analyzing the tangle of motives and interests involved, in both domestic and foreign policy, there was much truth in what his friend Charles G. Dawes wrote in his diary that winter: "Whatever the result to our Nation, the retention of the Philippines was inevitable from the first. No man, no party could have prevented it."

McKinley achieved his goals in the Treaty of Paris of December 1898. Spain departed from Cuba and ceded Puerto Rico to the United States as a war indemnity. The United States also acquired the Philippines and Guam, which, together with the acquisition of Hawaii that July, created a U.S. presence in the Pacific and Asia. The treaty set off a great debate in the United States. Numerous Republicans opposed it because of isolationist attitudes. Some objected on the grounds that the country could not acquire territory not intended for statehood or against the apparent will of their people. Many Democrats agreed with Republican opponents of the treaty, with an additional racism against acquiring and governing peoples of color. The president exerted all his power and, on February 6, 1899, achieved Senate treaty approval by the required two-thirds vote, plus one.

President McKinley emerged from the war and the peace settlement with enormous popularity. He traveled widely and used speeches and the press to cultivate support for these and other policies. Old issues such as free silver and simple tariff protection seemed bygones. His first term drew to a close with prosperity, a national sense of confidence, and international prestige.

There was no question of the president's renomination in 1900, and politicians and the press focused on who would be his running mate. Vice President Hobart had died in 1899, or the party would have renominated its winning ticket of 1896. No traditional Republicans either stood out or wanted the second spot. Attention soon focused on Theodore Roosevelt, hero of the Battle of San Juan Hill and now governor of New York. Roosevelt was a maverick, popular with the people but not with party regulars. They did not dislike his alleged reformism so much as his unpredictability, which boded ill for the national party for whose leaders no election was ever sure. McKinley had made Roosevelt assistant secretary of war in 1897 but kept some distance from him. Like other seasoned party leaders who had worked up the ladder, he found Roosevelt a trifle too young (forty-two in October 1900), nervous, and impulsive. Roosevelt outwardly respected his elders but never missed a chance for self-advertisement. He also seemed to represent the arrival of new issues in public life. The president saw this and declined to name any running mate. Nor would he oppose Roosevelt, which might be divisive, despite strong objections from Mark Hanna and other leaders who feared "Teddy's" personalism. Roosevelt wavered, believing that the vice presidency was a shelf from which no one arose. But he did not say "never" and in the end joined the 1900 Republican ticket in the hope of being McKinley's successor in 1904.

The Democrats renominated William Jennings Bryan. He meant to make the contest a referendum on overseas expansion, revisit the waning silver question, and in general champion the underdog. Amid prosperity and national satisfaction, this decision seemed to prove Thomas B. Reed's remark that Bryan would rather be wrong than president. McKinley spent most of the summer and fall in Canton. Roosevelt was a vivid campaigner, which offset some of the regular politicians' criticism of him and essentially made the campaign trail a one-man show.

The Republicans naturally emphasized prosperity and asked voters not to tamper with success. Yet one of the new issues grew out of that economic expansion; the economy was passing through the first wave of corporate mergers into what critics called trusts. The public began to see these as efforts to limit competition and as concentrations of power that would affect politics and other aspects of life.

This issue was not new to McKinley. As a congressman he had consistently denied any relationship between protection and monopoly or business combination because he thought that the huge home market promoted competition even with the tariff. But he supported competition. "I regard all such [combinations] as against public policy and opposed to fair and legitimate trade," he said in 1888. He had supported the Sherman Anti-Trust Act of 1890 as a measure "which strikes at trusts, or unlawful combinations of capital to raise prices according to their own sweet will, and extort undue profits from the mass of the people." But like many other people, he was uncertain about just how to regulate trusts without harming legitimate business and affecting prosperity. In the spring of 1899 he told Charles G. Dawes that he expected to raise the issue in the annual message to Congress in December. He did so and again in the annual message of December 1900, saying bluntly: "Restraints upon such combinations as are injurious and which are within Federal jurisdiction, should be promptly applied by the Congress."

The Republican platform of 1900 roundly condemned combinations that restricted trade, raised prices, or lessened competition. In his official letter accepting the party's nomination, which became a campaign document, McKinley was forthright in detailing the party's record and his own views regarding trusts: "They are dangerous conspiracies against the public good, and should be made the subject of prohibitory or penal legislation." McKinley knew what he wanted but was in uncertain legal and economic terrain. He was characteristically cautious but knew that action must come. The electoral results in November hardly surprised anyone. The president won 7,218,491 popular votes, a clear majority, to Bryan's 6,356,734 from the solid South and some western states. McKinley won the rest of the country, with 292 electoral votes to Bryan's 155, and carried both houses of Congress for the Republican party. The voters ratified the administration's policies and ideas as much as any election did.

McKinley returned to Washington that winter and was inaugurated a second time on March 4, 1901. He turned his attention to foreign policy issues such as planning an isthmian canal to connect the Atlantic and the Pacific Oceans. He continued to monitor events in Cuba and the Philippines. Since the end of hostilities, the U.S. armed forces in Cuba had been improving the country's infrastructure, public health, and education. The

Americans and Cubans cooperated uneasily, essentially from mutual necessity. The United States left the island in 1902 but with the right to intervene to maintain order under the Platt Amendment. The Philippines were a different story; Aguinaldo's forces opposed American acquisition. Eventually, 70,000 Americans soldiers were sent to fight in the Philippines in a tragic three-year guerrilla war. McKinley was determined to establish civil government in the islands and began to implement a comprehensive plan in 1900.

At home the president continued to modernize the armed forces and worked on a domestic agenda for the second term. He visited the southwestern states in early summer en route to San Francisco to launch the battleship USS *Ohio*. He anticipated returning home via Buffalo, where he would speak at the Pan American Exposition. But Ida fell ill and hovered near death in San Francisco. When she recovered sufficiently, they returned to Canton for her recuperation.

As fall approached the president prepared his rescheduled address at the exposition, which celebrated the products and cultures of the Western Hemisphere. Before leaving for Buffalo he received many guests, some of whom gently suggested that he should acquire more personal protection, given his numerous public appearances. He waved aside such ideas with surprise. "Why should I? No one would wish to hurt me." He and Ida and their party arrived in Buffalo on September 4 and visited the exposition and environs.

On the morning of September 5, McKinley spoke to a vast crowd of people in the central esplanade with a theme that captured national and world attention. He set the scene for his remarks with a brief survey of how much rapid communications and information had changed the world in recent years. The very place he stood illustrated this vividly: "Expositions are the timekeepers of progress. They record the world's advancement." The text that followed surprised many observers. "Isolation is no longer possible or desirable," he said. The country's booming economy needed outlets abroad for both present and future development. "Only a broad and enlightened policy will keep what we have. No other policy will get more." The country's leading protectionist then espoused international reciprocity, which was vital to the changed world order. "We must not repose in the fancied security that we can forever sell everything and buy little or nothing." Then came a noted departure from protection. "If, perchance, some of our tariffs are no longer needed for revenue or to encourage and protect our industries at home, why should they not be employed to extend and promote our markets abroad?"

Reaction to the speech was positive. Only a traditional protectionist such as McKinley could lead the country to new arrangements that reduced world trade barriers. Of course, he was not proposing free trade but mutually beneficial agreements among trading partners. These would lead to regional order, as in Latin America, which in turn would promote stability and economic growth everywhere. He conceived of a step-by-step process that would not disrupt world trade while reducing barriers and integrating economies. He understood that such a system would work to the advantage of his country, which had the largest potential for economic expansion. The speech thus offered concrete proposals that embodied both short- and long-term goals. McKinley knew that public opinion moved in steps, not strides, and that the party leaders would not easily modify a policy in which they believed and that had brought them victories. The subject had to be raised and would be debated, events had to take their course, and the reciprocity idea would expand as it seemed beneficial to the United States. Earlier he had told friends such as Robert M. LaFollette, with whom he had served in Congress, that he wanted to "round out his career by gaining for America a supremacy in the markets of the world, and this he hoped to do without weakening protection."

McKinley planned to meet the general public at a reception in the afternoon of Friday, September 6, a duty he always enjoyed. That morning he, Ida, and their guests boarded a special train to Niagara Falls. After viewing the falls and the sights near them, the presidential party returned to Buffalo. McKinley kissed Ida, tenderly bade her farewell, and sent her by carriage to the home of John G. Milburn, director of the exposition. The president, in good spirits, arrived at the elaborate Temple of Music on the exhibition grounds to greet a receiving line of well-wishers.

The afternoon was very warm and muggy. The procession of people entered the building through a door on the east wall, greeted the president as they moved past him, and then exited through a door on the west wall. While the event was concluding, a short, slender young man approached with a bandaged right hand, which concealed a gun. As McKinley reached for his left hand, Leon Czolgosz, an anarchist, shot him twice. A button on the president's coat deflected one bullet but the other penetrated the abdomen and lodged in his body with dire results. In the shock and confusion that followed, guards grabbed Czolgosz and roughly took him to the floor. McKinley said of the assassin, "Don't hurt him." Then he told his aides, "My wife, be careful how you tell her!"

An ambulance arrived within minutes of the shooting. As McKinley was rushed to the exposition clinic, he said calmly: "It must have been some poor misguided fellow." No specialist in gunshot wounds was readily available, but the president did receive much of the prescribed treatment. He was then taken to the exposition director's home to recuperate. Ida took the news surprisingly well and remained at his bedside. McKinley was in good spirits while he mended, and bulletins in the first few following days were guardedly optimistic, but gangrene set in and he was clearly doomed.

William McKinley died on September 14, 1901, a martyr to the anarchism then gaining prominence in the Western world. He received an elaborate state funeral, amid stunned public grief, and then was interred in Canton. A public subscription endowed a large mausoleum and memorial there, in which he, Ida, and their children were interred in 1907. Czolgosz was quickly tried and executed.

At the time of his death, President McKinley enjoyed widespread popularity and respect both as a national leader and as a person. McKinley left his successor and country a formidable legacy. He had enhanced the powers and the public perception of the presidency. He had developed a unified party with a national majority. His administration had restored the confidence and sense of direction that were crucial to sustaining the prosperity that returned after 1897. The currency question and its attendant sectionalism that had bedeviled the country and politicians for a generation was dead. He had begun to modify the protective system that he thought was the basis of prosperity with the reciprocity idea. He had outlined a firm policy on the trust issue, which symbolized public concern about some aspects of triumphant industrialism. He had followed a popular foreign policy with caution and concrete policies, such as preparing Cuba and the Philippines for self-rule as quickly as possible. Second terms are always problematical for any president, and his success in dealing with these and other issues was open, yet his ideas and actions matched the American mood.

William McKinley was an idealist in his belief in the nation's abilities and destiny. He was a realist in understanding the country's complexities and the difficulty of managing its often conflicting aspirations. He saw himself as an agent of democracy and the popular will and was not especially introspective about his own fate. "That's all a man can hope for during his lifetime, to set an example, and when he is dead to be an inspiration for history," he told friends in 1899. This was both the voice of that idealism and realism and a hopeful expression of his contributions to history.

Further Reading

The first substantial biography of McKinley was Charles S. Olcott, *The Life of William McKinley*, 2 vols. (Boston: Houghton, Mifflin Co., 1916), which remains valuable for primary materials. The first modern biography was Margaret Leech, *In the Days of McKinley* (New York: Harper Bros, 1959), which focuses on the administration and his personal life. The first complete modern life was H. Wayne Morgan, *William McKinley and His America* (Syracuse, N.Y.: Syracuse Univ. Press,1963; rev. ed, Kent, Ohio: Kent State Univ. Press, 2003). Lewis L. Gould, *The Presidency of William McKinley* (Lawrence: Univ. Press of Kansas, 1980), covers the administration in detail and is definitive. The best background study for overseas expansion is David F. Healy, *U.S. Expansionism* (Madison: Univ. of Wisconsin Press, 1970). The best examination of the origins of the war with Spain is John L. Offner, *An Unwanted War: The Diplomacy of the United States and Spain over Cuba, 1895–1898* (Chapel Hill: Univ. of North Carolina Press, 1992). The Cuban perspective is analyzed in Louis A. Perez Jr., *Cuba between Empires, 1878–1902* (Pittsburgh, Penn.: Univ. of Pittsburgh Press, 1983), and *Cuba: Between Reform and Revolution* (New York: Oxford Univ. Press, 1988; 2d ed., 1995). The best study of the war is David F. Trask, *The War with Spain in 1898* (New York: Free Press, 1981). A. Wesley Johns, *The Man Who Shot McKinley* (New York: A. S. Barnes, 1970), deals with the president's last days with a good deal of insight into his personality and his appeal to the American people. Jack Fisher, M.D., *Stolen Glory: The McKinley Assassination* (La Jolla, Calif.: Alamar Books, 2001), recounts the story and analyzes the treatment McKinley received. He also speculates on his chances of surviving with modern medical care. Richard L. McElroy's *William McKinley and Our America: A Pictorial History* (Canton, Ohio: Stark County Historical Society, 1996) contains many interesting photographs pertaining to McKinley, his career, and Ohio.

William Howard Taft

Twenty-seventh President of the United States, 1909–1913
Ninth Chief Justice of the United States Supreme Court, 1921–1930

JUDITH I. ANDERSON

After watching William Howard Taft grope his way "foggy and bewildered" through four years as president of the United States, journalist Charles Thompson dubbed him "the blundering politician, the honest greenhorn at the poker table." Theodore Roosevelt's attorney general, Charles Bonaparte, believed that Taft, as president, committed the most notable unbroken succession of "colossal blunders" in the history of American politics. Ushered into the presidency in 1908 with one of the greatest popular majorities in the nation's history, Taft was turned out of office in 1912 as a result of the nastiest internal revolt the Republican Party had as yet experienced. The ill fortune of his situation was most poignant to Taft himself; his love was the law, not politics, and he was never content except within the seclusion of the judge's bench. He was so fond of judicial work, he once said, that if he could be made a common pleas judge in Hamilton County, Ohio, he would be content to remain there all his life. He especially suffered when, as president, he was called on to appoint another man to be Chief Justice of the Supreme Court, the position he desired for himself most of his adult life and came close to obtaining more than once before becoming president in 1909.

Although Indiana Republican congressman James Watson remembered Taft "as nearly devoid of executive ability as any one of our presidents that could be named," he nonetheless confessed to loving the man: "No one, it seemed, was immune to his wholesome, warmhearted genial charm and modest, gentle character—he was probably the most likable man ever to hold the office of president." Conceding that he was frequently entirely out of patience with Taft's "lumbering and ineffective" political methods, Watson still considered Taft one of the finest men who ever lived anywhere. Such impressions go a long way toward suggesting why Taft so firmly secured the approbation and confidence of Presidents William McKinley and Theodore Roosevelt. Roosevelt, who had become Taft's closest friend, said, "You know, I think Taft has the most lovable personality I have ever come in contact with. I almost envy a man possessing a personality like Taft's. One loves him at first sight."

Taft was a hard worker, and his diligence vitally contributed to his success before he assumed the presidency. As secretary of war in Roosevelt's cabinet he had worked harder than any other officer. But when Roosevelt stepped aside, Taft was on his own. Neither lion nor fox, he was unable to comprehend the intricacies of the president's political role or to bully his way through as Roosevelt had. He trusted almost everyone, spoke his mind freely on most occasions, and tried to be friends with everyone. The innocent candor for which he had always been praised now became a serious liability. He openly talked of Congress, of promotions in the army, of his opinion of certain high public officers, as if his words were of no more significance than an ordinary citizen's. Most public men kept their private thoughts for their diaries, but Taft revealed his in public. Taft lacked the higher political wisdom that might have enabled him to avoid political disasters. Nellie Taft, who was a shrewd politician, often echoed the exasperation of such men as Henry Cabot Lodge and Henry Adams over her husband's "unfortunate shortcomings of not knowing much and of caring less about the way the game of politics is played."

William Howard Taft's mother, Louisa Torrey, and her sister Delia attended Miss Mary Lyon's Female Seminary at Holyoke, Massachusetts, founded in 1837, the first permanent American institution for the higher education of women. Their father, Samuel Torrey, indulged his wife and daughters and gave them the freedom to pursue a liberal education, even though the avenues available to women seeking independent careers in the mid-nineteenth century were severely limited.

In 1853 Louisa, then twenty-six years old, met Alphonso Taft, forty-three, while he was visiting friends in Millbury—in search of a wife. A New Englander by birth, he had emigrated to Ohio with his parents. For his education he went east to Yale and ranked third in the class of 1833.

He returned to Yale to study law but settled in Cincinnati, and by 1841 his law practice was well established. He married the pretty but frail Fanny Phelps; two sons were born to them, but she died in 1852 at the age of twenty-nine. Alphonso Taft had liberal-minded views about women and even called for their political and legal equality. Louisa's mother had always counseled her to take every advantage of opportunities, and Louisa thought Alphonso Taft presented an opportunity not only for achieving status and security but also for pursuing her own intellectual interests. Alphonso's marriage to Louisa, eighteen months after Fanny's death, was for both parties a matter of convenience. Yet their marriage was nevertheless considered very successful in the Victorian manner. In time Louisa bore "Mr. Taft," as she always referred to him, a daughter and three sons, one of whom was William, born September 15, 1857.

Enormously energetic, aggressively intellectual, and decidedly ambitious, Louisa not only raised six children but helped organize a kindergarten movement and an art association and contributed time to charities. She also founded a local book club, studied German, and participated in a French club. At the same time, she contributed to her husband's success in his legal practice and in local politics. When President Grant in 1875 appointed Alphonso Taft secretary of war and then in 1876, attorney general, Louisa was gratified to find herself in the midst of Washington political circles, where she was described as a lady of rare perception and of still rarer common sense. Louisa's hunger for travel led her to intercede boldly with President Chester Arthur on her husband's behalf, seeking his appointment as ambassador to Austria-Hungary. President Arthur granted her request, and in 1881 they left for Vienna.

She was in charge of the household, and she also coached the children in their studies. Louisa's relationship with William was always special and intense. Her first baby died of whooping cough shortly after his first birthday; her second, she was determined, would survive. Fortunately William was a stout baby, whose good health was aided by her nourishing solicitude. Once William entered school she became even more attentive, surveying every detail of his studies. Until her death, on the eve of his nomination as a candidate for president, she devotedly followed every step of his career, and though warmly affectionate, often gave him advice that was highly critical.

Alphonso Taft, in contrast, had no driving ambition to rise in the political sphere. Perhaps his most notable characteristic was his self-effacing and benign personality. He was described as "unostentatious, kindly and gentle." William Howard Taft was very much like his father; he shared his father's lovable traits and identified with his father's aspirations to be a lawyer and a judge, rather than a politician.

William, striving to fulfill his parents' desires and worried about his ability to live up to parental expectations, manifested his anxiety by over-eating. Chubby in grammar school, he had to endure the taunts of peers who called him "lubber." Taft studied more than the others in order to excel; for this he was also teased. Under his mother's supervision he suppressed the desire to play and became a model schoolboy.

Taft's high school performance was solid, and through extra effort he achieved second place in his senior class at Cincinnati's Woodward High School in 1874. Following his father and brother, Taft matriculated at Yale. There he rarely tired even at the most laborious chore, and by "steady, ponderous work," earned good grades. At graduation he again stood second in his class. Despite his even temperament and apparent placidity, he felt the effects of the strain.

Taft's brothers underwent the same parental pressures to succeed and suffered different, but no less serious, effects. His brother Peter earned the highest marks scored at Yale up to that time. But in 1878 he suffered a nervous breakdown and died in 1889 in a sanitarium at the age of forty-three. Tall and thin, Horace also exhausted himself through academic effort. Acute dyspepsia afflicted him in early manhood; he slept poorly and continually suffered severe headaches. Taft often mentioned his brother's "nervous temperament." Another brother, Henry Waters, also became a lawyer like William and Horace. He was described as "quiet, moody, and morbid," and afflicted with frequent depressions.

The emotional patterns Taft had developed as a child made him an ideal mate through whom Helen "Nellie" Herron could pursue her personal ambitions. She was the daughter of John Williamson Herron, a prominent Cincinnati lawyer, influential Republican, former state senator, and personal friend of President Rutherford B. Hayes. In 1877, at the age of seventeen, Nellie spent several weeks in the White House with her parents as the guest of the president. It was then, she told a *New York Times* reporter in 1912, that she fantasized becoming a First Lady herself. She vowed to marry only a man "destined to be president of the United States."

Nellie Herron was a fiercely independent girl and an exceptional student, who read, between household chores, such books as Carlyle's *Life of Schiller* and his *History of the French Revolution*. She persuaded her parents to allow her to attend Miami University in Oxford, Ohio, where she concentrated on chemistry and German. Meanwhile she was very much attracted by the atmosphere of her father's law office and after graduation spent much of her time there reading, studying, and assisting him with his work.

The Herrons and Tafts had been acquainted in Cincinnati when William and Nellie were children, but it was not until 1884, after Taft's graduation from law school that he began to court her in earnest. Nellie and her friends took their weekly study sessions in her living room "salon" very seriously; they read and discussed novels, poetry, philosophy, and history. Taft was invited to attend and soon became, as he wrote to Nellie in March 1884, her "humble but enthusiastic disciple each Sunday afternoon."

Throughout their courtship he was often unhappy because of her remoteness and her frequent pleasure trips, while he was left in Cincinnati to brood, as his sister Annie said, like "a mountain of misery." Neither then nor later did she show as much interest in him as he did in her. Even after their secret engagement in June 1888, Nellie alternated between moods of grudging kindness and frigid distance, yet he hoped that they might marry "in less than a year; if you continue to 'think' that you are reconciled."

Taft assured Nellie that his love "grew out of a friendship" and was "founded on a respect and admiration for your high character . . . and your intellectual superiority." When they married she would be, he wrote, his "senior partner" for life. Nellie possessed the strength he feared he lacked, and he was ready to subordinate himself to her. She came to the marriage with a directional blueprint for his life. For Nellie, marrying Taft was the next best thing to having a career of her own. They complemented each other, and he gave her a mandate to make of him what she could.

After graduation from Cincinnati Law School in 1880, Taft, then twenty-three, went to work for his father's law firm. Soon he was appointed assistant prosecutor of Hamilton County, a post he held from 1881 to 1883, prior to his marriage. He was next appointed to the position of collector of internal revenue, "a circumstance not of his seeking," Nellie noted in her *Recollections.* Taft had many qualities to recommend him: he was honest, personally engaging, extremely cooperative, ready to work, and loyal. Recalling these early days, Nellie wrote that, at the time she had decided on marriage, "Mr. Taft was making a very satisfactory progress in his career."

In 1887 Taft was extremely pleased to be appointed to the position of judge on the Ohio Superior Court, a post his father had once held. Now thirty, Taft discovered that the court was a "pleasant harbor." The work was congenial—hearing motions, writing opinions, presiding over the court in his judicial robes. His life was orderly and undisturbed. He was happy and so successful that he and his judicial friends began to discuss the possibilities of his appointment one day to the U.S. Supreme Court.

This goal became Taft's one consuming desire. In 1889 he urged Ohio governor Joseph Foraker to press his nomination with President Benjamin Harrison. Harrison refused to appoint so young and inexperienced a judge but did offer Taft the post of U.S. Solicitor General, a position Taft wished to decline, but which Nellie persuaded him to accept. Taft was apprehensive about his new job and told his father that he found it "rather overwhelming." Nellie admitted that Taft in farewell cast "regretful glances at his beloved bench," but she was "very glad because it gave Mr. Taft an opportunity for exactly the kind of work I wished him to do."

Taft felt when he accepted the solicitor generalship that he might not like his duties and feared he might not excel in them. Arguing cases in an open courtroom was something he did not enjoy, and the solicitor general's main task was to present government cases before the Supreme Court. "Well, I am in it now and I'll do the best I can," Taft confided to his father. His greatest difficulty lay "in holding the attention of the Supreme Court justices. They seem to think when I begin to talk that it is a good chance to . . . read . . . letters, to eat lunch, and to devote their attention to correcting proof." Nellie, as her mother-in-law Louisa before her, assumed the responsibility of coaching Taft in this new experience. She cautioned him not to cite too many precedents, not to talk too long. Taft never did become a compelling speaker, but he lost only two of his eighteen cases as solicitor general.

Nellie's idea of Taft's career lay in directions other than the judicial sphere, and she was thrilled when her husband began to associate with national political figures. In Washington Taft soon made the acquaintance of Theodore Roosevelt, then civil service commissioner. Their friendship, built on mutual trust and admiration, rapidly deepened. Although Nellie liked Washington and delighted in planning future triumphs, she was not completely satisfied with their immediate situation. They did not have sufficient income to maintain what she considered a proper lifestyle, and they had to borrow. Neither was Taft very satisfied with his job as solicitor general, and when a seat on the Sixth Federal Circuit Court of Appeals opened, which would mean returning to Cincinnati, he made inquiries. President Harrison promised him that post, and Taft, overjoyed, attempted to reconcile Nellie to the idea by pointing out that his closest competitor for the post had been the leading lawyer of the Ohio bar.

Nellie worried that, once cloistered in the courts, he might become "fixed in a groove for the rest of his life."

Taft sat on the Sixth Federal Circuit Court of Appeals from 1892 to 1900. During most of those same years (1896–1900,) he also was professor of law and dean of the University of Cincinnati Law School. Taft labored hard over his legal opinions, with the result that they tended to be thorough, however ponderous and dull. Secure and successful as a judge, Taft became greatly respected for his diligence. Given his conservative views and exceptional judicial record, Taft attracted the favorable attention of Republican leaders in Washington. By 1900 it was generally known in Republican circles that President McKinley was seriously considering Taft for the U.S. Supreme Court.

Neither Taft nor Nellie knew what was in store for them when a telegram from President McKinley arrived late in January 1900. The president had begun to consider Taft for a position other than one on the Supreme Court. McKinley wanted a tactful, honest man for an executive position in the Philippines. Sensing Taft's disappointment when he was offered the post, McKinley claimed that he would be "a better judge for this experience" and assured him that "if you give up this judicial office at my request you shall not suffer. If I last and the opportunity comes, I shall appoint you [to the Supreme Court]."

"I dreaded meeting Nellie," Taft recorded later, because he knew how much she counted upon returning to Washington society. "She met me at the door and her first question was, 'Well, are we going to Washington?'" Taft explained the situation, and, "after a moment's hesitation, she exclaimed, 'I think you should accept!'" Nellie later acknowledged that his resignation from the circuit court bench "was the hardest thing he ever did" but that the news of his appointment "gave me nothing but pleasure." She knew instantly that she "didn't want to miss a big and novel experience." Nellie began preparing immediately.

They sailed in April 1900 on the army transport USS *Hancock*. En route to the Philippines, they stopped in Japan, where Nellie decided to stay some time longer because she found the country enchanting. When Taft lumbered off the boat in Manila, he did not, apparently, make a spectacular impression on the American newsmen. One reporter interviewed him and wrote, "We ought to ship this splendid fellow back. It's a shame to spoil his illusion that folks the world over are just like the folks he knows out in Ohio. He makes me think of pies, hominy, fried chicken, [and] big red apples." Without Nellie for more than two months, Taft grew unhappy, and Nellie later admitted she had been "selfish to stay away so long having a good time." At last, with her children and a Japanese maid, she set out to join him.

Taft was sworn in as the civil governor of the Philippines on July 4, 1901. He feared that the Islands were "utterly incapable of self government," and his chief desire was, consequently, to help the Filipinos learn how to build a stable government. Meanwhile the Filipino people were overjoyed to see a civilian government installed. Establishing a civil government was, as it turned out, quite within Taft's competence as a lawyer. He was at work before half past eight every morning. At six he walked the two-and-one-half miles home. By May 1903, he had completed the "foundation work," as he called it, for the Criminal Code of Procedure, the Internal Revenue Act, a general incorporation act, and regulations for the settlement and sale of land.

Nellie was thoroughly contented in the Philippines, where they were the "first family," with a large estate and the thirty-five room palace at their disposal, and the luxury of a multitude of servants. She was immensely pleased at all the pomp and ceremony that attended her position. In contrast to her social discontent during the Ohio years, Nellie kept up a constant round of parties and gave dinners once a week for a cosmopolitan assemblage. She also took the opportunity for further travel by herself, visiting Peking, Canton, Shanghai, Hong Kong, and Nagasaki. Although the Tafts returned home in 1904, the Taft era in the Philippines actually extended to 1913, as a result of Taft's continuing close connection with the Philippines, first as secretary of war and then as president of the United States. Although his policies drew criticism from those opposed to American involvement there, Taft did hope for eventual self-government for the Philippines.

During his stint as governor of the Philippines, twice Taft was offered a position on the Supreme Court, and, though strongly tempted, he declined. His motives for turning down the president's invitations, proffered in October 1902 and again in January 1903, have perplexed many historians. On both occasions, the Filipino people's warm display of affection for Taft made him feel he could not abandon them. In addition to his sense of personal commitment to the Philippines, Taft was influenced by his wife. Nellie had no inclination to leave the Islands and return to the life of a judge's wife.

Their stay in the Philippines was not to last much longer however, for on March 27, 1903 Taft received an offer for a position that suited Nellie's tastes and ambitions. Roosevelt wanted Taft to become his secretary of war. Nellie was as eager for him to accept this post as she was discouraging of the offers to join the Supreme Court. The Cabinet was, as she later wrote, "in line with . . . the kind of career I wanted for him and expected him to have." Despite her insistence, Taft was hesitant because the appointment was likely to involve him in the 1904 presidential campaign, which, experience had taught him, "would be most distasteful to me, for I have no love for American politics." Taft was persuaded to accept the cabinet post, after twice rejecting Supreme Court appointments, because Nellie encouraged him, because Roosevelt called upon him as a friend for help, and because as secretary of war he would not be deserting the Filipinos.

From the beginning of his tenure as secretary of war, Taft's relationship with Theodore Roosevelt was very friendly. Taft became Roosevelt's confidant and troubleshooter, now doing full time what he had done occasionally while serving as governor of the Philippines. Roosevelt had all the worries and responsibilities, and Taft was content just to work for him.

Roosevelt, whom friends often described as the most competitive man alive, clearly enjoyed Taft's faithful friendship and was intrigued by his obvious lack of political ambition. Increasingly confident of Taft's ability to manage special assignments, Roosevelt placed more burdens on him. Taft was absent from Washington more than any other member of the cabinet. Taft, always "jovial, never excited, considerate and smiling," according to the prominent journalist Mark Sullivan, exclaimed, "I love my chief, and . . . I admire him from top to toe."

As the 1908 national election neared, Theodore Roosevelt, fifty years old and at the height of his national popularity, began to regret his declaration that after serving the remaining three years of McKinley's presidential term and one term of his own; he would not run again. In anticipation of the election Roosevelt was thus obliged to search for another presidential candidate, preferably one who would carry on his policies. Although some people doubted it was proper for Roosevelt to handpick his successor, he felt no reservations.

Secretary of State Elihu Root was Roosevelt's first choice, but Root said that he was "not willing to pay the price." Charles Hughes, Republican governor of New York, was another likely candidate, and many people expected Roosevelt to select him. Roosevelt instead turned to Taft, who had publicly endorsed the president's policies many times. Taft had a personality that easily made friends, and in addition, he came from Ohio, the birthplace of Presidents Grant, Hayes, Garfield, Benjamin Harrison, and McKinley.

One evening in May 1906, Taft told Nellie, "I went to the White House for a long talk with the president. . . . He thinks that I am the one to take his mantel." Though elated, Nellie began to harbor a deep distrust of Roosevelt's motives. She thought that he was using Taft as a stalking horse and planned ultimately to capture the nomination for himself; she could scarcely believe that Roosevelt would really relinquish such a position of unchallenged power and status.

Nellie began to groom Taft for the nomination. She feared that his lackluster speaking performances on behalf of Republican congressmen might affect Roosevelt's decision. Anxious that he do well, Nellie followed the press accounts of his speech-making, continually advising him. Taft complained about the congressional campaign grind in letters home. "Politics when I am in it makes me sick," he wrote.

Roosevelt turned to Nellie to prod Taft. In turn, she warned her husband, "You must be more encouraging." Desperately Taft turned to the one source of comfort left—his mother. Louisa had opposed from the beginning any talk of his candidacy. She cautioned him, "Roosevelt is a good fighter and enjoys it, but the malice of politics would make you miserable." She knew that Taft truly believed in his father's exhortation that "to be chief justice is more than to be president."

In the end, Roosevelt supported Taft for the Republican nomination in 1908 chiefly because, in his words, "I believe with all my soul that Taft . . . represents the principles for which I stand. His policies, . . . purposes, and ideals are the same as mine." Roosevelt coached and advised Taft in the weeks before the convention in Chicago. But Taft said to reporters, "I'd rather not say what I think of happenings in Chicago. Besides I am the man least interested." When the convention assembled at the Chicago Coliseum, reporters complained that it would be a colorless affair and that the delegates sat "like mourners at a funeral," determined to nominate whomever Roosevelt named. Every mention of the president's name brought a wave of enthusiastic tribute to the otherwise lackluster convention. Seven candidates were placed in nomination, but Taft quickly garnered 702 votes and thus became the Republican candidate.

As the balloting in Chicago was taking place, Taft, in Washington, seemed uninterested. Nellie, however, was tense and nervous, even distrustful of what Roosevelt might do. Their son Charlie came in with the bulletin announcing Taft's nomination. Nellie's face turned pale; sitting "white as marble and motionless," she read it with visible effort. But she was quickly "aglow with excitement." "Oh Will!" she cried, while kissing him. At that Taft beamed and seemed "as happy as a big boy."

Taft's first desire was for some recreation to take his mind off the campaign ahead. At a resort in Hot Springs, Virginia, he took up golf, which later became his major means of escape from the demands of the presidency. He also began the regular horseback riding he was to enjoy so much when he became president. Roosevelt had discouraged Taft from riding because he felt it was "dangerous for him and cruelty to the horse."

The Democrats again nominated William Jennings Bryan, in what was to be his third presidential race. Nellie was overjoyed at the prospect of confronting Bryan but Taft remained fearful. "The next four months are going to be a kind of nightmare for me," he remarked wanly.

The campaign proved to be for Taft the "awful agony" he had anticipated. He was such a listless candidate that his campaign managers, anxious to hide from the public the truth of Taft's reluctance to enter the fray, often wrote press announcements for him. Roosevelt initially planned to avoid further involvement in the campaign once Taft had been nominated, but he soon saw the danger in leaving everything up to Taft. The "hardest and most aggressive hitting" was needed, Roosevelt urged. "Do not answer Bryan; attack him!" When Taft wouldn't, Roosevelt excused Taft's refusal to tangle with Bryan by saying that "he hates to fight unless it is necessary. . . . There isn't a mean streak in the man's make-up."

Not only was Taft an indifferent campaigner, he also seemed unable to cope with political details. Roosevelt had, as one reporter expressed it, "to watch over Taft like a hen over her chickens." Taft, happily relieved to have Roosevelt actively interceding, appealed almost daily to him for guidance. Nellie's counsel was continually forthcoming too and was often frantic about some potentially damaging campaign utterance he had inadvertently made.

Enraged by Roosevelt's tactics, Bryan complained about having two opponents to battle. "As Mr. Taft is alive and able to speak for himself," he snapped, "it is hardly necessary for Mr. Roosevelt to tell us what Mr. Taft will do." Despite Taft's passivity, most pundits expected from the start that the Republicans would be victorious. The public was quite ready to believe that if Roosevelt thought Taft his proper successor, then he must be acceptable.

Taft's victory was overwhelming. He carried all but three states outside the solidly Democratic South. "We have beaten them to a frazzle," Roosevelt exulted. "I was never so happy in my life," was Nellie's simple response. Nellie was proud of Taft, but even more proud of what she began henceforth to refer to more frequently as her own "very active participation in my husband's career." Yet Nellie also had some unsettling premonitions: "Mr. Taft calls me the politician of the family," she had explained to a New York reporter in June. "His own ambitions always have been towards the judiciary. But I have persuaded him to remain in politics. Perhaps I may regret it."As inauguration day drew nearer, Taft's apprehensions became more public. Even his personality began to change. Roosevelt noticed Taft's altered manner and mused, "something has come over Will, he is not the same man."

Despite favorable predictions, late on the eve of the inauguration dark clouds descended on Washington. A furious snow and sleet storm shredded the bunting and flags set out for the ceremonies. Breaking precedent, Nellie joined Taft in the drive from the Capitol to the reviewing stand. "I had my way and in spite of protests took my place at my husband's side. For me that drive was the proudest and happiest event of Inauguration Day."

In notable contrast to Nellie's joyful countenance during that drive from the Capitol, Taft's face was grave and downcast. Not once on the entire trip did he look from the carriage, nor did he once bow or wave his hat. As White House usher Ike Hoover described it, the new president, upon his return to the White House from the reviewing stand, threw himself into a large comfortable chair, stretched out to his full length, and said, "I am president now, and tired of being kicked around."

Except for Roosevelt in 1904, Taft received the largest plurality in the popular vote up to that time. Americans in 1909, said the *Washington Post,* were a prosperous, united, and a happy people, and being so, had taken the large good-natured president to their hearts. After seven years of the Roosevelt administration, many people were ready for a period of less storm and stress. Roosevelt retired to Sagamore Hill, his country estate at Oyster Bay, New York, to prepare for an African safari. The former president's trip was generally felt to be well-timed. The country said farewell to Teddy and settled back to enjoy a period of progressive government by quieter means.

Every president enjoys a honeymoon period, with the press and with the opposition party, a time allowing him to become accustomed to his new duties. The new president was not sanguine; this "sweet music" will not last, he soberly calculated. It did not, indeed, but no one expected the change to come quite so quickly. Attempting later to account for the brevity of Taft's term of grace, Ray Stannard Baker acutely perceived that the country's disillusionment arose because the people had known very little about their new chief executive before electing him. Taft was just a "large, dim, charming personality hovering somewhere" in the background.

On the eve of his departure for Africa, Roosevelt betrayed some foreboding: "He means well and he'll do his best. But he's weak. They'll get him. They'll lean against him." Unlike Roosevelt, Taft was no starter, no pusher; he saw no grand visions and disliked pioneering. Roosevelt thrived on stress and discontent, whereas Taft could not deal with tumultuous discord and was not excited by the idea of change. Roosevelt later conceded that he might have made a mistake in choosing Taft. He lacked "the gift of leadership," was "too easily influenced by the men around him," and did "not really grasp progressive principles."

Archie Butt, Taft's White House aide, observed that he had "never known a man to dislike discord as much as the president." He "hates to be at odds with people, and a row of any kind is repugnant to him." Taft's older half-brother Charles, greatly disturbed by Taft's weakness in the hands of cabinet members, exclaimed, "It makes me sick, Archie, the way the president lets his cabinet run riot with him. All he would have to do is fire one of them and the others would . . . toe the line."

This overriding wish to avoid confrontations was the main reason for Taft's meager success in obtaining effective legislation, with so many attempts resulting in futile compromises. Previously, for example, Taft had strongly supported the graduated federal income tax sponsored by the progressives, but once he became the chief executive he began to waiver. By 1911 he had abandoned the measure altogether. He told his brother Horace that he was "afraid of the discussion" and the "criticism" that would follow if there were a division over the constitutionality of the tax.

Criticism was the one thing Taft could not endure, and it overwhelmed him once he became president. He soon discovered that reporters no longer regarded him as simply a pleasant source of information about government programs and intentions. And once scarred by their barbs, he became wary and viewed them as potential enemies. They were not long in recognizing the change. "The old cordiality and friendliness were gone," Oscar King Davis wrote in the *New York Times,* "and there was in its place a reserve that amounted almost to coldness."

For Taft every piece of legislation that he sponsored or signed was potentially a political danger. As he prepared to sign the Panama Canal Act in 1912, for example, his thoughts turned to his customary regret: "I shall create enemies in signing the bill, but that is what one usually does and makes no friends. That is what politics is." Once out of office, Taft remarked, in an address entitled "The President": "One of the results of my observation in the presidency is that the position is not a place to be enjoyed by a sensitive man."

His unhappiness was sufficiently manifest to those around him. The White House staff, accustomed to a cheerful Secretary of War Taft lunching each day comfortably with President Roosevelt, found him much altered. On occasion the public also caught glimpses of Taft's changed personality. Stories circulated about his bitter denunciations of men he had come to regard, for some fancied grievance, as his enemies. His temper, the *Washington Post* observed, now showed in explosive flashes.

Throughout his four years in the White House, Taft often betrayed his desire to be a one-term president, fearing he might be forced into a second term. The chief source of his unhappiness was his painful self-awareness of his limitations in the office he had assumed. "The White House is a bigger proposition than one imagines," he remarked shortly after his election; he continually ate more, as if to balance the scale.

From his adolescent years, Taft's weight had increased in proportion to his discontent. First he felt family pressure to excel at Yale; later, other burdens arrived with various appointive offices that he filled in government services, first in the Philippines and then in Washington. Finally, with the manifold problems of the presidency he reached his maximum weight. At twenty years he weighed 220 pounds. When he was fifty-three and in the second year of his presidency, he scaled over 355 pounds. Anecdotes, jokes, and cartoons inspired by Taft's weight were innumerable. All Washington talked about the bathtub—reported to be the size of a small swimming pool—which had to be installed for him at the White House. Several times, it was said, he had gotten stuck in the regular one, and on each occasion two men had been called in to heave him out. Taft also had a specially built Ford sedan with an extra-wide door. Dentist and barber chairs also presented a hazard for him. Horace Taft recalled entering a theater with his brother one night, who, after taking his seat, looked up smiling and said, "Horace, if this theater burns, it has got to burn around me." Nearly all of America learned the anecdote of how Taft, after a horseback trip to a mountain resort in the Philippines, wired Secretary of War Elihu Root, "Stood trip well. Rode horseback twenty-five miles to five thousand foot elevation," only to receive the query by return cable: "How is the horse?"

After becoming president, Taft apparently was reluctant to curb his eating, his one sure source of comfort while suffering in the White House. He sensed that the heavy responsibilities were one cause of his weight problem, for he said that he would probably eat less once he returned to private life. Nellie tried to manage his diet, but his failure to eat as she wished only raised further anxieties. He had thus another incentive for escape to the countryside on his private train, when he could flee Washington and his "persecutors," and, of course, eat as he pleased. Before departure, he had his train well stocked with all his favorite delicacies.

While at home, he used the excuse of exercise to get away from his duties. He golfed and rode horseback daily with Archie Butt, who was proud to have done "something in the way of keeping him from lapsing into a semi-comatose state."

Taft's excessive weight actually impaired his ability to carry on the routine functions of the presidency. On several occasions, in the middle of affairs of state, he closed his eyes and took a catnap. Once he fell asleep as Joe Cannon, Speaker of the House, was leaning over his chair talking to him. Even though Taft was aware of the humiliating consequences of his drowsiness, he was happy to escape in slumber. Nellie dubbed him "Sleeping Beauty."

Taft regularly fled the White House by vacationing at his summer home in Beverly, Massachusetts. But even when he was not officially on vacation, many thought he acted as though he were. In order to escape from the anxieties of his office, Taft also accepted unimportant invitations to travel away from Washington, the farther the better. In his biography of Taft, Edward Cotton noted that the president was happiest when traveling on his special train. Scarcely installed in office, he went "on the road for all the world like a traveling salesman." He attended numerous college commencements, class reunions, state fairs, and miscellaneous banquets. Taft made so many excursions he humorously concluded that the major part of the work of a president was to increase the gate receipts at fairs.

But several short journeys were nothing compared to the long ones Taft took to seek relief from his anxieties. From September through November of 1909 Taft made a swing around the whole country and was feted at banquets everywhere the train stopped. He enjoyed Boston codfish and beans, Chicago steaks, Kansas short ribs, Colorado cantaloupes, Montana venison, Seattle salmon and oysters, New Mexico chili con carne, Texas wild duck, New Orleans red snapper, and Virginia wild turkey. At the conclusion of his first nationwide tour, Taft admitted that after being gone so long "your conscience begins to prick you and then your duties grow mountain high so that you cannot look over them at all. That is my feeling now. It is a somewhat strenuous life to eat and talk and talk and eat, but there are other things . . . even more burdensome."

Angered by the absentee president, the Eastern press attacked. After the first long trip had exhausted the president's $25,000 traveling allowance for 1910, Congress hotly debated whether or not to increase it. Political cartoonists exploited the opportunity: one cartoon portrayed Taft looking at a picture of the White House inquiring, "Where have I seen that place before?" Another depicted the White House refashioned into a lo-comotive engine with a bell and a smokestack. The caption read, "The President Comes Home: One Way to Keep Him There."

Nellie Taft, after Roosevelt the chief architect of Taft's political career, played a somewhat different role once she was in the White House, ceas-ing to prod her husband so much and instead concentrating on politics, entertainment, and White House management. To Ike Hoover, chief usher in the White House, it seemed that shortly after her arrival she was plan-ning "to revolutionize the place." Although Nellie's enthusiasm for read-justing White House routine caused considerable consternation among the permanent staff, under her management the presidential mansion was running quietly and orderly, in sharp contrast to the way it operated when occupied by the Roosevelts.

Immediately after moving into the White House, Nellie began redeco-rating the living quarters in the oriental style of which she had grown so fond during their sojourn in the Philippines. And she decided that what Washington needed most was some of the lovely cherry trees she had seen in Japan. When the mayor of Tokyo heard that she planned to purchase some, he sent a gift of two thousand Japanese cherry trees, accompanied by a special agent.

Nellie Taft had always relished pomp and pageantry, and the Red Room at the White House became her favorite place to "hold court." One of her first decrees was that the entire White House staff dress in fancy uni-forms. "I decided," she wrote, "to have, at all hours, footmen in livery at the White House door." Nellie ordered an automobile for herself, which was even more expensive than the president's—a large, green limousine upon which was emblazoned the shield of the nation.

The White House was Nellie's chosen domain, and she intended to make her influence felt. She did not have many intimate friends in Wash-ington; the *Washington Post* suggested that this was because she spent most of her time running the White House and "assisting [the president] in his work." Ike Hoover said that Nellie's parties were spectacular, and there were twice as many social affairs in the Taft administration than previously. Already impressed by Nellie's executive ability, Archie Butt expressed no surprise that everything was done on a grand scale and in the best form. Nellie made a point of inviting artists, musicians, and writ-ers to dinner, favoring them with Tiffany gold medals as souvenirs. For Nellie, the culmination of her social ambitions was their elaborate silver wedding anniversary party, held in June 1911. She sent out six thousand invitations, and for months Washington buzzed with nothing but plans for the spectacular event. After the party was over, one observer proclaimed it "the most brilliant function ever held in that historic mansion."

Unlike most first ladies, Nellie did not confine her influence to the social sphere. Indeed, she presumed to sit in on many of the important political conferences held in the mansion, and her unprecedented role soon caused a great deal of talk within the White House. Ike Hoover felt that she possessed a "keen discernment" in such matters and acted as if she had been accustomed to taking part all her life. Sometimes when Taft was unsure of his ground, she would carry on the conversation for him, with much success. "Mrs. Taft seemed always to be present and taking a leading part in the discussions," Ike Hoover observed.

Nellie would not suffer being cast in the background. When President Taft on occasion gave a stag dinner for various congressmen, Nellie, hating not to be at the center of all the political talk, arranged to have her dinner served in a lobby closely adjoining the state dining room so that she could hear the voices through the door. Nellie was aware that her continual advice and reproaches to the president were gossiped about. In self-defense, she countered, "I confess only to a lively interest in my husband's work, which I experienced from the beginning of our association."

At an Associated Press banquet in New York in May 1910, Taft responded to a toast offered to both him and his wife by thanking the master of ceremonies, "for including the real president in his toast." On a latter occasion he told a group of reporters, "I am no politician." Then turning toward Nellie, he acknowledged, "There is the politician of the family. If she had only let me alone I should now be dozing on the Circuit Court Bench."

The reform or progressive wing of the Republican party had nominated Taft at Roosevelt's command. The conservative or Old Guard Republicans had accepted him because they thought he was preferable to the unpredictable Roosevelt. The progressive leaders had expected Taft's active support of their policies. But President Taft, they soon discovered, had no intention of becoming continually embroiled in the dispute between progressives and conservatives. During the campaign Taft had led many progressives to believe that he would aid their attempt to topple powerful Joe Cannon, who had been Speaker of the House for many years. Cannon arrogantly challenged and freely insulted the progressives in Congress and out. It was not long after the inauguration, however, that Taft assumed a neutral pose. To the progressives' dismay, Taft even went so far as to seek reconciliation with "Uncle Joe" and his supporters. When the progressives failed in their attempt to recapture the House from Cannon's iron-fisted control in March 1909, Taft uneasily justified his about-face to the Republican insurgent leader by appealing to the need for party unity. Progressive Democratic and House leader Champ Clark, recalling their defeat in the rules fight, said his colleagues were "astounded and angered" at Taft's desertion. "We got a bloody licking," Clark wrote, and we "never forgave him."

Standing primarily as a symbol of the power of big business, the tariff issue aroused people both emotionally and politically, and one of the more dramatic episodes in Taft's administration revolved around it. A high protective tariff, devised to protect American industries against foreign competition, had been supported as a major policy by the seven Republican presidents since the Civil War. But by 1908 there was much sentiment throughout the country for the downward revision of tariff rates, which many felt were responsible for the high cost of living.

Taft was made to believe that the demands for tariff revision could no longer be ignored. During his presidential campaign he pledged a "substantial revision downward." Roosevelt, acutely aware of political danger, had shied away from the debate and he warned Taft during the campaign to "move with great caution" on the tariff issue.

After his inauguration Taft called a special congressional session to consider the tariff, but he lacked the disposition and the will to oversee the tariff bill during the heated and protracted congressional debates ahead. "The great tug will begin [soon]," he lamented, and will be "one of the crises in my life."

The struggle between revisionists and protectionists took place in the Senate, where Nelson Aldrich, representing big business, was determined to revise the rates upward. The wrangling began. At first Taft indicated that he had to have a downward revision or he would "veto the bill." But rather than exercise his power and influence, Taft began soon to incline toward a reconciliation of the disputants.

When the bill reached committee, Taft found that he had been, as Champ Clark put it, "served up." The tariff was reduced in only six insignificant items. The press condemned the tariff for favoring industrialists and letting the heaviest burden fall on consumers. Taft publicly claimed that he had done all he could to convince the conservatives to accept lower rates. Now he was willing to let Congress settle the matter. Taft was both surprised and appalled by the "ruthless selfishness" exhibited in the tariff-making process. Although many felt that Taft could have done much more to influence the final bill, the public did not initially direct its anger at him. Instead, low tariff advocates looked to the president to exercise his veto power.

To avoid criticism, Taft tried to escape by making the first of two very long trips. He started out on the sixty-seven day, forty-four city trip on September 15, 1909, feeling in "rare good humor." His optimistic mood was short-lived. It was characteristic of Taft's political sense that he now chose to eulogize the Payne-Aldrich tariff in Minnesota, a state in which anger against the tariff was intense. Incredulous, Minnesotans heard the president exclaim in a speech at Winona: "I am bound to say that I think the Payne Tariff Bill is the best tariff bill that the Republican party ever passed." The response to his speech from Minnesota to the East Coast was quick and negative. Taft's refusal to veto the Payne-Aldrich Tariff perhaps did him more harm than any other of his official acts. He later compounded the damage by apologetically explaining that he had just "dashed off the Winona speech hastily between stations" and had barely had time to consider it. In the congressional elections of 1910 the Republican party felt the first painful effects of Taft's acceptance of the Payne-Aldrich Tariff. The large Republican majority of 1908 was suddenly reduced to a minority.

Taft began to talk either of not running in 1912 or of being defeated if he did. Archie Butt noticed lines coming into Taft's face, "deep, deep lines," and he told his sister-in-law that Taft "looks much older than he did six months ago, and has lost much of his joyous and happy manner." The poignancy of Taft's situation became especially clear when in December 1910 he appointed Edward Douglas White to be the new chief justice for the Supreme Court. As he signed the document he grew wistful: "There is nothing I would have loved more than being chief justice."

Although Taft shirked some presidential duties, such as pressing Congress for a lower tariff bill, and was confounded by several issues, it would be a gross misrepresentation to say that his administration was devoid of accomplishment. One of his greatest successes was the Postal Savings System, which was to protect the average citizens' savings because they were often lost in periodic bank failures. Another of Taft's favorite projects was the arbitration treaties with England and France, which were signed in August 1911, to deal peacefully with disagreements that might arise. During his years in office many postal employees were placed under civil service regulations. Taft believed strongly in placement and promotion by merit. With Taft's assistance, Congress strengthened the Interstate Commerce Commission with the Mann-Elkins Act of 1910, extending the power of the Interstate Commerce Commission (ICC) to regulate telephone and telegraph rates. Taft supported a law establishing the eight-hour workday for persons doing work under federal contracts. In the name of economy Taft abolished four hundred positions in the Department of Treasury. He reorganized the customs service and made large cuts in the military services.

During Taft's administration the Department of Commerce and Labor was divided, and the Federal Children's Bureau was established. Arizona and New Mexico were admitted to statehood. The Sixteenth Amendment was passed, making possible the federal personal income tax; and the Seventeenth Amendment, establishing the direct election of U.S. senators by voters, was finally passed too. Also during Taft's presidency, Roosevelt conservation policies were regularized and his Food and Drug acts strengthened.

Taft was seldom around to take sides in a political battle and exercised little leadership over Congress and therefore failed to drive many of his programs through. More important, he could not keep his party united. Consequently, contemporaries such as Arthur Wallace Dunn, author of *From Harrison to Harding: A Personal Narrative,* have commented that it is hard to write about Taft's four years in the White House without seeming to be severely critical. Even his devoted aide, Archie Butt, commented, "It is hard not to be critical when one sees mistake after mistake being made which may as well be avoided." In many ways, Butt thought, "He is the best man I have ever known, too honest for the presidency, possibly, and possibly too good-natured or too trusting or too something."

Personally, Taft most enjoyed studying the various pardon cases that reached his desk. He took great delight in writing his opinions. He was also extremely proud of his six new Supreme Court appointments and the numerous lower court selections that he made.

In the angry progressive onslaught against Taft, little attention was paid to the fact that his administration initiated eighty antitrust suits. Taft aggressively prosecuted the trusts because he liked to get involved in issues that came before the courts rather than the legislature. More trust prosecutions may be attributed to Taft's administration than to Roosevelt's, though the two major Supreme Court decisions during these years, against the Standard Oil and tobacco trusts, had been initiated under Roosevelt.

Taft, far more than Roosevelt, gave vigorous encouragement to foreign trade. Uncle Joe Cannon said of Roosevelt, "I think if the truth be known, [he] rather despised trade." Taft was reviving McKinley's desire to see American commercial supremacy throughout the world. In the Far East, Taft and his secretary of state, Philander Knox, sustained the open door policy; their interest was not the protection of China but the development of overseas markets and the wish to gain financial influence. Taft also acted forcefully to protect American foreign investments and foreign markets in Latin America. In 1911, for example, the State Department arranged for American bankers to reorganize Nicaragua's finances when revolutionaries threatened to take over the Nicaraguan government. Taft's critics called his policies "dollar diplomacy."

Even before Taft took office, Roosevelt expressed reservations about his hand-picked successor. And while in Africa, he received numerous reports about Taft's problems. Roosevelt became enraged by news of Taft's courting the conservative faction of the Republican party. As president, Roosevelt had skillfully used conservative leaders for his own ends. The difference is, he said, that Mr. Taft "gets their assistance at the price of going their way." Roosevelt was also indignant that Taft did not sufficiently lean on the protectionists in Congress to get an honest tariff revision. The Ballinger-Pinchot affair additionally annoyed Roosevelt, because Gifford Pinchot was one of his closest friends and because the former president began to think that Taft was betraying his policies.

Taft did approve legislation for irrigation projects and the preservation of more forest and mineral land. As Secretary of the Interior he appointed Richard A. Ballinger, a corporate lawyer who wanted to open some federally protected land in the West to private enterprise. This brought him into a clash with Gifford Pinchot, the ardent head of the National Forest Service and a dedicated conservationist. Pinchot was one of the few Roosevelt appointees whom Taft retained in his administration. President Taft and Secretary Ballinger believed that Roosevelt and Pinchot had probably acted illegally in placing so much land irreversibly in the public domain, and in reaction they decided to make some of the land available for private ownership.

In August 1909 Louis Glavis, a field agent of the General Land Office, accused Ballinger of allowing the banking giant J. P. Morgan and the mining magnate David Guggenheim to get control of certain reserved coal lands in Alaska. Pinchot supported Glavis and leaked the charges to the press, including an allegation that Ballinger had personally profited from the sale. In doing so, Pinchot was criticizing the president by implication. Ballinger proceeded independently to fire Glavis for insubordination. Very soon nationwide attention was focused on the controversy.

Taft wished to avoid becoming involved. He asked Attorney General Wickersham to look into the matter — an unusual request, because he was directing one cabinet member to investigate another. Taft concluded that

Ballinger was innocent of any wrongdoing. After that, he avoided the problem. Pinchot became outspoken in his contempt for the president's inaction and rushed to Roosevelt to describe Taft's action as a betrayal of his conservation program. The news stunned Roosevelt, who was returning from Africa by way of Europe. Reports that Roosevelt had sent for Pinchot to join him signaled his sharp displeasure with Taft.

The whole matter irritated and depressed the president. Realizing that he was not handling it as Roosevelt would have, he argued, "I cannot do things that way. I will let them go on and by and by the people will see who is right and who is wrong." Then Taft added irritably, "I get rather tired of hearing from his friends that I am not carrying out his policies." President Taft's "good nature and kindliness" were fine qualities, *The Nation* conceded, but a president needs "a great deal more strength in dealing with situations like the Pinchot-Ballinger imbroglio." The *New York Times* argued that this hostility further pointed up how "loosely, inadequately, and poorly organized" was Taft's administration.

In March 1911, about a year after the trouble started, Taft finally bowed to Nellie, his brother Charles, and his cabinet and reluctantly accepted Ballinger's resignation. In contrast to his much happier days as secretary of war, Taft soon considered newspaper and magazine writers as his implacable enemies. On one occasion, Nellie, disturbed by his hypersensitivity, tried to point out his folly in ignoring all critical papers: "You will never know what the other side is doing if you only read the *Sun* and the *Tribune* [those papers that support you]." The president answered simply, "I don't care what the other side is doing."

The rumors that all was not right with the Roosevelt-Taft friendship moved near to open confirmation after 1911. In distant Africa, Roosevelt avoided making any public statements that might have reflected poorly on Taft. Once back in the United States, he found it more difficult to remain quiet and impartial. Some observers think that genuine hostility on Roosevelt's part emerged after Taft had selected his cabinet. Of the five cabinet members that Taft finally did replace, Roosevelt particularly resented the dismissal of Interior Secretary James Garfield. The son of the assassinated president was, along with Gifford Pinchot, especially close to Roosevelt. Many contemporaries pointed to the Taft administration's prosecution of the U.S. Steel Corporation as the main source of discord. The suit charged U.S. Steel with monopolistic behavior, in part because it had purchased Tennessee Coal and Iron Company—a merger to which President Roosevelt had given his blessing. Roosevelt felt he was being made to look like a "knave" or "fool" by the government's suit. Taft had been a cabinet member at the time, Roosevelt charged, and had been "emphatic" in his commendation of the merger. Bringing suit now, Roosevelt declared, was "small, mean and foolish."

There is no question that Taft was distinctly uncomfortable in trying to find his own way as president and insecure in his strange, new relationship with Roosevelt. Meanwhile, Roosevelt in his early fifties was certainly very young to be retired, and he began to yearn again for the power he had so much enjoyed. Predictably, he was drawn back into politics upon his return from Africa. The only obstacle in his path was the subordinate he had guided into the presidency.

From August 23 to September 11, 1910, Roosevelt made a sixteen-state trip west, giving speeches and outlining his "New Nationalism" policies. The former president received twenty-five invitations a day to speak, more than two thousand in all. The newspapers generally called Roosevelt's speaking tour a great success. Conservative Republicans were downcast, insurgent Republicans, elated. The newspapers exploited the rift between Taft and Roosevelt. Taft soon felt that Roosevelt had "thrown down the gauntlet." "I have doubted up to the present time," he told Archie Butt, "whether he really intended to fight my administration or not, but he sees no one but my enemies."

Gradually Taft's unhappiness turned to bitterness: "I shall always be grateful for what he did for me," he explained, "but since he has come back he has seared me to the very soul." Unable to explain Roosevelt's attitude in any other way, Taft accepted Nellie's argument that Roosevelt had planned all along to run for the presidency in 1912.

By mid-1911 many others realized that Roosevelt was planning to contest Taft's renomination by the Republican party. Taft did not want a second term, but Roosevelt's "New Nationalism" seemed radical to Taft, and he began to reconsider. Yet the idea of a combat greatly disheartened him. "It is hard, very hard," Taft moaned, "to see a devoted friendship going to pieces like a rope of sand." In reaction Taft began to pull himself together: "He made me president and not deputy, and I have to be president."

On February 21, 1912, Roosevelt took public aim at Taft. "My hat is in the ring," he said. "The fight is on and I am stripped to the buff." Taft at times seemed to be no more interested personally in the contest for the nomination in 1912 than he had been in 1908. A direct primary, allowing the people to voice an opinion on a preference for candidates on their party's ticket, had been instituted in Wisconsin in 1905, and by 1912 ten states had primary laws. Roosevelt entered his name in these primaries, thus beginning his offensive. Taft refused to respond, despite attacks on his administration from the Roosevelt camp.

Old Guard Republicans began to urge Taft to strike back. His cabinet tried to persuade him that it was his duty to reply to Roosevelt's charges. When Roosevelt attacked the sanctity of judges, Taft was finally galvanized to resist. This time, he said, Roosevelt had "gone too far." Taft decided finally to stay in the campaign for the express purpose of defeating Roosevelt, whom he now saw as "a great danger and menace to the country."

After weeks of silence, Taft chose Boston as the place to respond to Roosevelt. "I am here to reply to an old and true friend. I do not want to fight Theodore Roosevelt, but then sometimes a man in a corner fights. . . . I don't like to fight. I am a peaceful man. But he has got me up against the wall and if I have any manhood at all I have got to fight." He avoided Roosevelt's criticisms and instead responded to his "radical" pronouncements. He spoke for two hours, refuting Roosevelt's charges one by one. Repeatedly the anguished president told the crowd, "This wrenches my soul." But it was his duty to counter Roosevelt's radical demands, he insisted, "in the name of the Constitution of the United States."

Roosevelt was delighted over Taft's being stirred into action. The following night he delivered what the *New York Times* called a "merciless denunciation of President Taft." Roosevelt charged that owing to a "quality of feebleness," the president had yielded to the bosses and the privileged interests. "It is a bad trait to bite the hand that feeds you," Roosevelt charged. Roosevelt called Taft an "apostate," a "flubdub," a "floppy-souled creature," a "puzzlewit," a "fat head," and a "man with brains of about three guinea-pig power."

The political issues that Roosevelt raised in each new speech were alone enough to anger Taft, but when his old friend made personal attacks it hurt him unbearably. For Taft the widening gulf between them was a cause only for weeping. Once, between speeches on the presidential train, Taft "slumped over with his head between his hands" and told Louis Seibold of the *New York World*, "Roosevelt was my closest friend." And then he bowed his head and covered his eyes and cried.

The effect of the strain on Taft became evident when he said the wrong thing in the wrong place on even more numerous occasions. He continued the campaign by declaring his newfound resolution to fight Roosevelt for the nomination, but the metaphors he chose were singularly inept: "I was a man of straw, but I have been a man of straw long enough." At Hyattsville, Maryland, Taft shouted to the crowd, "I am a man of peace and I don't want to fight. But . . . a rat in a corner will fight."

As president, Taft had one big advantage over Roosevelt—federal patronage—and the Taft men proceeded to use it to secure a number of delegates. Nonetheless, Roosevelt won six primaries and had 281 delegates to Taft's 71. Roosevelt was just 80 votes short of a majority when the Republican convention opened in Chicago on June 16, 1912.

The night before the convention, Roosevelt held a meeting in the five thousand–seat theater, to which twenty thousand people tried to gain entrance. There Roosevelt, never one to shun hyperbole, thundered, "We fight . . . for the good of mankind, fearless of the future . . . we stand at Armageddon, and we battle for the Lord."

Victor Rosewater, Republican national committeeman, called the convention to order, standing at the rostrum protected by barbed wire concealed under the bunting on the railings around the platform. One thousand policemen with nightsticks strolled around the hall, prepared for any eventuality. Amidst jeers and catcalls, he began the keynote address. The crowd listened to his appeal for harmony in "stony-silence." The reception was no better for other regular Republicans. Old Guard Republicans who, though dissatisfied with Taft, were intent on preventing Roosevelt from getting the nomination engineered the convention. Taft again took almost no active part in organizing the convention or securing the nomination. With the Old Guard in control of the convention machinery, the seats in dispute were awarded to the Taft delegates. Roosevelt, for example, had won the California primary by more than 70,000 votes, yet the committee gave the two contested seats to Taft. Fistfights broke out on the floor. When order was restored, former vice president Charles Fairbanks read the traditional, conservative platform. It was followed by scant applause. The spectators stayed to hoot as the remaining delegates on the floor, amid a wilderness of chairs vacated by Roosevelt supporters, went through the final motions.

Roosevelt refused to accept defeat. He and his enthusiastic followers bolted the convention and formed a third party, called the Progressive, or Bull Moose, after Roosevelt's earlier exclamations to newsmen, "I'm feeling like a bull moose!" The Progressive convention was held in the Chicago Coliseum and was attended by two thousand delegates. The New York contingent marched up and down the aisles singing "Onward Christian Soldiers." Roosevelt delivered an hour-long speech entitled "Confessions of Faith." Hiram Johnson of California was chosen as Roosevelt's running mate. The party platform, containing a wide variety of reform measures, was entitled "A Contract with the People." The Progressive convention then adjourned to the hymn, "Praise God from whom all blessings flow."

The only question now, said Senator Chauncey Depew about the shattered Republican party, "is which corpse gets the most flowers."

When the Democrats met for their convention in Baltimore in June 1912, most were confident that the man they nominated would become the next president of the United States. The balloting for the nominee went on for some time before there was a winner — Mrs. Taft was so concerned about the outcome that she broke all precedent by attending the convention. And on the seventh day of the convention, Woodrow Wilson became the Democratic nominee.

Although Taft dreaded "the awful agony of a campaign," he felt it a duty to his Republican friends and to the country to counterweight the "socialistic" advances of his opponents. "Mr. Roosevelt has planned," he asserted, "a vast system of state socialism, a government of men unrestrained by laws." Yet Taft bristled at being called an extremist by his opponents, a label which Roosevelt and Wilson gave him. "Though I am a conservative," he proclaimed, "I am not a reactionary or a trilobite."

Taft just drifted along with the campaign. He expected to lose and secretly hoped he would. "The truth is," he confided to a friend, "I am not very happy in this renomination and reelection business. . . . I am not going to squeal or run away. But after it is all over I shall be glad to retire and let another take the burden." It was nearly certain that Roosevelt would not win, and that defeat was now Taft's main objective.

Concerned Republican regulars dispatched a committee to the White House to admonish Taft and urge him to take a more active part in the campaign. "I have been told that I ought to do this, ought to do that, ought to do the other; that I ought to say this, ought to say that, ought to say the other, that I do not keep myself in the headlines; that there is this or that trick I might turn to my advantage. I know it," Taft added in frustration, "but I can't do it."

As Taft retreated, the real contest was left to Theodore Roosevelt and Woodrow Wilson. Wilson praised Taft as a delightful person but condemned him as an "unserviceable president." The Republicans under Taft's leadership, Wilson charged, were a "Know-nothing, Do-nothing party which had allowed the ship of state to drift about for four years without a pilot." But it was Roosevelt whom Wilson went after in earnest, faulting him for too often promising but not delivering the millennium. Wilson told the people, "I do not want to promise you heaven unless I can bring it to you."

Disgusted with Taft's inaction, Roosevelt announced that he was dropping Taft from any further consideration during the campaign and focusing on Woodrow Wilson. Replying to an enthusiast in Massachusetts who shouted "Tell us about Taft," Roosevelt sneered, "I never discuss dead issues."

When the results of the 1912 presidential election were in, Taft and Roosevelt were soundly defeated, with Roosevelt having disastrously split the Republican vote. Wilson received 6,286,214 popular votes, Roosevelt 4,126,020, and Taft 3,483,922. The electoral vote was 435 for Wilson, 88 for Roosevelt, and 8 for Taft. Taft won only two minor states—Utah and Vermont—the worst defeat ever suffered by a president.

Taft was greatly relieved both that the ordeal of the election and his presidency were over and that Roosevelt had not won. He spoke from his heart when he said, "The people of the United States do not owe me another election. I don't carry in my heart the slightest resentment against the people or any bitterness of spirit with respect to their views of my administration." Although magazines like *The Nation* insisted that Taft "brought his fate upon himself," the calmness, the stoicism, and the good humor with which he accepted his defeat impressed all.

Taft assured Nellie and other friends, "Don't for a moment suppose that I am cast down or humiliated, or in any way . . . suffering from disappointment. The truth is I am glad that it is all over. . . . The nearer I get to the inauguration of my successor, the greater relief I feel."

On March 4, 1913, the last day of his term, associates marveled over "the cheerful optimism" Taft displayed, in marked contrast to his mood on his own inauguration day. "I'll be glad to be going," he told the president-elect, "this is the loneliest place in the world." The contrast between the two men was striking that day. Wilson appeared solemn and stiff; Taft, cheerful and relaxed. Viewing them on their drive to the Capitol for the inaugural ceremonies, Francis McHale wrote that one might have mistaken Taft for the president elect, for he was "smiling and radiant."

Nellie Taft's mood was quite different from her husband's on the final day of his presidential term. Sometimes hopeful that Taft would miraculously be reelected, she had during the campaign begun to make tentative plans for a second term. Taft had decided to invite the Wilsons to stay at the White House on inauguration eve. Nellie was, however, not feeling convivial and sharply vetoed his plan.

According to Ike Hoover's account of their departure day, Nellie wandered aimlessly around the second floor of the White House. The atmosphere was funereal. The staff just stood by and waited for her to leave. They could not begin any preparations for the Wilsons until she had gone. Finally Nellie put on her hat and furs and came down in the elevator. She was visibly affected and walked out the door without saying farewell to anyone. The servants who witnessed her departure were moved to sympathy: "Her feelings were so evident that practically no one even attempted to say good-by."

Upon leaving the White House, Nellie and the former president moved to New Haven, Connecticut. The fifty-five-year-old Taft had accepted an appointment as professor at Yale Law School. There he regained a zest for life, came to be immensely popular with his students, and within eight months showed visible signs of his relief by reducing his weight from 350 to 270 pounds. Taft enjoyed life on campus; coached a debating team, avidly followed sporting events, and frequently spoke to campus, service, and community organizations. He wrote articles for popular magazines such as the *Saturday Evening Post* and traveled extensively as a lecturer. Taft fully expected to be "a permanent resident of New Haven . . . and to live and die a professor." It was not to be his destiny.

Shortly after his election to the presidency in 1920, Warren G. Harding of Ohio invited Taft to the White House for breakfast. (Harding had made Taft's nomination speech at the Republican Convention in 1912.) There President Harding suddenly blurted out over breakfast, "By the way, I want to ask you, would you accept a position on the Supreme Bench because if you would, I'll put you on that court." Taft, slightly startled, admitted that it had been and still remained "the ambition of my life." Harding had the opportunity when Chief Justice Edward D. White died in June 1921. Taft was named to fill the vacancy and confirmed by the U.S. Senate as chief justice of the United States, a position which was, he said, "the crowning joy and honor of his life."

"It was a great pity," Arthur Wallace Dunn wrote, that "a splendid jurist was not allowed to carry out the ambitions of his life" in the first place. The bench, Taft came to know with a special relief, is "the only place in the country that is free from severe criticism by the press." The only ex-president ever to serve as Supreme Court Justice, Taft sat, as William Allen White has put it, "like one of the high gods of the world, a smiling Buddha, placid, wise, gentle, sweet."

Although the chief justice had incessant labor and great responsibility, Taft could hardly wait to begin his duties. He worked with energy and determination, clearing his docket as he had never been able to clear his presidential desk. "The truth is that in my present life I don't remember that I even was president," Taft wrote with satisfaction. The critics, too, forgot Taft the president, for as Norman Hapgood, editor of *Collier's* magazine, said, "All the world knows that he made a splendid chief justice."

Respected for his honesty, generosity, and good humor, William Howard Taft is the only American to serve as both president and Supreme Court justice. He contrasted the two positions by describing the presidency as "my storm" and his term as chief justice as "the crowning joy and honor of my life." Library of Congress.

Justice Louis Brandeis once said to the noted jurist Felix Frankfurter, "It's very difficult for me to understand why a man who is so good as chief justice . . . could have been so bad as president. How do you explain that?" "The explanation is very simple," Frankfurter replied. "He loathed being president and being chief justice was all happiness for him." As a judicial architect, legal scholar Alpheus T. Mason asserts, he was without peer.

Taft took on so much of the burden of writing the Court's opinions that his health eventually suffered. In June 1929 it took a serious downturn, and in September he forewent his seventy-second birthday celebration. Friends noted with alarm that his mind was growing weary and his chuckle growing fainter. Taft realized it too, and on February 2, 1930, he sent his resignation to President Herbert Hoover.

Taft died in his sleep at home in March 8,1930, in his seventy-third year. His coffin lay in state in the Capitol rotunda; he was attired in the robes of the office of chief justice. William Howard Taft was buried in a simple ceremony at Arlington National Cemetery, the first president to be so honored.

Taft left Nellie a $475,000 estate, including their two homes, and she lived on for thirteen more years. Her greatest satisfaction came with the success of her three children. Robert Taft, U.S. senator from Ohio for fifteen years, was a three-time contender for the Republican presidential nomination. He was known as "Mr. Republican." Their second-born son, Charles Taft, culminated his political career as mayor of Cincinnati from 1955 to 1957. Daughter Helen earned a Ph.D. in history from Yale in 1924, a law degree from George Washington University in 1937, authored two history books, and was a dean and acting president of Bryn Mawr College.

Content with her children and grandchildren, but most especially with the cherished memories of her full years as first lady, Nellie died in Washington on May 22, 1943, one week before her eighty-second birthday. She was buried beside her husband in Arlington National Cemetery.

Further Reading

The most important biography of William Howard Taft is Henry F. Pringle's *The Life and Times of William Howard Taft*, 2 vols. (New York: Holt, Rinehart, & Winston, 1939). Recent studies of Taft and his career include Alpheus T. Mason, *William Howard Taft: Chief Justice* (New York: Harcourt, Brace, & World, 1964); Donald F. Anderson, *William Howard Taft: A Conservative's Conception of the Presidency* (Ithaca, N.Y.: Cornell Univ. Press, 1968); and Paolo Coletta, *The Presidency of William Howard Taft* (Lawrence: Univ. Press of Kansas, 1973).

Many insights into Taft's personality are furnished by contemporary figures. These include family members, political acquaintances, White House staff personnel, and journalists: Oscar King Davis, *William Howard Taft: The Man of the Hour* (Philadelphia: P. W. Ziegler, 1908); Arthur W. Dunn, *From Harrison to Harding: A Personal Narrative Covering a Third of a Century, 1888–1921,* 2 vols. (New York: G. P. Putnam's Sons, 1922); Irwin Hood Hoover, *Forty-two Years in the White House* (Boston: Houghton, Mifflin, 1934); Horace Dutton Taft, *Memories and Opinions* (New York: Macmillan Company, 1940); Nellie Herron Taft, *Recollections of Full Years* (New York: Dodd, Mead, 1917); and Charles W. Thompson, *Presidents I've Known and Two Near Presidents* (Indianapolis: Bobbs-Merrill, 1929).

Archibald W. Butt, Taft's White House aide, is the most valuable source of information for the presidential years. Both the *Letters of Archie Butt,* 2 vols. (Garden City, N.J.: Doubleday, Page, 1924), and *Taft and Roosevelt: The Intimate Letters of Archie Butt,* 2 vols. (Garden City, N.J.: Doubleday, Doran, 1930), consist of letters written in diary-like form that chronicle Taft's experiences in the White House. The Papers of William Howard Taft in the Manuscript Division of the Library of Congress are a 700,000-piece collection including the addresses and articles by Taft; letterbooks containing materials covering his years as secretary of war, president, and professor of law at Yale University; family correspondence; correspondence with friends; family diaries; and legal papers. The Taft Papers have recently become available on microfilm from the Library of Congress.

Warren G. Harding

Twenty-ninth President of the United States, 1921–1923

THOMAS C. SOSNOWSKI

*M*arion, Ohio, enjoyed the national spotlight one last time when President Herbert Hoover and other dignitaries arrived on June 16, 1931, to dedicate a memorial for Warren G. Harding. The hometown of the twenty-ninth president of the United States had been a political focal point during his two-and-one-half-year tenure, but that ended abruptly on August 2, 1923, with the president's death by cardiac arrest in San Francisco. Work soon commenced on his mausoleum in Marion, and the attractive memorial was ready for dedication in 1927, when the remains of the president and the first lady were transferred there. However, the town had to wait another four years for the much-anticipated dedication and its last hurrah on the national scene. Calvin Coolidge, Harding's vice president and successor, was responsible for the delay; by tradition, tombs of presidents are solemnly dedicated by the current president, but Coolidge was unwilling to travel to Ohio for the ceremony because of the scandals associated with his predecessor. Consequently, it had to wait until Coolidge retired from office in March 1929 and his successor, Herbert Hoover, agreed to travel to Marion.

The American people deeply mourned Harding at the time of his death, in an outpouring of grief similar to that for Abraham Lincoln almost six decades earlier. However, while architects and laborers constructed his tomb, the four years following Harding's death were full of investigations and exposures of scandals involving various members of his administration, leading to the imprisonment of the first cabinet member in U.S. history. In addition, numerous allegations were made against him personally, including accusations of his fathering of an illegitimate child. President Coolidge was appalled. Thus, within months of his death, the beloved Harding became heavily maligned.

The election of Warren Gamaliel Harding to the presidency in 1920 symbolized to Americans that affluence and family were not necessary ingredients for success in federal politics. Warren G. Harding—the descendant of pioneer Ohioans from America's heartland, son of George T. Harding, a self-styled homeopathic physician chronically in debt, and Phoebe Dickerson Harding, a midwife—would take up the office once held by George Washington.

Born in the hamlet of Blooming Grove on November 2, 1865, Warren Harding grew up under the strong influence of central Ohio. In 1873 George Harding decided to move with his wife and children to the larger village of Caledonia, Ohio. Here, among a larger population of potential patients, he hoped for greater financial security. Unfortunately, Dr. Harding focused his attention not only on his practice and his large family but also on financial investments that were almost always ill-chosen and poorly managed. He also loved to barter and trade with locals. Instead of the financial security he sought for the family, the opposite was usually the case. This situation continued throughout his life, and later his successful son, Warren, had to assist him occasionally.

Warren's mother was a more positive influence than his father during his formative years. For the mother, raising a family of eight children in the country was taxing, demanding hard work and great stamina, yet Phoebe Harding always remained a gentle, caring, devoted spouse and mother. She complemented George's profession, while trying to counteract his financial misadventures, by becoming a midwife. Although George was a Baptist, Phoebe was a devout Methodist who raised the Harding children in a strict Christian household. She taught Warren the alphabet before he was four, and soon thereafter how to read by using the Bible and copies of a local newspaper, the *Marion County Sentinel*. In adulthood Warren Harding never ceased being deeply devoted to his mother. Every Sunday morning, until her death in 1910, he either brought her flowers or saw to it that a florist delivered some to her, and the top of his desk at the White House never lacked her photograph.

The young Harding attended the local elementary school, and by the age of ten was working part-time at the village newspaper where he gained some knowledge of the printing business. In his teens he worked as a laborer helping to grade the roadbed of the Toledo and Central Railroad. Despite the uncomfortable financial position of the family, at the age of fourteen Harding was able to attend Iberia College, sometimes called Central Ohio College. Here he participated in organized debates and honed his talents for public speaking, which were recognized when he graduated with a bachelor of science degree in the spring of 1882 and had the honor of presenting the commencement address to his class of three students. Afterward, he returned to a new home, for his parents had moved again, to the booming county seat of Marion.

Armed with his degree (one whose quality educators would seriously question a century later), the young Harding began to search for appropriate employment. His first professional appointment was in teaching at a school only two miles from Marion. Quickly he discovered that his talents lay elsewhere, so he resigned his position at the end of the fall semester. After reading law for a short time (at his father's insistence), he tried his hand at selling insurance. Neither was meant for him. While he continued to search for a career, he kept himself busy by playing in a local band as the first B-cornetist and by actively supporting and attending functions of the Republican party. By the end of 1884, he and two acquaintances decided to purchase one of Marion's newspapers, the financially unstable *Star*, for three hundred dollars. The paper had never been successful and was the object of derision because of its irregularity of publication and lack of professionalism. Nonetheless, at the age of nineteen the future president had found an outlet for his talents and energies. Here he worked hard, prospered, and in succeeding decades became an acknowledged leader of the community.

The eventual success of the *Star* was not apparent in the months after its purchase. The new managers had to find a niche for their paper because the Democratic-oriented *Mirror* and the Republican influenced *Independent* already served Marion. They chose a nonpartisan editorial path, which in late-nineteenth-century Ohio was an unusually difficult, if not impossible task. Harding and his colleagues worked feverishly at improving the *Star* itself. They collected news from the town and carefully cribbed information from other newspapers, especially those on the east coast. Over several months they increased the regular coverage of national and international news and by the summer of 1885 successfully contracted with the Associated Press to receive news directly by wire. Within one year, Harding claimed that his newspaper had a circulation twice that of either of the other ones in Marion. The young editor, known fondly in the office as W.G., was on his road to the American dream.

As Marion continued to prosper, so did the *Star*. Its subscription rate increased, in spite of, or maybe because of, the rivalry between the other two newspapers in town. Harding was also able to assume full ownership during this time by buying out one colleague and outwitting the other at poker. With increasing fame and good fortune, he began to become more active in hometown social and political activities. He joined the Knights of Pythias and later became a member of civic groups such as the Rotary, the Elks, and the Marion Chamber of Commerce. The Republican party became more and more his political focus, and by 1888 he had gone to the state convention in Columbus as the delegate of Marion country. He was pleased with the election of Republican Benjamin Harrison to the presidency in November but dismayed that his favorite governor, Joseph Foraker of Cincinnati, lost to his Democratic opponent, James Campbell, the following year. It was then that Harding suffered what his father called a nervous breakdown, which made it difficult for him to work and participate in his favored activities. As a result, Warren went to Michigan's Battle Creek Sanitarium, directed by the famed Doctor Kellogg, whose discipline and vegetarian diet provided him a rest and a much needed opportunity to lose some weight. After about two months, he returned to Marion, although he would admit himself to the Sanitarium several more times in the future.

In his mid-twenties Harding turned his attention to marriage. There appeared to be only two problems in his search for the right spouse. The "old" families considered Harding an interloper and an upstart; his family was relatively new to Marion and his father had never gained the financial and professional success he desired. And there was a persistent rumor about his ancestry—that one of his ancestors was an African American. Even a trace of African blood was considered a blight upon any white person. The rumor was resurrected several times during his public career, although it was never proven true. Undeterred by these biases, Harding took notice of Florence Kling, daughter of one of the most respected and richest members of the community, Amos Kling. She encouraged Warren's advances and pursued him openly. Mr. Kling vigorously opposed their relationship and engagement. Florence ignored her father, and on July 8, 1891, she and Warren celebrated their nuptials in the new home they designed and built on Mount Vernon Avenue.

The new Mrs. Harding came to the marriage with some baggage that was considered unusual, if not scandalous, in the late-nineteenth century. Five years older than her husband, Florence had attended the Cincinnati Conservatory of Music, where she specialized in the piano. Upon her return to Marion, she fell in love with Henry (Pete) DeWolfe, son of a local entrepreneur. Amos Kling strongly opposed their plans to marry, but nineteen-year-old Florence eloped in 1880. A son, Eugene Marshall, was the result of this union. However, her husband, an alcoholic, could never hold a job and apparently did little to support his family. After three years, Florence appealed to the courts for a legal separation and custody of her child. Eventually, she rented an apartment and taught piano to support herself and her son without any assistance from her parents.

Throughout the 1890s both the *Star* and Harding's public career prospered despite unsettled times in many parts of the United States. The Panic of 1893 spread across much of the country, but Marion did not seem to suffer as badly as other communities. The newspaper involved itself in local politics and civic affairs, even to the point of muckraking—fighting corrupt business practices related to public works programs. Editor Harding also maintained his rivalry with the Republican *Independent,* which eventually ceased publication, especially after the *Star* secured the right to publish official city documents, an arrangement that appears to have provided it with an important financial base. Thereafter, Harding's newspaper dropped its independent editorial stance and openly supported the Republican party. In 1899 he declared, with appropriate partisan support, his candidacy for the vacant state Senate seat from his district. During this hotly contested campaign, he first met lawyer Harry M. Daugherty at a rally in Richwood, Ohio. Daugherty would later become a significant force in Warren Harding's life, including serving as attorney general during the Harding presidency. The November election brought Harding his first major political success, with a majority of more than 1500 votes, thus commencing a political career that would be crowned with the presidency twenty-one years later.

Warren G. Harding's victory made him an acknowledged leader of the Republican party in Marion County. The junior state senator would bring to his new post a reputation for honesty in an era too often characterized by political graft, corruption, and bossism. Party rivalries were bitter and loud in Ohio, and parties themselves were objects of fierce internecine warfare in the 1890s. The Republican party saw a long struggle for leadership between Joseph Foraker and Mark Hanna, the Cleveland industrialist and friend of William McKinley.

Harding traveled to Columbus for the opening of the Ohio General Assembly in early 1900 and to take his oath of office. The Senate met only in alternate years, unless the governor called a special session. Here Harding developed his skills as a man of harmony—despite his devotion to the Republican party, he did not enjoy intra- and interpartisan battles. Politics, it seemed to him, was an opportunity to bring people together, to find a common ground. His belief in progress and the ability of Americans to improve the quality of life for all was a common theme in his speeches then and in the future. Nonetheless, in the real world of Ohio politics, Harding had quite a challenge. Despite the domination of the Republicans in the General Assembly, their party was still rent with the ongoing struggle between the Hanna and Foraker factions. Harding worked carefully and skillfully to compromise differences between the two and was able to gain respect, even grudgingly, from most of his colleagues. Because of the policies of partisan politics at the time, state senators seldom served more than one two-year term. Such inexperience made them more malleable and increased the power of political bosses. However the Republican leadership liked Harding, so as his initial term drew toward its conclusion, they suspended this rule and permitted his renomination. Harding easily won a second term, during which he served as majority floor leader.

America at the turn of the twentieth century was a nation of continual industrialization, immigration, political bossism, and graft. Party bosses dominated Cleveland, Toledo, and especially Cincinnati to their own ends. They used political patronage and the franchise system to provide needed municipal services such as public transportation and rubbish removal. The most obvious example of this corruption was George Cox, who controlled Cincinnati and indeed Hamilton County without even holding public office. To most, he was a shadowy figure who publicly supported and promoted the Cincinnati Red Stockings, his favorite professional baseball team. Only those in state and local politics really knew the extent of Boss Cox's control and that he secretly dictated city policies and appointments. In the late 1890s, a harbinger of good news was the arrival of political reformers, later called progressives, who crusaded against the entrenched establishment. First came Samuel Jones of Toledo, better known as "Golden Rule" Jones. He changed the political complexion of the town and made it a model of Progressivism. The successful businessman and former U.S. congressman Tom L. Johnson, whose progressive programs from 1901 to 1909 transformed Cleveland into "the best governed city in the United States," followed his example.

In the face of the Progressive challenge, the political bosses increased efforts in Columbus to maintain control of the state and its cities. Throughout the first years of the twentieth century, the Ohio General Assembly supported the bosses by undermining home rule in the cities. For example, it voted to restrict the powers of municipal government in Cleveland as a way of circumventing Mayor Johnson's prestige and successes. Harding supported these measures despite his earlier activity as the chair of the Municipal Corporations Committee, where he endorsed home rule of Ohio's cities.

Another issue dominating the state and national scene, especially since the 1890s, was Prohibition. With increased immigration encouraged by industrialization after the Civil War, especially in the decade prior to the beginning of World War I, American cities saw the formation of ethnic communities, where the customs and languages of immigrant groups predominated. For many of these people, the use of alcoholic beverages was traditional at both meals and recreation. Many Americans condemned such activities and encouraged the temperance movement in part to control and acculturate these aliens. Others argued convincingly that liquor was not only deleterious to people's health, but it also hindered punctual and diligent work habits and was a source of financial woes and violence among families.

The Anti-Saloon League, founded at Oberlin in 1893, under the leadership of Wayne B. Wheeler became the best organized lobby in the state. No public figure could avoid the issue. Rural Ohio was usually conservative and Protestant, and its populace tended to support Prohibition vigorously. Ohioans in urban centers and towns, such as Marion, were ordinarily more liberal and opposed to Prohibition.

Harding had already invested in a Marion brewery and personally enjoyed whiskey, especially while playing cards. Yet he had to be careful not to alienate his strong rural support, a most significant part of his senatorial district, while maintaining the "wet" support of Marion—a delicate balance to say the least. As a result, he said little on the issue. Nonetheless, when a county-option issue came to a vote in the Senate, he voted in favor of it because of his important rural majority. At the same time, he knew the issue would fail because of the dominance of "wets" in that chamber and in the General Assembly as a whole.

Well into his second term in 1903, Harding realized that he had to seek another office if he were to remain in the forefront of Ohio politics. By a strange set of circumstances, the governorship seemed open and Harding publicly stated his interest in securing it. However, by the time of the convention, the leadership of the Republican party caucused and agreed to nominate Myron Herrick, a successful Cleveland banker and supporter of Hanna, for this position. Foraker's Cincinnati political machine had only the lieutenant governorship to offer and, after some debate, blessed Warren G. Harding as its compromise candidate. The campaign that followed was one of the most colorful in Ohio history, in large part because the Democratic candidate was Tom Johnson, who traveled around the state in his imported automobile, the "Red Devil." A group of supporters followed after Johnson, erecting a large tent, similar to circuses, to attract audiences wherever they could be found. An advocate of Henry George's single-tax plan, Johnson attacked the power and corruption of big business and denounced the present taxation system, which favored them. His message gained both significant support and spirited opposition in the state. At election time Ohioans declined such a dramatic change; the Herrick-Harding ticket won by a plurality of more than 113,000.

The position of lieutenant governor, similar to that of the vice president of the United States, was a rather powerless one. With only two required constitutional duties—presiding over the state Senate and waiting for the governor to die—the lieutenant governor could be a minor political fixture in Columbus, often unknown to most of the citizenry. During his two-year term in the capital, Harding apparently used his time to develop political friendships, which would be useful in seeking other positions. However, as his term came to a close, he decided to withdraw from politics and return to his editorship of the *Star,* especially as his wife Florence became critically ill, suffering from a kidney disease that brought her to the brink of death several times. Dr. Charles Sawyer, with careful treatment, helped her to regain her health. The Hardings' professional relationship with him quickly became a personal friendship.

The *Star* was reorganized, and although Harding occasionally wrote editorials for it, he did not guide it as closely as he had in the past. In fact, it was flourishing—in a sense mirroring the growth and prosperity of Marion itself. The loyal and trustworthy staff that he created meant that it could do well with only an occasional nudge from the proprietor-publisher. Harding in this way was free to indulge occasionally in a favored pastime—travel. While in public office, he relished trips to Washington and Florida. Now he could organize a dream trip to Europe. James and Carrie Phillips, friends from Marion, joined Warren and Florence on their February to April 1909 trip. This was probably when Harding and Mrs. Phillips developed a special interest in one another. The extent of their relationship is unclear, but the discovery of letters between them in the 1960s led to unpleasant encounters between Harding biographer, Francis Russell, and the Harding family. As the result of an agreement between the Ohio Historical Society and the Harding family, the letters will remain sealed until well into the twenty-first century. And without these sources, it is difficult to assess this friendship.

Some contend that the Phillips's friendship was preparatory to a second dalliance that lasted longer and had more serious repercussions after Harding's death. Nan Britton, born in 1896, became infatuated with the *Star*'s editor during her student years at the local high school and apparently attended many of Harding's public events in the area. She claimed that she began an affair with him after she completed high school and that this relationship continued until he reached the White House. The result, she asserted, was a daughter, Elizabeth Ann, born in October 1919, one year before he was elected president. Harding did not acknowledge this liaison at any time, nor did he make any adjustments in his will, the final form having been prepared immediately before his journey to Alaska and the West Coast in 1923, which ended in his death.

Nan Britton unsuccessfully attempted to secure a financial settlement from the Harding family, especially after the death of Florence Harding in 1924, but to no avail. As a result, she wrote a 439-page best-seller, *The President's Daughter*, which described in detail her supposed relationship with Marion's most famous citizen. It must be pointed out that Britton's book and her public statements are the only apparent sources and that the alleged corroborating evidence is circumstantial and could easily be read several ways. Some biographers, such as Francis Russell, believe her story unequivocally, and others, such as Robert Ferrell, do not. The stories in *The President's Daughter* and its 1932 sequel *Honesty or Politics* are believable but unsubstantiated. Most of the materials would have been available to anyone with some knowledge of the Harding family—that is, anyone who lived in Marion. As a result, Britton's claims could not be accepted in court, nor was it possible to verify them in an age that had not invented DNA technology.

From 1908 until 1914, Warren G. Harding did not hold any public office, but he remained an active voice in the Republican party. His withdrawal from politics proved fortuitous because it made it possible for him to distance himself from the mantle of Joseph Foraker, who now served as one of Ohio's two U.S. senators. Even before serious accusations of corruption were made against Foraker, Harding had decided to abandon his longtime political mentor and protector.

Meanwhile in Washington, President Theodore Roosevelt, after serving out the assassinated William McKinley's term and then winning an election of his own in 1904, decided against running again in 1908. Ultimately he pointed to his secretary of war, William Howard Taft, as his successor. The Cincinnati native, who at one time admired publicly the order that George Cox organized in Cincinnati, became the adversary of Senator Foraker, who hoped to secure the Republican presidential candidacy in 1908 for himself. With the deaths of his bitter party rivals McKinley and Hanna, Foraker in fact thought himself the logical and rightful successor. Harding, however, read the political tea leaves differently and threw his support behind Taft. This decision, regarded by Foraker as an appalling betrayal, encouraged other Ohio Republicans to follow suit. Soon there were accusations about Senator Foraker's close relationship with the Standard Oil Company and John D. Rockefeller and even the acceptance of a $50,000 bribe. Foraker's political power and his longtime ambition for gaining the White House disappeared.

With the election of William Howard Taft as president in 1908 and a Republican majority in the Ohio General Assembly, Harding's name was put forward as a possible candidate for U.S. senator. Before the approval of the Seventeenth Amendment to the Constitution, the General Assembly chose the two senators who represented the state in Washington. Foraker still wanted the position, but various powers around the state did not agree. To some, Harding seemed a better choice—an experienced, well-liked man not badly tainted by any of the political machines. Harding's candidacy did not last long; the legislature selected Theodore Burton, an Ohio congressman.

Harding graciously supported his political rival, which must have given him extra points with the party leadership—enough that he was nominated for the governorship in 1910. With Harry Daugherty managing his campaign, Harding traveled extensively around the state, giving dozens of speeches, especially in the rural areas. In many of these villages and towns, he was already a familiar figure because he had often participated in the Chautauqua programs, giving his set speech on one of his favorite Americans, Alexander Hamilton. At the same time, among its national leaders, the Republican party saw the development of a major schism that spilled downward to the state level. Taft, once the protégé of Theodore Roosevelt and now the target of the former president's wrath, endorsed measures that appeared to support the old-line, non-Progressive members of the party. Harding lost the election, largely due to the split in the Republican party. Even Marion County voted Democratic. This did not bode well for the Republicans in the 1912 presidential election. Harding pulled back from active politics for a while, although he remained in the Taft wing of the party.

In 1912 Harding was selected as a delegate to the Republican National Convention in Chicago, and his reward was a chance for national exposure when he was called upon to place President Taft's name in nomination for a second term. Honored, Harding ascended to the podium, commenced his address with its tributes to Taft, and faced a chorus of catcalls and boos. Furious, Harding lost his temper, raised his voice as he continued to read his prepared text, only to be drowned out by cries of "We want Teddy!"

The campaign that followed was brutal—with Theodore Roosevelt bolting from the party and becoming a candidate from the new Progressive or Bull Moose party. Venomous rhetoric from Roosevelt dominated and only served to fracture the GOP and undermine the power of the Republicans. Harding, through the editorial pages of the Marion *Star,* characterized the former president as ruthless and the greatest impostor of all times. Democrats, led by their presidential candidate, New Jersey governor Woodrow Wilson, felt assured of victory. They were correct, securing the White House and a majority in Congress in the November elections. Even Ohio was on the winning side and did not support its native son Taft. Political prospects for Harding seemed limited, even though he eventually was able to effect some conciliation with Roosevelt and his supporters.

A new and important development in 1913 was the ratification of the Seventeenth Amendment to the U.S. Constitution, which required that senators be subject to the popular vote, not that of the state legislature. A Progressive measure, it was encouraged as a means to undermine the power of the political bosses and to democratize the upper house of the national Congress. In a similar vein, Ohioans voted to convene a state constitutional convention in 1912. Every twenty years, as required by the Constitution of 1851, voters had to decide whether to review the state's fundamental document. The last convention, in 1873, presented a new constitution, which the voters rejected. Whereas voters did not agree to a convention in 1891, the lesson of 1873 was not lost on the 1912 gathering, where the delegates proposed forty-one amendments—not a constitution—most of which were Progressive measures. Voters approved thirty-three, among them the requirement for direct primaries, one more anti-boss tool. No longer could the leadership caucus choose candidates for the party; now voters participated personally in this selection process. These two Progressive measures—one national and the other state—came together in the 1914 senatorial campaign in Ohio.

The incumbent senator, Republican Theodore Burton, selected by the party leadership in 1908, decided not to face the voters in 1914. Harding seized the opportunity and made his bid for the Republican candidacy in the primaries. His friend Harry Daugherty later claimed that he gave the necessary push, but we cannot always rely on his sometimes doubtful declarations. Although publicly tarnished, Joseph Foraker also entered the contest. Harding, who had the backing of the party, was successful, winning a plurality of votes (41 percent to 35 percent) against Foraker, who came in a strong second.

The Democrats chose Timothy Hogan, former attorney general of the state, whose career was crowned with successful forays against election fraud. His reputation was impeccable among Progressives and the old order. Many pundits thought he would have few problems on the road to the Senate, but unfortunately he suffered from what many Ohioans considered a severe disability—his Roman Catholic affiliation. Harding never used this situation to his advantage, but many Americans of that time, including some of Harding's supporters, feared this denomination. They denounced its growing importance, which stemmed from heavy immigration from eastern and central Europe. Victory by a 100,000-vote majority blessed Harding's efforts, as he secured 52 percent of the votes cast to Hogan's 42 percent. Warren Harding's political future was secured for the next six years as he and Florence journeyed to Washington, D.C.

Harding truly seemed to enjoy Washington, although most historians could not refer to the aspect of his public life as distinguished. During his term he sponsored more than 130 bills; almost all of them were Ohio specific and usually private, such as securing a military pension for a constituent. Also, he was notoriously absent from the Senate chambers for roll-call votes—almost half of the time. Most probably he did not participate at that decision-making level many times because he did not want to antagonize his colleagues. Indeed, the junior senator from Ohio strongly preferred not to alienate anyone, and his votes on important issues seem to reflect that characteristic.

Senator Harding, a charming and congenial man, came to be liked by the powerful, the influential, and the up-and-coming of Washington, Republicans and Democrats alike. The country-club spirit of the Senate, companionable but competitive golf outings, and social events of the capital all provided opportunities for making friends, which Warren did with ease. Among them he soon counted future president Franklin D. Roosevelt, then serving as President Woodrow Wilson's assistant secretary of the navy; Senators James Wadsworth Jr. from Ohio and Albert B. Fall from New Mexico; and Oscar Underwood, who had been Wilson's floor leader in the House.

Washington provided a different social venue for the Hardings, and a new and exhilarating scene replaced the more restrictive atmosphere of Marion. The District and their newly built two-story Georgian style residence on Wyoming Avenue became their new focal point, and both of them enjoyed it immensely. Added to the family social register were Nicholas and Alice Roosevelt Longworth. Nick Longworth, a congressman from Ohio, had married Theodore Roosevelt's eldest child, known in capital circles as "Princess Alice." The Hardings frequently visited the Longworth home for card parties, always one of Warren's favorite pastimes. The friendship between the couples symbolized a reconciliation, or at least a truce, between branches of the Republican Party.

Another set of friends was Edward (Ned) and Evalyn McLean, whom the Hardings met over cards at the Longworths'. He was the heir to the *Washington Post* fortune, she the daughter of an Irish immigrant who had amassed vast wealth in the Colorado gold fields. Evalyn thought Warren "a stunning man" and Florence a delightful woman, but to her the small-town Ohio couple also seemed to lack certain social refinements. Unfortunately, Florence Harding was frequently in poor health and hence often unable to enjoy this new situation. Her kidney ailment returned shortly after the Hardings arrived in Washington. Soon falling critically ill, only under the care of Dr. Sawyer, called in from Marion, and the insistent attention of friends like Evalyn McLean did she recover.

Less than a year before Harding came to Washington, the assassination of the heir to the Austrian Empire's throne in June 1914 had provided the spark that ignited World War I. President Wilson called upon all Americans to remain "impartial in thought as well as in deed." The United States declared itself neutral, but the shadow of this brutal, bloody war in Europe stretched across the Atlantic and continued to be a major problem. That problem became significant during the presidential election of 1916. Democrats nominated Wilson for a second term. He portrayed himself as the "peace president" and ran on the slogan "He kept us out of war." Ethnic America, notably German Americans, supported Wilson's efforts. The Republicans nominated Charles Evans Hughes of New York, whose close ties to Theodore Roosevelt, who had been arguing that war with Germany was inevitable, seemed to place him in the prowar camp. Wilson won narrowly over Hughes.

Perhaps the president knew that remaining out of the global conflict was almost impossible, but he cherished that hope almost until the last moment. Although the diplomatic situation seemed to improve somewhat after the November 1916 elections, it deteriorated rapidly after the beginning of 1917. One month after he took his second oath of office, President Wilson called on Congress to declare war against Germany, emphasizing, "The world must be made safe for democracy." On April 6, Harding voted in the majority for the entrance of the United States into the Great War. He also supported Theodore Roosevelt's hope to organize new "Rough Riders," whom the former president would personally lead in Europe and so quickly make an American military imprint on this conflict. Harding added an amendment to a draft bill to permit Roosevelt to raise his volunteer units. Both houses of Congress passed the bill with the Harding amendment. Wilson signed the bill into law but made it absolutely clear that he would not permit the formation of new Rough Rider units, even though Roosevelt already had received tens of thousands of applications.

During the country's eighteen months in the war, Harding ordinarily supported measures that might ensure victory for the Allies. The establishment of several government agencies to regulate the economy and to assist the military was congruent with his views of American greatness—anything else would have appeared unpatriotic. He was even willing to accept temporarily the concentration of more power in the hands of the president, because efficiency and rapid decision-making action could ensure success. At the same time he was unwilling to vote for tax increases that singled out large corporations because he felt that they were the bulwark of the economy. To him such a practice would only undercut American prosperity.

As the congressional elections of 1918 came closer, Democrats and Republicans put aside the spirit of unity and girded themselves for political battle. Wilson, in an effort to win votes for Democratic candidates, argued that a Republican victory would embarrass the nation abroad at a crucial time in world affairs. Republicans hoped to gain the majority in Congress and thus better position themselves to influence postwar developments and decisions. At election time they were successful, winning majorities in both houses. Many Republicans, among them Roosevelt and his supporters, were furious that Wilson would equate loss of national honor abroad with a Republican victory at home. Roosevelt's close friend Henry Cabot Lodge of Massachusetts, the Senate Foreign Relations Committee's powerful chairman, declared, "I never thought I could hate a man as much as I hate Wilson." Lodge became Wilson's implacable foe, and after the war Harding became an adherent of Lodge's diplomatic perspectives.

World War I ended with the signing of an armistice on November 11, 1918. American casualties totaled more than 112,000 dead and 230,000 wounded, heavy losses for so brief a period of combat. The great powers of Europe, which had been fighting for three years before the Americans arrived, saw more than six million of their young men perish and millions more return home as human wreckage. The almost incomprehensible death toll affecting both combatants and noncombatants alike made many Americans replace their idealism with cynicism and reaction. One noted journalist said that it would have been just as reprehensible to have shot American soldiers in cold blood on Broadway Avenue in New York City as it was to have subjected them to the trenches of the western front. The atrocities and deaths also drew many Americans further away from supporting the United States as an integral player in international geopolitics and back to the traditional stance of isolating the United States from world affairs and conflicts.

Woodrow Wilson, the former Princeton political science professor, did not perceive these changes and sailed to Europe, and the Paris Peace Conference, where the Allies welcomed him like a messiah—roaring crowds, soaring platitudes, with bridges, squares, and other parts of their landscape later named in his honor. With the end of the Great War, Harding and his colleagues in the Senate had in many ways a new world to face. Dramatic changes on the international scene and the question of what role the United States should play in it henceforth concerned many Americans in and out of government. Wilson chose not to involve senators—Democrats or Republicans—in the Peace Conference, which he hoped to direct exclusively or at least to influence heavily. Because the U.S. Constitution specifies that no treaty is binding until approved by the Senate, this decision was both insulting and diplomatically dangerous. Nor did Wilson include on the peace delegation any distinguished Republicans, such as Lodge or Taft, although that party now held the majority both in the Senate and in the House of Representatives.

Before the Great War had ended, many Americans succumbed to the hysteria of germanophobia and the Red Scare. The propaganda of the Committee on Public Information and other government agencies set up by Wilson to publicize and popularize the war often misled the citizenry to think of Germany, the leading enemy of the Allies, as a land of barbarians. Simultaneously, the Bolshevik Revolution in Russia and the establishment of a Communist regime by Lenin, who promised soon to export the revolution worldwide, instilled a fear of socialism and leftist radicalism in the American republic. Americans in 1919 witnessed numerous major labor strikes — from Seattle and its general strike to Boston and its police strike – and these were blamed, perhaps incorrectly, on these undesirables.

Harding's Ohio was not left untouched by these developments. Towns such as New Berlin and Osnaburg demonstrated their patriotism by changing their names to North Canton and East Canton respectively. Driven by the same motive, bands and orchestras refused to play the works of Beethoven and Bach, cooks offered servings of "liberty cabbage" instead of sauerkraut, and taverns in Cincinnati stopped serving pretzels. Harding found it difficult to remain neutral on these issues, and at times he was forced to make public statements. Because of the large German-American population in the state, he lauded the German language press and asserted that it often affirmed its patriotism and support of the federal government even during the Great War. It is noteworthy that his father-in-law could speak German, as did many other Ohioans in the early twentieth century. As for socialism, he expressed his discomfort and concern, preferring his innate conservatism. By 1919, Harding emerged as a fervent, not rabid, nationalist—America First was the popular new ideology, and the League of Nations was its major opponent.

After the delegates at the Paris Peace Conference signed the Treaty of Versailles on June 28, 1919, President Wilson brought it home and shared its contents with America. Many objected to its terms, and many Republicans additionally saw it as an opportunity to lash out politically at the president. Harding joined numerous colleagues, led by Lodge, in denouncing the treaty or aspects of it, especially the establishment of the League of Nations. In mid-August 1919, Harding and other senators journeyed to the White House to discuss the treaty and the League of Nations. Harding came away from the meeting believing that the president had evaded answering some of his deepest concerns about the league. On September 11, in one of his few major Senate speeches, he denounced Wilsonian progressive internationalism and outlined his doubts about the league and reservations about the treaty. Facing formidable opposition, Wilson launched a crusade by train across the country to invigorate Americans to support his cause, but the president's paralytic stroke brought his crusade to a close some six weeks later. The Treaty of Versailles was put to numerous votes in the Senate between November 1919 and March 1920, and each time various combinations of Republican and Democratic senators rejected it. Harding and the isolationists basked in victory.

War in Europe notwithstanding, Congress had to deal with two perennial political issues: Prohibition and women's suffrage. Although Florence Harding delighted in her first opportunity to vote in 1920, her husband had tried to maintain a neutral position during the debates about the proposed women's suffrage constitutional amendment. He was sufficiently politic to allay the fears of the suffragists so that they thought he was on their side. Nonetheless he wanted to maintain old-fashioned male support. When it became clear that there was a substantial majority of Ohioans favoring this issue, he supported the Nineteenth Amendment.

Prohibition created other difficulties for the Ohio senator. The harmonizer Harding obfuscated by voting affirmatively for the proposed Eighteenth Amendment in order to keep the Anti-Saloon League and his rural constituency satisfied, while privately hoping that when it was sent to the states for ratification a three-quarters majority of states would not be possible. He misjudged the power of Prohibition forces and the spirit of idealism so powerful in the United States near the end of the Great War. The "Noble Experiment" and the "Roaring Twenties" commenced simultaneously, as the United States went dry in January 1920.

While these scenarios played out, Harding found himself the leading Republican in the Buckeye State. The Taft presidential debacle in 1912 tarnished that branch of the "brotherhood," and even other notables such as Frank Willis, governor of Ohio after James Cox's first term failed in his reelection bid in 1916. During the three years that followed the 1916 presidential and gubernatorial elections, Harding monitored the political scene carefully. Whether or not he really *wanted* the presidency will never be certain. Perhaps not even his prime booster, Florence Harding, was ready for this step. However, as an astute politician, Harding carefully assessed the situation and made certain to use what he could to his advantage. His friend Harry Daugherty surely kept this Marionite in the political forefront, although later many would consider him a Daugherty marionette. Shortly before Christmas in 1919, Harding made a formal announcement of his desire to seek the Oval Office (actually Daugherty leaked this information to the press earlier). Indicative of the Buckeye State's political significance is that the Democratic Governor Cox was also regarded as a potential presidential or vice-presidential candidate. Once again, Ohio was going to play a pivotal role in national politics.

Before the Chicago convention, Harding assessed and reassessed his chances often while deploying and redeploying his boosters and supporters around the nation. Harding's only real Republican opponent was General

Leonard Wood, the former army chief of staff and a protégé of Theodore Roosevelt whose Republican fervor apparently denied him military leadership in Europe under Wilson. The demise of the infamous bosses, whether by natural selection or by Progressive prescription, substantially changed the ambiance of the convention, where Harding received additional support from various sectors of the party including the old leadership of the Senate.

Early in the balloting, there was a deadlock among the frontrunners, General Wood, Governor Frank Lowden of Illinois, and Senator Hiram Johnson, a progressive from California. After several ballots in which Harding remained at the bottom of the list, the convention adjourned for the evening—leading to numerous caucuses among party leaders in suite 404–406 of the Blackstone Hotel, and to the expression "smoke-filled room." Lodge and others feared that unless a compromise candidate was found soon, another schism similar to the 1912 Bull Moose rupture would plague the party. The next day started off slowly again with the deadlock still remaining—Harding usually gaining a few votes during each subsequent ballot. On the ninth ballot he took the lead, and on the tenth he finally received a healthy majority and was declared the Republican candidate. His quip was pure Harding: "I feel like a man who goes in on a pair of eights and comes out with aces full!" Governor Calvin Coolidge of Massachusetts, who enjoyed great popularity because of his firm handling of the Boston police strike the previous year, received the nomination for vice president.

With the convention ordeal over, Harding turned to heavy campaigning against fellow Ohioan, Governor James M. Cox, his Democratic opponent. Harding began campaigning in July and, whether by design or default, proposed to emulate the front-porch style of William McKinley, with his Mt. Vernon Avenue home in Marion as the focal point. This folksy approach appealed to rural and small-town America. Cox traveled the country, pursuing the White House at a frenetic pace one observer called "campaigning all over the lot, in a sweat."

The Democratic platform advanced the League of Nations "as the surest, if not the only, practicable means of maintaining the permanent peace of the world," and Cox made the need for American participation in it a central campaign theme. Harding replied that it was time:

> To safeguard America first;
> To stabilize American first;
> To prosper America first;

> To think of America first;
> To exalt America first;
> To live for and revere America first.

Harding's economic conservatism and America First Nationalism, contrasted with Cox's progressivism and internationalism, mirrored the desires of many—from big business, which wanted to see a reduction in wartime taxes, to hyphenated Americans, who were angered over the boundary reconfigurations designed at the Peace Conference with the approval of the Democrat Wilson. Harding promised that Americans would find in him a reliable statesman who understood their anxieties in the aftermath of Wilson's international progressivism and the dreadful human toll of the World War. "America's present need is not heroics but healing," he told a Boston audience, "not nostrums but normalcy; not revolution but restoration; not surgery but serenity."

Republican leaders could sense victory as long as Harding acted in a gentlemanly manner and gave his daily political homilies from his front porch. By September, more than 600,000 people had trekked to Marion to see and hear him. Now the leading Republican in the United States, he did what he liked to do best—harmonize and conciliate instead of creating discord and antagonism. He did not want to return to the rough style of politics that he had experienced so much during his public life. In a sense, he hoped to give to politics an image that suited his personality—the essence of congeniality and friendliness. In Harding, rural and small-town America enjoyed one more chance to represent the nation.

Two other factors added interest to the campaign. The Nineteenth Amendment was one. Ratified during the campaign months, it meant that the enfranchisement of women nationwide would commence with this election; Florence Harding and millions of other women were going to get their first chance to vote. The race card was the other; shortly before the election, some Democrats, in an effort to destroy Harding, released some rumors to the public purporting that he had African American ancestry. Nonetheless, Warren Harding easily won with more than 60 percent of the popular vote, the largest popular majority for a president to that time, although it must be pointed out that many of those eligible to participate in the election did not exercise that right. In the Electoral College, Harding received 404 votes to Cox's 127. Franklin D. Roosevelt, Cox's running mate, quipped after the landslide defeat, "Thank God we are both comparatively youthful."

This success took place on Warren Harding's fifty-fifth birthday, November 2. He and Florence had voted that morning in Marion, and then

Warren Harding and his wife, Florence, voted on Election Day 1920 in their home town of Marion, Ohio, she for the first time thanks to the Nineteenth Amendment. Harding then journeyed to Columbus to play golf and await the election returns. He easily won the 1920 election with more than 60 percent of the popular vote. Ohio Historical Society.

he journeyed to Columbus to play golf with Harry Daugherty. A birthday party on his front porch greeted him upon his return home, and then came the exhilarating news of victory. "I have been on the square with you [the people of Marion]," he told gathered friends and neighbors, and now "I want to be on the square with all the world."

• • •

With four months until his oath of office on March 4, 1921, Harding had a great deal of time to plan and prepare, but especially to select his cabinet. As expected, various factions in his party emerged with celerity after a show of unity during the campaign. Each had its own agenda and its own preference for candidates. Though Henry Cabot Lodge expected the president-elect to defer to his "betters," Harding wanted to create his own cabinet. He wanted men with talent and experience who shared his conservatism, and he intended to use the "spoils of office" to reward his boosters too.

His first appointee was New Yorker Charles Evans Hughes, the 1916 unsuccessful presidential candidate. A man of great talent and experience, he would serve as secretary of state under Harding and Coolidge, and in 1930 he became chief justice of the United States. Some of the old leadership were not pleased with this choice, but they saved their real opposition for Harding's next appointment: Herbert Hoover as secretary of commerce. Here was a respected administrator under Wilson who directed food programs in the United States and afterwards relief efforts in starving, wartorn Europe. A successful mining engineer and businessman with roots in Iowa and residence in California, he fit easily into Harding's image of a talented cabinet member while adding trans-Mississippi balance. According to Andrew Sinclair, one of Harding's biographers, the Republican leadership balked and tried to block this appointment. However, they simultaneously proposed Andrew Mellon, one of the richest men in the world, as the secretary of the Treasury. Although he was not Harding's choice— likely Brig. Gen. Charles Gates Dawes of Illinois was—the president-elect proposed a compromise reflective of his character. If the leadership accepted his choice, he would return the favor. The harmonizer won. As for Dawes, he later became the first director of the Budget Bureau, negotiator par excellence in Europe during the Ruhr River crisis, and recipient of the 1925 Nobel Peace Prize. Other appointments of note were Henry Wallace of Iowa as secretary of agriculture, an important choice in an era of declining farm prices. The Department of Labor was offered to James Davis, like Hoover an exemplar of the Horatio Alger mythology and Social Darwinism, whose résumé included employment as an iron puddler in his youth.

Harding also made several decisions that eventually undermined the credibility of his administration. First, his fellow Ohioan, Harry Daugherty, booster and self-styled political expert, accepted the attorney general slot. Albert B. Fall of New Mexico, whom Harding chose to direct the Department of the Interior, was the only U.S. senator chosen for this exclusive presidential club. A Roosevelt Republican and southwestern rancher, Fall had become a friend of the Ohio politician when Harding served in the Senate, but Fall's connections with the petroleum industry did make him suspect and proved to be his undoing after Harding's death. Added to these choices were Jess Smith, a Washington Court House, Ohio, friend of Daugherty, who took a position in the Department of Justice, and Charles Forbes, a relatively new friend from a recent Hawaii expedition, who was picked to direct the Veterans' Bureau. The actions of these men would severely undermine Harding's plans for a government of talent and experts. Nonetheless, one could not gainsay the quality of the majority of his administration—Harding largely satisfied his desire for talent and experience, while balancing it with political and social considerations. Once he completed most of this work, he took one more vacation in Florida to visit friends and enjoy some golf.

Rested and tanned, the president-elect returned to Marion to prepare for his grand move to Washington. He checked on his *Star* and arranged to rent his house for the next four years. The city honored him at 10:00 A.M. on March 2, 1921, by closing down its schools and business establishments. After farewells to his friends, he gave one last porch appearance for the townspeople. The grand inauguration took place two days later in Washington. The differences that day between the seemingly healthy Harding and the sickly, fragile Wilson were apparent to all. Harding offered an upbeat inaugural speech but promised nothing new, only the apparent reversal of programs and policies, both domestic and foreign, dear to the outgoing president. After the festivities, visitors to the nation's capital noticed a change in the atmosphere at 1600 Pennsylvania Avenue. The Hardings opened their "home" and its gardens to the citizenry more than did the Wilsons, who seemed to have created a barrier of secrecy, especially during the second administration—perhaps because of the war and the president's illness. Harding also paid close attention to his correspondence and even attempted to answer much of it himself, despite the fact that he had a diligent personal secretary, George Christian, a fellow Marionite. One century after James Monroe's presidency, Warren Gamaliel Harding hoped to create a new Era of Good feelings. He wanted to reunite the citizenry after the divisive forces and circumstances that rent the country after the Great War and to end financial and diplomatic burdens that it had created.

Presidential honeymoons are not necessarily long, and such was the situation for Harding. Economic problems plagued him, especially because the year of the inauguration was one of continuing recession in the United States. Most seriously affected were the farmers, many of whom looked upon him for support after the inactivity of Wilson. To the anger of the congressional farm block, little assistance was forthcoming. Farmers remained discontented because they faced one of the worst depressions in their lifetimes—obviously the return to normalcy was not working for them and some readjustment would have to be made.

Other sectors of the economy suffered too, in large part because of industrial readjustment and military demobilization. Strong leadership and some independence of action can be seen occasionally from Harding, yet he was often captive to his own economic philosophy and popular opinion. Traditional economists of that era argued that governments must balance their budgets and that the economy must endure periodic boom-and-bust cycles, without government intervention, to correct itself and, in Darwinian fashion, shake off the weak and unproductive. Hoover and Secretary of the Treasury Mellon certainly supported such traditional economic theory. By 1922 it appeared to have been the correct decision, as the recession ended and the nation entered a period of remarkable growth. From 1922 to 1929 and the onset of the Great Depression, unemployment never exceeded 5 percent, the gross national product grew at an annual rate of 5.5 percent, and real wages rose about 15 percent.

To aid in balancing the federal budget and to more efficiently manage it, President Harding established the Bureau of Budget, which placed formal budgetary restraints on federal expenditures for the first time. Because he committed himself strongly to reducing the national debt and federal expenses, he was unable to support any measure that gave bonuses to World War I veterans. They argued that they should be compensated for the differential between their military pay and that of Americans who remained in civilian life during the war, working in industry and enjoying the benefits of overtime pay. He vetoed the bonus bill because another outlay of federal monies was not in his or Mellon's plan. The president also pushed for reduction in taxes while reducing the national debt. Mellon's revenue act slashed the high income taxes of the rich that Progressives had pushed through Congress during the World War. However, any proposal for federal aid to the disadvantaged had to wait until the calamity of the Great Depression.

Harding also had to face labor problems, always difficult to resolve, but even more so during the business-oriented twenties. Members of the cabinet, such as Daugherty and Mellon, backed by middle- and upper-class opinion, were hostile to unions and increased strength for organized labor. There were strikes in several sectors of the economy—from textiles and the coal mines, America's two largest industries, to the railroads and the steel industry. Wage reductions often sparked these disturbances. Coal miners went on strike, but the results were not satisfactory because the recommendations of a special commission in charge of investigating these problems were never followed. Harding also had to face problems with the railroads because of changes in the rules governing salaries and benefits—leading to violence and the destruction of property. Only a bitter injunction ended this work stoppage. The result was that some important sectors of labor were unhappy with his policies, although at least there was a more humane work schedule for the steel workers. At the behest of Hoover, Harding attempted to convince leaders of the iron and steel industries to reduce employees' workday to eight hours. The president experienced great resistance from them, although before his death the twelve-hour work day in the steel industry had ended.

America of the 1920s sought normalcy, and in foreign affairs that meant isolationism. Harding was left with a vexing problem remaining from the Wilson administration: what to do with the Treaty of Versailles and the League of Nations. Although early in his senatorial career he had expressed his support of some form of internationalism in U.S. foreign policy, he changed that with the end of the war. Because the United States had not signed the peace treaty, it was still officially at war with Germany in 1921. Harding sent a message to Congress requesting a joint resolution that would declare a termination of the conflict. Congress obliged in July, then Secretary of State Hughes arranged a formal end to the war with a separate U.S.-German treaty by the end of the year. The United States also decided to pull back from international involvements by way of the League of Nations. During the recent campaign he had expressed both support for a "world association . . . that will discourage or tend to prevent war" and opposition to the League of Nations as defined by the Versailles Treaty. The United States never joined the League, although unofficial observers were sent to its meetings at Geneva, and the federal government often cooperated with the work of this international organization. Harding did push for American participation in the World Court, but he could never secure enough votes in the Senate for ratification.

Despite a desire to have the country detached from international affairs, Harding responded to calls for disarmament. Not only would that be a policy with wide popular support after the excesses of the war, but it also would fit into Harding and Mellon's plan to cut taxes and to reduce the federal budget and the national debt. Harding and Secretary of State Hughes proposed a conference in Washington where the great powers could discuss slowing the arms race, particularly naval armaments. Scheduled to begin, fittingly, on the third anniversary of Armistice Day, November 11, 1921, officials postponed the Conference for the Limitation of Armament one day to allow the interment of an unknown soldier and the dedication of his tomb with great solemnity, pomp, and panoply at Arlington Cemetery. The arrival of foreign dignitaries added greatly to this national day of recognition.

The conference convened the following day, and during its opening speeches the secretary of state proposed not only a stoppage in the construction of battleships and other major naval vessels but also a substantial reduction in their overall number. This came much to the surprise of the delegates, because the United States, Britain, and Japan were then involved in major naval buildups. After months of negotiations, these three plus France and Italy agreed to stop naval construction and to cut back on their fleets according to a ratio formula. Although there were really no means to enforce this agreement, many in the United States and other countries lauded it as a major success on the road to international peace. Other agreements of the 1920s were similar—much verbiage but little enforcement strength, only a desperate hope for peace and no repeat of the Great War. In the spirit of the postwar years, Harding had scored a noticeable diplomatic victory through Hughes.

Harding subscribed in some way to the xenophobia that captivated many Americans during the World War and in the subsequent years. Germanophobia was only one aspect of it. Many began to denounce the open immigration policy, believing that the country could no longer accommodate the millions that arrived each year. Efforts to curb immigration by means of a literacy test failed under the Cleveland administration in the 1890s and the Taft administration of the 1910s, but that proposal came forward again during the World War years and passed over a presidential veto. Pressure to restrict immigration remained, although some industrialists saw such a program as detrimental to their needs for cheap labor. Despite their support in the election of 1920, Harding signed the first quota bill of the 1920s to limit the arrival of those "huddled masses." The law limited immigration in any year to 3 percent of the number of each nationality according to the 1910 census.

The historic image of Harding as weak and malleable, perhaps created by Daugherty and popularized by the scandals involving various members of his administration that surfaced after his death, do not appear altogether valid. For example, Harding traveled to Birmingham, Alabama, in the heart of the solid Democratic South, to accept an honorary degree from the University of Alabama. On October 26, 1921, he became the first president since the Civil War to speak out on Southern soil for minority rights. "I want to see the time come," he proclaimed to a segregated audience of some 20,000 whites and 10,000 blacks, "when black men will regard themselves as full participants in the benefits and duties of American citizenship." He continued: "We cannot go on, as we have gone on for more than half a century, with one great section of our population, as many people as the entire population of some significant countries of Europe, set off from real contribution to solving national issues, because of a division on race lines." He also spoke strongly about the necessity of giving blacks additional economic and educational opportunities and recognized the right of many of them to register to vote. Prior to the New Deal of the 1930s, blacks usually voted for Lincoln's Grand Old Party, if given the chance. The president did not call for complete equality, however, because segregation had been declared constitutional by the U.S. Supreme Court in the *Plessy v. Ferguson* case of 1896. Total equality was not his theme, but a dramatic improvement in the position of African Americans in the South and a recognition of their voting rights, which should be enforced without bias. Still, this was an audacious speech and a daring effort by a Republican president in the Jim Crow South.

Harding was moved to pardon some so-called political prisoners from World War I, incarcerated because of their pacifism and nonviolent antiwar activities. The prime exemplar was Eugene V. Debs, the leader of the Socialist party and a labor organizer who first gained national prominence during the Pullman strike of 1894. After his arrest in Canton, Ohio, for denouncing the war, he was found guilty of violating the Espionage Act and sentenced to ten years in federal prison. Woodrow Wilson, even Harry Daugherty, and many others opposed the least show of clemency, yet Harding acted differently. The president released him, perhaps moved by correspondence from his former *Star* worker, Norman Thomas, the noted socialist, who appealed personally to Harding. Interestingly, the president required Debs to visit him at the White House after his release from the Atlanta prison and never to divulge the contents of their conversation. Harding also ordered the Justice Department to review clemency petitions for other political prisoners on a case-by-case basis.

Harding obviously felt a certain compulsion to share his political victory with some close friends, especially a few whose company he enjoyed. These appointees became known as the Ohio Gang—men such as Harry Daugherty, Albert Fall, Charles Forbes, and Jess Smith. Their "little house on K

Street" in Washington, D.C., served as clubhouse and headquarters, where they gathered to play poker and drink some illegal beverages, sometimes with the president. They also betrayed the president and the nation's trust. Soon congressional committees, following up on the rumors of graft and corruption among some in the Harding administration, brought the Ohio Gang's activities to national attention. A shocked and depressed Harding had been unaware of their chicanery and treachery.

Albert B. Fall was not a conservationist, despite the fact that he directed the Department of the Interior, which oversaw national parks and forest as well as other natural resource reserves. In 1921 he persuaded his friend Secretary of the Navy Edwin Denby to transfer the control of some strategic naval oil reserves at Teapot Dome, Wyoming, and Elk Hill, California, to his department. Fall then secretly leased them to two important oil entrepreneurs for a payoff of nearly $400,000. He persuaded Harding to believe that these measures were in the best interests of the U.S. government, but the president did not know about the bribery that preceded these leases. A special Senate investigation was organized in 1922 to examine these transfers, and in January 1923 the president accepted Fall's resignation, not suspecting the worst, which he was spared by his sudden death that summer. In 1929 Albert Fall was convicted of bribery and sent to prison.

Harding experienced a real taste of scandal related to the Veterans' Bureau, a new government agency created in 1921. Its director, Charles Forbes, met the Hardings while on vacation in Hawaii during Warren's senatorial career. They were impressed with the then-director of public utilities on the islands, especially after his gracious treatment. Later he became one of Harding's boosters in the state of Washington during his presidential bid. Once Forbes took control of the Veterans' Bureau, he quickly realized its financial possibilities. Whereas other departments of the federal government faced significant reductions, his did not—in fact during the fiscal year 1923, it was allotted approximately one-fifth of the government budget. The United States could not forget its veterans, so many of them still suffering from the effects of the World War. Forbes took advantage of that national concern, pocketing millions of dollars. He secured kickbacks not only in the purchase of hospital sites and construction of facilities but also in the sale of surplus military-medical supplies from the war. As soon as Harding heard about this, he demanded Forbes's resignation. One journalist claimed that Harding confronted Forbes in 1923, literally shook him, and shouted vulgarities at him. Later Forbes faced trial and ultimately punishment for fraud, conspiracy, and bribery. His defense attorney committed suicide.

Other problems surrounded Jess Smith, the confidant of Harry Daugherty who gave him a job in the Justice Department. Both were from Washington Court House, Ohio, a community some forty miles south of Columbus. Daugherty was the ever-aggressive politician, whereas Smith was the follower, taking advantage of whatever scraps fell in his direction. Because the attorney general's wife was in bad health and demanded special treatment, she did not live in the District, so Smith shared Daugherty's apartment, keeping it in order and providing him with food and beverages for entertainment. While in Washington, Smith misused the Daugherty connection for his own political and social gains; for example, he enjoyed the chauffeur service entitled only to the attorney general. Further, he was accused of suggesting preferences in presidential pardons. On Memorial Day 1923, after Harding told Daugherty to remove Smith not only from the Department of Justice but also from a yet-to-be announced presidential voyage to the West Coast, Smith committed suicide in Daugherty's apartment. As a result, it is not surprising that President Harding reputedly said shortly afterwards to William Allen White, one of the noted journalists of the 1920s: "My God, this is a hell of job! I have no trouble with my enemies . . . but my friends, they're the ones that keep me walking the floor at nights!"

In 1923 Harding planned an extensive trip to the West Coast to galvanize public support, to gain support of the farm bloc, and to create a solid base for his 1924 reelection campaign. The two-month excursion would include a railroad trip to Washington state, a Pacific voyage along the Inward Passage to Alaska, forays into the territory's inland, and stopovers in Oregon and California before returning to Washington. The trip would demand numerous speeches and public appearances, which his staff thought would present no problem for the president because he always enjoyed displaying his oratorical skills.

By this time, however, some of Harding's health problems were apparent, a secret carefully confined to his inner circle. He was diagnosed with high blood pressure, which he passed off as a family trait of no real consequence. Only a few years earlier had medical researchers "discovered" the heart attack and began to understand it. Unfortunately, Dr. Charles Sawyer, who held the title of brigadier general as White House physician, was not acquainted with this recent medical advance and could not prescribe in any reasonable manner what was necessary to improve or to maintain the president's health.

The grand journey began at Union Station in Washington, D.C., on June 20, 1923, with the president in poor spirits due to the scandals. After several health crises during the trip, Dr. Sawyer diagnosed Harding as suffering from some sort of food poisoning. Nonetheless, the tour continued and wended its way to Alaska. Harding enjoyed the trip immensely, although physically he was not prepared for it. Yet he found it difficult to slow down and especially to cancel public appearances. Any sign of physical weakness was not to be broadcast to his fellow Americans. He always wanted to appear in control and ready to reassure the citizenry, but upon his arrival in San Francisco on Sunday, July 29, his heart problems at last subdued his physical activities.

Bulletins from the Palace Hotel in San Francisco sounded hopeful, and at times the president seemed to be on the mend. During the evening of August 2, Florence read him a complimentary article about his presidency, which pleased him. After this, she and his nurse excused themselves for personal or professional reasons for several minutes. During their absence, he had a heart attack and died immediately. Dr. Sawyer said it was a cerebral hemorrhage, but Dr. Ray Lyman Wilbur, director of the medical program at Stanford University, who also attended the president, knew otherwise. Florence Harding was quickly in mourning, and soon the nation followed her.

The funeral cortege to Washington and then to Marion where a temporary burial place was arranged led to a general mourning of the American public. The First Lady, despite her own physical frailties, lived up to the obligations of a presidential widow—not an easy task in both the nation's capital and her hometown. With dignity she persevered, while the new president, Calvin Coolidge, prepared to take over the Oval Office. Upon her return to the White House after the funeral ceremonies in Marion, she collected her husband's papers and examined them to some extent. In the tradition of others before her, Florence Harding decided to destroy some and preserve others. How much she incinerated, historians will never know, but biographer Francis Russell accused her of a wholesale destruction of his records so as to misrepresent her husband to his country. Although the hearth was hot with paper ash, her actions were not unusual in the American political tradition. The sickly First Lady outlived her husband by fifteen months and succumbed to her persistent kidney ailment in November 1924.

Within months after Harding's death, his "friends"—such as Forbes, Fall, and Daugherty—found their public careers subject to the scrutiny of congressional committees. Forbes and Fall were sent to prison, whereas the former attorney general, although faced with trials, invoked the Fifth Amendment and was never incarcerated. He published his memoirs, or reminiscences of his relationship with the deceased president, in which he glorified his role as a power broker in the cabinet and understated that of the president. As if this were not enough for the reputation of a man who believed in harmony and the necessity of conciliation, Harding posthumously faced the onslaughts of those who wanted to undermine his character for a variety of reasons. A former agent in the Department of Justice, Gaston Means, published his infamous *Strange Death of President Harding*, which asserted that the First Lady, supposedly aware of the deceased president's putative scandalous affairs, poisoned her husband. Because of conflicts in diagnosing the reasons for the president's death, many Americans were willing to expect the worst, especially after the Teapot Dome scandal. And then Nan Britton claimed to have given birth to "his" daughter, Elizabeth Ann, in 1919. What remained of the reputation of the much beloved president in the summer of 1923 was thoroughly destroyed, and American historians still consider him the worst of U.S. presidents.

Warren G. Harding was in many ways "the available man," an expression that Andrew Sinclair used as the title of his biography of the twenty-ninth president. Harding was a politician, but not a leader, who took advantage of situations presented to him—and this one can easily see in his campaign for the Ohio state senate, the lieutenant governorship, and even the U.S. Senate. He usually received the strong support of his spouse, Florence Harding, who apparently delighted in her various public roles despite her poor health.

The documents that remain suggest strongly that he preferred not to change the course of events but to follow them and to participate actively in their unfolding. He wanted to bring people together and detested the animosity created by the debate over the Treaty of Versailles and the related issue of American membership in the League of Nations. The Senate wanted a compliant president, and by 1923 it was apparent that they had lost. Harding had proposed U.S. membership in the World Court at The Hague, but this was another battle he lost with the upper chamber. It wished to direct foreign policy and not react to the pronouncements of the chief executive. One can criticize the Washington Naval Conference as being ineffective, but in the fractious spirit of the postwar world, that gathering was an accomplishment. Harding tried to improve the lot of iron-workers and steelworkers and to a much lesser extent that of the farmers. The creation of the Office of Budget and his appointment of Charles Gates Dawes was truly a progressive measure that brought some fiscal sanity to the federal government. Finally, it is easy to attack the quality of *some* of his appointments, but on the other hand, one can see the quality that he also selected—from William Howard Taft as Chief Justice of the United

States to Herbert Hoover and Charles Evans Hughes as the secretaries of Commerce and State respectively. In a number of situations, Harding demonstrated leadership and that he was no Daugherty marionette.

As for his personal life, one cannot be certain about the validity of the claims of Francis Russell and Nan Britton. The former willingly accepted at face value the claims of the latter and his disagreements with the president's heirs over the Carrie Phillips's letters led him to suspect the worst. However, in the case of Britton, one can easily assume that she took advantage of a ripe situation as Harding's reputation became besmirched and she suffered financial and social problems because of her scandalous status as an unwed mother.

The president who appeared much beloved in his lifetime for his folksiness and political homilies became much maligned within months of his death. The harmonizer never had an opportunity to bring out the facts about his presidency and to write his memoirs. As a result, it took four years in his tomb and memorial to await a proper presidential solemnity and dedication. At the turn of the following century, it is unfortunate that the worst is still believed, except in Marion where "their" citizen is honored and respected.

Further Reading

Research on the twenty-ninth president and his times should begin with a careful examination of *Warren G. Harding: A Bibliography,* comp. Richard G. Frederick (Westport, Conn.: Greenwood Press, 1992), a thorough catalog of primary and secondary sources. Serious research focuses on the Ohio Historical Center in Columbus, where most of the president's papers are stored. However, much of this archival material has been microfilmed and is available through Scholarly Resources of Wilmington, Delaware. Further basic catalog information can be accessed via the Internet: <www.whitehouse.gov/history/presidents/wh29.html> is a good place to start. The C-Span videotape series on U.S. presidents is a careful visual introduction to Harding and to his home in Marion, Ohio: *Life Portrait of Warren G. Harding* (West Lafayette, Ind.: C-Span archives, 2000; videotape 151625). It includes interviews with two noted historians and the curator of the Harding Museum and Memorial.

One of the best-known biographies on Harding is Francis Russell, *The Shadow of Blooming Grove: Warren G. Harding in His Times* (New York:

McGraw-Hill, 1968), but it maintains a traditional view of him as the worst U.S. president while at times attempting to be sympathetic. Russell, as others, underestimates Harding's efforts to control his own presidency. An improvement over Russell's work is Andrew Sinclair, *The Available Man: The Life behind the Masks of Warren Gamaliel Harding* (New York: Macmillian, 1965). This work is more sympathetic toward Harding, but it remains quite critical. Other sources, filled with stories about smoke-filled rooms and lots of forbidden beverages abound and continue to fascinate the public, but these are not necessarily objective. One example is Charles L. Mee Jr., *Ohio Gang* (New York: M. Evans and Co., 1981). More balanced approaches are found in Eugene P. Trani and David L. Wilson, *The Presidency of Warren G. Harding* (Lawrence: Univ. of Kansas Press, 1977), and Robert H. Ferrell, *The Strange Deaths of President Harding* (Columbia: Univ. of Missiouri Press, 1996), which refute, through solid research, some of the worst scandals and unpleasantries that surrounded the Harding administration. This book is required for all scholars of the Harding era.

Any study of the twenty-ninth president will unfortunately include some of the traditional literature and interpretations. One can expect the unsympathetic and incorrect image in Carl Sferrazza Anthony's *Florence Harding: The First Lady, the Jazz Age, and the Death of America's Most Scandalous President* (New York: William Morrow, 1998). To examine the origin of the poison theory—that is, that the First Lady killed her husband because of his immoral behavior—one must read *The Strange Death of President Harding* by Gaston B. Means as told to May Dixon Thacker (New York: Guild Publishing, 1930). It is a fascinating fabrication by a former investigator in the Department of Justice. The story of a malleable president in the hands of his attorney general can be found in Harry M. Daugherty, *Inside Story of the Harding Tragedy* (1932, reprint; Boston: Western Islands, 1975). Finally the "source" of information on Harding's reputed affair with a young lady from Marion is Nan Britton, *President's Daughter* (New York: Elizabeth Ann Guild, 1927). However, it has not been properly corroborated by reliable sources, and therefore one should be wary of using it. The same treatment should be accorded to Britton's other book, *Honesty or Politics* (New York: Elizabeth Ann Guild, 1932). One should remember that she was looking for money and maybe status, even of the infamous variety.

The Authors

JUDITH I. ANDERSON, California State Polytechnic University at Pomona, is the author of *William Howard Taft: An Intimate History* (1981).

GEORGE W. GEIB, Butler University, has published extensively on the subjects of midwestern regional studies, the state of Indiana, the city of Indianapolis (including *Indianapolis: Hoosiers' Circle City* [1981]), as well as scholarly articles about Benjamin Harrison.

ARI HOOGENBOOM, Emeritus, Brooklyn College and Graduate Center, City University of New York, is the author of *The Presidency of Rutherford B. Hayes* (1988), *Rutherford B. Hayes: Warrior and President* (1995), *Rutherford B. Hayes: "One of the Good Colonels"* (1999), and *A History of the ICC: From Panacea to Palliative* (1976, with Olive Hoogenboom).

H. WAYNE MORGAN, Emeritus, University of Oklahoma, is the author of numerous books, including *William McKinley and His America* (1963, 2003) and *From Hayes to McKinley: National Party Politics, 1877–1896* (1969).

JOHN B. SHAW, Emeritus, Hiram College. His publications include *Crete and James: Personal Letters of Lucretia and James Garfield* (1994).

BROOKS D. SIMPSON, Arizona State University, is the author of *Let Us Have Peace: Ulysses S. Grant and the Politics of War and Reconstruction* (1991), *The Political Education of Henry Adams* (1996), *America's Civil War* (1996), *The Reconstruction Presidents* (1998), and *Ulysses S. Grant: Triumph Over Adversity* (2000).

THOMAS C. SOSNOWSKI, Kent State University, Stark Campus, teaches and writes about Ohio history and regional history. His research interests also focus on the émigrés of the French Revolution who sought refuge in the United States.

KENNETH R. STEVENS, Texas Christian University, served as a consultant on William Henry Harrison for the PBS production "The American President" and has published *Border Diplomacy* (1989); "The Triumph of Old

Tip: William Henry Harrison and the Election of 1840," which appeared in *Traces* (1990); and *William Henry Harrison: A Bibliography* (1998). He also is coeditor of the *Diplomatic Papers of Daniel Webster* (1983, 1987).

PHILIP WEEKS, Kent State University, Stark Campus. His books include *Subjugation and Dishonor* (1981), *Land of Liberty: A United States History* (1985), *The American Indian Experience* (1988), *Farewell, My Nation: The United States and the American Indian in the Nineteenth Century* (1990, 2001), and *"They Made Us Many Promises"* (2002).

Index

Calhoun, William J., 199
Canada, 4–5
Cannon, Joe, 226, 228–29, 231
Carnegie, Andrew, 48, 166
Carter, Jimmy, 112
Castillo, C·novas del, 197
Chambers, John, 36
Chandler, Zachariah, 104
Chase, Salmon P., 67–68, 93, 123–24, 129, 131
Christian, George, 264
Civil Rights Act (1866), 66
Civil service reform, 109, 136, 152–53, 161
Civil War, 46, 62, 65, 95; at Antietam, 181; Army of Northern Virginia in, 95, 125; Army of Tennessee in, 56, 59; Army of the Cumberland in, 124–26; Army of the Ohio in, 56, 120; Army of the Potomac in, 95–97, 123; Army of the Shenandoah in, 96; Army of West Virginia in, 96; at Bull Run, 121, 124; at Chickamauga, 125–26, 138; at Fallen Timbers, 11, 16; 40th Ohio in, 120–21; 42d Ohio in, 119–122; at Middle Creek, 121, 122; 7th Ohio Regiment of Volunteers in, 118; 70th Indiana in, 146–47; at Shiloh, 56–57, 122; 20th Ohio in, 122, 146; 23rd Ohio Volunteer Infantry in, 114, 181–82; veterans of, 164; at Vicksburg, 57–59; at Winchester, 181
Clark, Champ, 229
Clarkson, James, 161–62
Clay, Green, 21
Clay, Henry, 25, 27–28, 30, 32, 35–37, 43–45, 90, 93
Claybaugh, Joseph, 143
Clemmer, Mary, 135
Cleveland, Grover, 112–13, 153–56, 167, 190; administration of, 162, 188, 196–97, 267
Coburn, John, 147
Codman, John, 37
Colfax, Schuyler, 75, 128
Conkling, Roscoe, 81, 103, 106, 109, 135–36
Constitution to the United States of America, the, 100, 104, 106–108, 178, 231, 259; Fifteenth Amendment, 69, 72, 99, 152–53, 161; Fifth Amendment, 271;

Fourteenth Amendment, 66–67; Nineteenth Amendment, 261; Seventeenth Amendment, 252–53; Thirteenth Amendment, 46
Coolidge, Calvin, 134, 243–44, 260, 263, 271
Corbin, Abel, 71
Cordova, José María, 28
Cortelyou, George B., 196
Cotton, Edward, 226
Cox, George, 175, 248, 252
Cox, Jacob Dolson, 95, 117–19, 126
Cox, James, 259–61
Crawford, William H., 23
Credit Mobilier scandal, 75, 129
Croghan, George, 22, 24, 33
Custer, George Armstrong, 79
Czolgosz, Leon, 209–10

Darneille, Isaac, 14
Daugherty, Harry M., 247, 252, 254, 259, 262–63, 265, 268; mentioned, 267, 270, 273
Davis, David, 105
Davis, James, 263
Davis, Oscar King, 224
Dawes, Charles Gates, 205, 207, 263, 272
Dawes General Allotment (Severalty) Act (1887), 111
Debs, Eugene V., 268
December Confederates, 147
Declaration of Independence, the, 10, 98
Denby, Edwin, 269
Dent, Fred, 52
Dent, Julia. See Grant, Julia
Denton, William, 116
Depew, Chauncey, 155, 237
Desha, Joseph, 23
Dewey, George, 203
DeWolfe, Eugene Marshall, 247
DeWolfe, Henry (Pete), 247
Dimmick, Mary Lord, 168
Dorsey, Stephen W., 137
DuBois, W. E. B., 178
Dudley, William W., 157
Dunn, Arthur Wallace, 231, 239

Early, Jubal, 64, 96
Edison, Thomas, 48